Methods, Sex a

MW01038248

Social research yields knowledge which powerfully affects our daily lives. The 'facts' it generates shape not just how we see ourselves and others, but also whether or not we see the existing status quo as normal, just and legitimate. Everyone, particularly students of the social sciences, should therefore examine and question the methods used by social researchers to produce such knowledge. This book will help them to do so, focusing chiefly on research into human sexuality and madness, it introduces and critically assesses everything from survey methods to participant observation, opens up broader philosophical debates about the nature of knowledge, and highlights issues surrounding the ethics and politics of research.

Medical and social researchers in the nineteenth and twentieth centuries both reproduced and helped to construct a vision of 'normal' sexuality. This research provides a clear example of the links between everyday life and scientific thinking and those between social research and social power. Taking this as a starting point, the book then looks at the research community and the research process in more detail before moving on to examine the main techniques used in social research: the use of official statistics, the survey method, interviewing, laboratory observation, ethnography, the use of documentary sources and textual analysis. By exploring both technical and conceptual problems in the work of researchers like Freud and Kinsey, and by considering the difficulties faced by researchers concerned with phenomena such as rape, witch hunts and prostitution, this book makes methodological issues both interesting and accessible.

Julia O'Connell Davidson is Lecturer in Sociology and **Derek Layder** is Reader in Sociology at the University of Leicester.

Methods, Sex and Madness

Julia O'Connell Davidson and
Derek Layder

London and New York

First published 1994
by Routledge
11 New Fetter Lane, London EC4P 4EE

Simultaneously published in the USA and Canada
by Routledge
29 West 35th Street, New York, NY 10001

© 1994 Julia O'Connell Davidson and Derek Layder

Typeset in Times by LaserScript, Mitcham, Surrey
Printed and bound in Great Britain by
Mackays of Chatham PLC, Chatham, Kent

British Library Cataloguing in Publication Data
A catalogue record for this book is available from the British Library.

Library of Congress Cataloging in Publication Data
Davidson, Julia O'Connell, 1960–
  Methods, sex and madness/Julia O'Connell Davidson and
  Derek Layder.
    p. cm.
  Includes bibliographical references and index.
  ISBN 0–415–09763–0: $50.00 – ISBN 0–415–09764–9 (pbk.): $16.50
  1. Sexology – Research. 2. Mental illness – Research. I. Layder, Derek
  II. Title.
HQ60.D38   1994
306.7'072 – dc20   94-5596
                                                                        CIP

ISBN 0–415–09763–0 (hbk)
ISBN 0–415–09764–9 (pbk)

For June, Dawn, Charmagne and Dot,
with thanks – Julia O'Connell Davidson

Contents

Figures

Preface and acknowledgements

Understanding the philosophical, methodological and political issues surrounding social research is central not only to doing good research, but also to evaluating research done by others. But despite its critical importance to all social science disciplines, methodology is a not a subject which typically makes the heart beat faster. Most social science students take some form of compulsory course on research methods, but few would claim to have been rivetted by either the lectures or the reading matter presented to them. Our aim is to provide a very general introduction to the main techniques used by social researchers and the philosophical and methodological problems associated with them, but to do so in a reasonably engaging way. We do this primarily through a focus on research into human sexuality and madness. Most people find these areas interesting and virtually the entire array of research methods and techniques of investigation have been, and are, used to explore them. A focus on sex and madness therefore allows us to introduce and critically appraise everything from survey methods to participant observation, as well as to open up wider philosophical issues about the nature of knowledge, and to highlight questions about the ethics and politics of research.

Furthermore, as Chapter 1 shows, the relationship between everyday thinking and scientific investigation is well illustrated by nineteenth- and twentieth-century medical and social research into sexuality. On the one hand, popular beliefs about sex are shaped by the findings of such research, on the other, research into sexuality is powerfully influenced by the moral and normative values of the society in which it is undertaken. The centrality of concepts of 'normal sexuality' to common-sense thinking and the construction of gender identities also make it vital to question the reliability and validity of research upon which such concepts are based, as well as to examine the philosophical and moral assumptions which underpin research in these areas. The book's focus on how knowledge about sexuality and madness is produced should help students to follow recent debates about the extent to which both sexuality and madness are socially constructed phenomena and, indeed, to take a more critical approach to all social scientific knowledge.

The book is organised as follows. The first chapter is concerned with the relationship between scientific and everyday thinking. It argues against those philosophers and methodologists who believe that scientific methods necessarily and automatically produce value-free, objective knowledge about the social world. It challenges the idea of 'scientific' and 'common-sense' thinking as two completely separate, even antagonistic, ways of knowing about the world and suggests that the relationship between the two is far more intimate. Through a consideration of nineteenth- and twentieth-century research into human sexuality, it further argues that there is a strong relationship between social power and social research, but concludes that despite this political dimension and the powerful link between 'scientific' and 'everyday' thinking, critical investigation is not an impossibility. Chapter 2 then outlines the dimensions of social research which distinguish it from other ways of knowing about the social world, and presents our general views on how to go about doing better research.

The next six chapters are devoted to looking at specific research sources and methods in more detail. We look at the use of official statistics in social research, the survey method, interviewing techniques, observational and ethnographic techniques and the use of documentary sources. A number of themes recurr throughout:

• The impact of the researcher's pre-existing moral, political and theoretical assumptions on the research design and the analysis of findings;
• The feminist critique of orthodox methods;
• The ways in which the social identity of the researcher (in terms of gender, class and 'racialisation') impacts on the research process and the data gathered.

Throughout this book we will refer to the 'racialised' identity of researchers and research subjects rather than using the term 'race'. We reject the idea of 'race' as a biological fact and follow Small (1994) in using the term 'racialised' identity to recognise 'the social identities often embraced by groups which we call 'Black' and 'white'. Such identities are not fixed, are influenced by a host of other factors (such as class, gender, religion) but remain a primary organising feature of social relations' (Small 1994, see also Small 1991a and b).

The final chapter draws together the book's themes through an examination of the methodological issues confronting one of the authors who is currently undertaking a small scale ethnographic study of prostitution. The book as a whole aims to show that there is no one, single best technique of investigation and that particular research techniques are not, of themselves, good or bad, conservative or progressive, feminist or masculinist. We argue that the key to good research is to apply techniques properly, and that all methods, quantitative and qualitative, can be used either to support the existing status quo or to challenge inequality and oppression.

We would like to thank the following people for reading and commenting upon chapters of this book and/or drawing relevant material to our attention: Stephen Small, Leigh Pinsent, John Scott, Dawn Halford, Harry Collins, Dot Cope, Steve Wagg, Della Cavanagh, Dean Huggins and Laura Brace. We are also grateful to Karsten Grummitt, who read and commented on the entire manuscript.

Chapter 1

Social research and everyday life

> Germain Garnier, christened Marie . . . was a well-built young man with a thick red beard, who, until the age of fifteen . . . had lived and dressed like a girl, showing 'no mark of masculinity'. Then once, in the heat of puberty, the girl jumped across a ditch while chasing pigs through a wheatfield: 'at that very moment the genitalia and the male rod came to be developed in him, having ruptured the ligaments by which they had been held enclosed'. Marie, soon to be Marie no longer, hastened home to her/his mother, who consulted physicians and surgeons, all of whom assured the somewhat shaken woman that her daughter had become her son.
>
> (Laqueur 1990: 127)

This story, told in the sixteenth century, reflected the centuries old belief that 'women had the same genitals as men except that . . . "theirs are inside the body and not outside it"' (Laqueur 1990: 4). If girls were too boisterous, their vagina, uterus and ovaries, which were imagined as an interior penis, scrotum and testicles, might simply fall out, transforming them into males. In *Making Sex*, Laqueur shows how for thousands of years it was common-sense knowledge that there was but one sex, that the female body was an inverted male body. Since around the eighteenth century, however, common sense has postulated the existence of two 'opposite' sexes, female and male, and that the difference between the two is biologically defined, fixed and immutable. Until the eighteenth or nineteenth century, it was also common-sense knowledge that women could not conceive unless they experienced orgasm during sexual inter- course (how else could they release the seed from their inverted testicles?), many people also believed that venereal disease could be cured by sexual contact with an uncontaminated partner – an idea which was sometimes offered as a defence by men who were on trial for the rape of young children (Simpson 1987). Common-sense knowledge about madness has also changed over the centuries. Gods, demons and devils, rather than an unhappy childhood, a disease or a genetic predisposition, were once the assumed 'cause' of bizarre or erratic behaviour and moods.

Where does such taken-for-granted, common-sense knowledge come from and what is its relation to 'scientific' enquiry? Looking back at the tragic consequences of common-sense beliefs that venereal diseases could be transmitted outwards or that a pregnant woman could not possibly have been raped but must have fully participated and enjoyed the act, it is tempting to see scientific knowledge as quite separate from, and infinitely superior to, everyday thinking. One version of the history of the natural sciences certainly presents the scientist, from Galileo on, as engaged in a heroic struggle against the benighted ignorance of lay people, and there are social scientists who conceive of their profession in much the same way. The twentieth century has seen an ever-expanding trail of 'experts' who draw on social science research to explain to the unenlightened how to behave at job interviews, how to be a more effective manager, teacher or social worker; how they should bring up children, make a marriage last, or cope with bereavement; how to recognise, avoid or deal with alcoholism, annorexia nervosa, depression, stress and a myriad of other afflictions. In short, both social scientific and natural science research can be presented as sweeping away 'old wives tales' and the prejudiced 'mumbo jumbo' that is common sense to reveal the hard, objective truths beneath it. What we aim to show in this chapter is that the relationship between scientific and everyday thinking is rather more complex than this.

This book is about the research methods used by social scientists and aims to equip the reader with a basic knowledge of the most commonly employed research techniques. But it is not simply a 'how to do it' manual. The book is also concerned with the methodological and philosophical problems associated with social research techniques, for an appreciation of these problems helps us to take a more critical approach to the knowledge which comes from social research. The book as a whole aims, therefore, to challenge the notion of 'scientific' and 'common-sense' thinking as two completely separate, even antagonistic, ways of knowing about the world. It suggests that the relationship between the two is far more intimate. Social scientists draw on their stock of everyday, taken-for-granted knowledge to conduct research, and the findings of social scientific research seep back into the pool of common-sense knowledge. Because of this interplay between scientific knowledge and everyday thinking, there is also a strong relationship between social power and social research and this political dimension of research (especially gender politics) is another of the themes addressed throughout this book. Though the same case could be made in relation to any field of sociological or psychological enquiry, whether it be 'racialisation', work and industry, health, education or whatever, the remainder of this chapter illustrates these points through a consideration of research into human sexuality.

COMMON-SENSE AND 'SCIENTIFIC' CONSTRUCTIONS OF 'NORMAL' SEXUALITY

Through a combination of medical, biological, psychological and social research, sexology (the science of sex) appears to have transformed everyday thinking about human sexuality, liberating us from many of the more repressive religious and traditional beliefs about gender roles as well as about how often we should have sex, with whom, when, where and in what position. Sexologists thrust their work upon us through the medium of sex manuals, popular magazines throb with their advice and agony aunts grind their message into the inhibited, the virginal and the guilty. Ever wider audiences now rub up against their ideas in television programmes like *The Good Sex Guide*, and the refrain to the sexologists liberation song is to be found in popular books and films, like Madonna's *Sex* and *Nine and a Half Weeks*. Nowadays, it is not only acceptable, but demanded, that women should enjoy sex. Surveys tell us that masturbation, far from being practised solely by a small minority of enfeebled moral degenerates, is an almost universal pleasure. Certain 'beastly and monstrous' techniques condemned as mortal sin by St Thomas Aquinas in the thirteenth century are now highly recommended as 'foreplay'. Oral intercourse, we are told 'cannot fail to . . . improve the intensity of the orgasm. . . . It is worth any time and patience making oneself really proficient at it' (Chartham 1971: 71). A hint of S & M is high fashion. Agony aunts tell wives who have discovered their husbands have a penchant for cross-dressing that there is no reason to worry, a lot of men get thrills this way.

From the vantage point of the 1990s, one could be forgiven for thinking that common-sense thought has taken a passive role in its relationship with sexology – that it has simply lain back and allowed itself to be penetrated by the ideas and research findings of a hard science. If the historical development of Western ideas about human sexuality is considered in a little more depth, however, the interplay between scientific and everyday thinking looks rather different. And, as always, looking at the history of ideas tells us something about the history of power relations. We see who has been in a position to define the research agenda, to conduct the research and to disseminate their ideas, as well as links between society's prevailing distribution of power and advantage and the way in which research findings are interpreted.

Sex and the Christian moralists

For centuries in Europe, strictures and advice on sexual behaviour were provided primarily by the Church and theologians. In a world created by God, everything had a purpose, and the early Christian moralists held that sexuality was given by God for the purpose of procreation. For theologians like St Thomas Aquinas, it followed from this that natural sex was sex within marriage for the purpose of begetting children. Anything else was not only sinful, but also transgressed natural laws by violating the true purpose of human sexuality (Ruse 1988: 184). From this line of reasoning, a 'hierarchy of sin' could be developed. All lust was immoral and, even within marriage, copulation for pleasure alone was a mortal sin. Moreover:

> Intercourse between husband and wife was supposed to take place in the 'natural' position, the wife stretched out on her back with the man on top. All other positions were considered scandalous and 'unnatural'. The one known as *retro* or *more canino* was unnatural because it was the way animals performed. The position *mulier super virum* was at variance with male and female characters, the woman being passive 'by nature' and the man active.
>
> (Flandrin 1985: 120)

But some vices were worse still. They conflicted 'with the natural pattern of sexuality for the benefit of the species' (Aquinas, cited in Ruse 1988). In ascending order of heinousness, these were masturbation, bestiality, homosexuality and, as Aquinas put it, acts where 'the natural style of intercourse is not observed, as regards the proper organ or according to other rather beastly and monstrous techniques' (cited in Ruse 1988). Through reference to the scriptures and to the natural world, then, Christianity presented sexuality in terms of a moral dualism. There was good sex, which was natural and sanctified by God, and there was bad sex, which was both unnatural and immoral. There were, of course, dissenters from such views, even a few who defended homosexuality, but until the nineteenth century, everyday thinking about human sexuality was powerfully shaped by the Church's twin dualisms – moral/immoral, natural/unnatural sex. Towards the end of the nineteenth century, however, there was, as Weeks puts it, a:

sustained effort to put all this on to a new 'scientific' footing: to isolate and individualise the specific characteristics of sexuality, to detail its normal paths and morbid variations, to emphasise its power and to speculate on its effects.

(1985: 66)

Sex and nineteenth-century science

The philosopher Bertrand Russell (1976) holds that the scientific world-view which emerged during the eighteenth century is distinguished from pre-scientific thought by its demand that statements of fact be based on observation, not on unsupported authority (such as the Bible); by its insistence that the physical world is a self-acting, self-perpetuating system, not one driven by gods or men; and by the dethronement of the idea that everything in the world has a God-given 'purpose'. Science thus answers epistemological questions (philosophical questions about how claims to knowledge can be proved or grounded, what will count as 'facts') in a very different way to religious or magical thought, and it might therefore be expected that a scientific approach to the study of sexuality would signal dramatic change. Scientific claims about human sexuality would now have to be based upon observation and rigorous empirical studies, not upon readings from the scriptures. From the mid-nineteenth century on, human sexuality became part of the field of study first of biological and medical science and then of psychoanalysis. But though the new scientists of sex would all have wished to make a sharp distinction between their own 'scientific' approach and traditional, superstitious or religious thinking on the matter, what is most striking is the way in which they invariably reproduced the basic dichotomy between 'natural' and 'unnatural', 'normal' and 'abnormal', 'good' and 'bad' sex that existed in theological and religious thought, and how similar their views were on which sexual activities fell on which side of this great divide.

In his second book, *The Descent of Man, and Selection in Relation to Sex*, published in 1871, Darwin argued that for a species to survive, it needed not only to adapt to its environment, but also to reproduce effectively. Biological scientists went on to explore the dynamics of sexual selection in the animal kingdom, and applied their findings to the human world. What these scientists discovered in the animal kingdom was 'evidence' that existing social norms and gender roles were perfectly suited to the survival of the species, while sexual activities that society frowned upon were dysfunctional and unnatural. Was this a fortuitous coincidence, or did these men's existing moral and normative values affect their research agenda, shape their observations and the way in which they interpreted them? This tradition has recently enjoyed something of a revival in the work of sociobiologists who use similar methods to produce equally conservative claims about human sexuality. Ethological studies of animals in their natural habitats are used to support assertions about the 'natural' order of the sexes. We are told that human males are 'naturally' promiscuous, dominant and territorial because male baboons have 'harems' of female baboons, male lions 'dominate' female lions, sticklebacks 'aggressively' defend space. There is little to add to Weeks' comment on such analyses:

> What is happening here is the attribution of highly coloured social explanations to animal behaviour. Why should groupings of female animals be seen as harems? They could equally well be seen, for all the counter-evidence available, as prototypes of women's consciousness-raising groups. To say that perhaps evokes a smile. But so should the circular argument by which explanations drawn from human experience are attributed to animals and then used to justify social divisions in the present.
>
> (Weeks 1986: 51)

As well as biological scientists, those working in the field of medicine applied new and rigorous methods of enquiry to contribute to the growing body of scientific knowledge about human sexuality. Again, what now seems most conspicuous is the way in which 'science' merely embellished common-sense knowledge, especially in so far as the essential 'nature' of man and woman was concerned. Laqueur notes that 'Sometime in the eighteenth century, sex as we know it was invented' (1990: 149). The ovaries and the uterus were 'discovered' and a model of male and female as biologically and incommensurably different was developed. These organs, in particular the ovaries, were seen to be the controlling organs of the female body:

> the ovaries . . . are the most powerful agents in all the commotions of her system . . . on them rest her intellectual standing in society, her physical perfection . . . all that is great, noble and beautiful, all that is voluptuous, tender and endearing . . . her devotedness, her perpetual

vigilance, forecast, and all those qualities of mind and disposition which inspire respect and love and fit her as the safest counsellor and friend of man, spring from the ovaries.

(Dr W. W. Bliss, 1870, cited in Ehrenreich and English 1976: 33)

Reproduction was woman's central purpose in life and the reproductive organs dominated her entire physical, emotional and psychological being, so much so that almost all ill health (mental or physical) could be traced to the womb or ovaries, and any kind of 'unfeminine' behaviour, whether excessive work or exercise, masturbation, reading or voting, threatened to seriously damage those organs (see Ehrenreich and English 1976). To preserve her health, a woman needed to conserve her energies. She should not develop other bodily organs (particularly not her brain) or engage in any vigorous activity, she should be passive in the sexual act itself, otherwise her energies would be sapped and her reproductive organs would atrophy. Thus a scientific justification was provided for the passive role that had previously been ordained by God. Of course, this 'conservation of energy' theory was hardly liberating for men either. Medicine taught that masturbation and excessive sexual activity depleted the body's energies and thus provided 'scientific' backing for religious strictures on the subject, but men did not suffer the grotesque fate that befell thousands of women as a consequence of the new 'scientific' knowledge. The surgical removal of the clitoris as a treatment for 'nymphomania' was recommended by some doctors (Ehrenreich and English 1976: 39) and:

Bilateral ovariotomy – the removal of healthy ovaries – made its appearance in the early 1870s and became an instant success to cure a wide variety of 'behavioural pathologies': hysteria, excessive sexual desires, and more mundane aches and pains whose origins could not be shown to lie elsewhere.

(Laqueur 1990: 176)

But where women were constructed as passive and passionless, man's 'natural' state was one of activity, and his sexual life was no exception. Too much restraint, as well as too little, could be harmful. The work of the early sexologists (scientists of sex) drew on and reinforced this notion of innate and incontravertible differences between male and female sexuality. Havelock Ellis's contribution in *Studies in the Psychology of Sex* (1897) was to show how women were not only naturally passive, but also masochistic. Again, their 'nature' had biological roots. After describing some extremely vicious attacks on young children and claiming that it is easy 'to trace in women a delight in experiencing physical pain when inflicted by a lover, and an eagerness to accept subjection to his will', Havelock Ellis explains that 'The psychological satisfaction which women tend to feel in a certain degree of pain in love is strictly co-ordinated with a physical fact. Women possess a minor degree of sensibility in the sexual region' (Ellis 1987: 523).

In the last half of the nineteenth century the sexologists also began to define, list and classify sexual 'abnormalities' and the pathologies that give rise to them. They concentrated primarily upon 'venereal disease, sexual psycho-pathology (the major "abberations" and their connection with "degeneracy") and eugenics' (Bejin 1985a: 181). Best known of these early pioneers is Krafft-Ebing whose 1886 study, *Psychopathia Sexualis*, provides a catalogue of sexual 'perversities' illustrated with real life case studies. Once again, the congruence between medical and traditional thought was striking. Homosexuality, condemned as immoral and unnatural by religious thinkers, was identified by medicine as a 'mental disease'. Men and women who failed to find sexual bliss in 'normal' coitus and engaged in other practices, such as oral sex, were 'masochistic' and masochism was found to be 'a pathological over-growth of specifically feminine elements' (Krafft-Ebing 1914: 152). To conceive of such sexual activities as a manifestation of 'ill health' rather than as 'sin' is often held to be a more liberal approach. People are not, after all, generally seen as personally or morally responsible for their sicknesses. But one has only to consider some of the 'treatments' and 'cures' that have been imposed upon homosexual men this century (from electric shock aversion therapy to castration) to see that the practical consequences of being judged 'sick' instead of 'sinful' are not always so very different.

Disseminating scientific knowledge about sex

If science draws on society's stock of taken-for-granted knowledge about the world to define its research agenda and to classify and inter-pret its observations, how does scientific knowledge feed back into everyday thinking? So far as sex is concerned, the general public appears to have an almost unquenchable thirst for knowledge. Today, as in the past, those who research or write about sex claim to be imme-diately inundated with requests for help with sexual problems, letters asking whether given sexual practices are normal or not, even un-solicited videotapes of couples in coitus (all such contributions from readers of this book should be sent to the authors). The amount of printed matter devoted to sex further indicates that people's appetite for advice on how to have 'good' sex is insatiable. Until the early years of this century, such advice was largely reserved for men (being passive recepticles, of course, women needed only moral, not practical guidance), but increasingly, 'scientific' knowledge about human sexuality has been fed to wider audiences.

In 1918, Beatrice Webb, the renowned liberal 'socialist' and feminist, insisted that evil came from ignorance and made the case for sex education for children. They should learn about the reproductive organs and be informed that 'reproductive processes should not be carried on without the sanction of matrimony' and told the precise age at which it is 'right' to engage in such processes: 'research . . . proves that first babies born when the mother is twenty-three are better than first babies born when the mother is either under or over twenty-three' (Webb 1987: 498). Webb takes from 'science' the idea of some kind of bodily 'energy' that is linked to the reproductive organs and explains that such 'energies' are particularly intense and troubling to girls between the ages of fourteen and twenty. She recommends that growing girls displace this 'energy' by taking plenty of exercise, eating plain food, sleeping next to an open window and taking a daily cold bath. Webb also warns mothers about 'certain abnormal activities of the reproductive organs' (1987: 500). These turn out to be masturbation. Once again 'thorough daily cleanliness' ('brisk' applications of soap and a 'plunge into a cold bath') is the prophylactic and should this fail, the child:

> should be put into a warm sleeping suit, and brought up to sleep with hands outside the bed clothes. To children old enough . . . one could explain that it is very exhausting, makes them dull and stupid, and is a waste of the powers given them for the good of the world, for the good of their children.
>
> (Webb 1987: 501)

This message of sexual restraint proved to be an enduring theme in sex education. A 1956 book aimed at a child audience explains that being 'civilised' makes us more intelligent but physically weaker than our forebears and young men and women should therefore 'wait until they are about twenty before they get married . . . by . . . that age the girl is strong enough to have babies without any trouble, and the boy is strong enough to look after his wife and baby' (Matthews 1956: 33). Restraint is also a moral imperative:

We can, of course, behave like animals and have sexual intercourse just because it gives us pleasure, just as we can eat a whole box of chocolates in one afternoon because we enjoy it. If we are greedy about eating chocolates we can't do much more than make ourselves sick. If, however, we are greedy about sexual intercourse, then we are doing one of the most selfish and wrong things we can possibly do. . . . Sexual intercourse between a husband and wife who want children is a very great thing . . . but we must *never* look upon it as an amusement which we can enjoy whenever we want it.

(Matthews 1956: 37)

Children thus learned from doctors, reformers and sexologists that 'good' sex was penetrative sex between people aged twenty plus, primarily for the purpose of procreation and always within marriage. The experts also had words of wisdom for women. Marie Stopes got the ball rolling with *Married Love*, published in 1918. Following its publication, she received hundreds of letters asking for advice, was invited to lecture school children on sex by the Welsh Education board and to write another book directed towards medical practitioners (Rose 1992: 119). Designed for educated middle-class wives – Dr Stopes was anxious about the survival of the 'white race' and disapproved of the 'thriftless, illiterate and careless' lower classes who undermined the Empire by producing too many weak and handicapped children – *Married Love* was seen as a radical book. It asserted that women were capable of passion, though only under specific circumstances. Stopes revealed that women have a 'spontaneous sex drive', but unlike men, theirs is governed by a 'law of Periodicity and Recurrence' which in turn is linked to the menstrual cycle (see Stopes 1987). Husbands should be sensitive to the ebbs and flows of their wives' desire, and, more shocking still, Stopes insisted that husbands should take steps to arouse the woman sufficiently to ensure that 'a secretion of mucus lubricates the opening of the vagina' (Rose 1992: 113). Women (or at least educated, white, middle-class women) were capable of experiencing, and entitled to, pleasure and passion – their husbands had a responsibility to bring them to orgasm – but 'good' sex was still penetrative sex within marriage, and it was still the man's role to control and orchestrate the act. Indeed, Stopes' views on gender roles were far from revolutionary; 'man is still essentially the hunter, the one who experiences the desires and thrills of the chase, and dreams ever of coming unawares upon Diana in the woodlands' (cited in Rose 1992: 117). This notion of the male sexual impulse as 'naturally' a desire to hunt, possess and dominate was also central to Van de Velde's *Ideal Marriage* of 1928. With sales of over a million and a good reputation amongst the medical profession, this was possibly the most influential sex manual until the 1970s, and it fed to a very wide audience Havelock Ellis's 'concept of courtship and the biologically inevitable association between love and pain' (Jackson 1987: 62–3).

Sex and psychoanalysis

Another highly influential approach to sexology which emerged at the turn of the century was psychoanalysis – indeed many Freudians would proclaim psychoanalysis as the only true science of sex. It was through his studies of the origins of hysteria and neurosis that Freud came to develop his theory of psychosexual development and then to develop a theory of human sexuality. Put extremely crudely, Freud held that sexual energy and drives do not suddenly appear at puberty, but are present soon after birth. Freud was not suggesting that children have full and lusty sexual urges like adult desires, but simply that they take pleasure and interest in their bodies and physical sensations. In childhood, the focus of these interests changes as the individual passes through the set stages of psychosexual development; oral, anal, phallic, latent, genital. A person's future sexual orientation, as well as their future psychological well being, depends on how the various crises associated with each stage of development are resolved. So far as sexuality is concerned, a person should ideally progress from infantile pleasures (associated with teeth, breasts, anus, their own sexual organs and so on) to mature sexual pleasures that derive from intercourse between man and woman. The key dichotomy in psychoanalytic thought is therefore between 'infantile' and 'mature' sexuality, rather than 'moral' and 'immoral' or 'normal' and 'pathological' sexuality. For example, Freud insisted that homosexuality 'is nothing to be ashamed of, no vice, no degradation, it cannot be classified as an illness' (cited in Isay 1993: 3). Instead, homosexuality had its origins in the individual's childhood. The Oedipal dilemma and castration complex associated with the phallic stage of development had been inadequately resolved. It was a case of arrested or incomplete development.

Freud's theories may sound bizarre when presented in this truncated form, but they should not and cannot be simply dismissed. Not only is it essential to recognise that psychoanalytic theory has had an enormous impact on our everyday thinking, but also, as Weeks observes 'like so many other of the great intellectual preoccupations of the twentieth century (Marxism, democracy and nationalism spring to mind), it has different meanings in different contexts' (1986: 61). Though Freud himself may have been far from progressive so far as sexual politics were concerned, because psychoanalysis involved 'a radical re-examination of the concept of sexuality' others have recently been able to reinterpret Freud in such a way as to 'challenge the orthodoxies of the sexual tradition' (Weeks 1986: 61). Having acknowledged the richness, diversity and flexibility of the psychoanalytic tradition, however, it must be noted that in Freud's own work, a basic dualism between 'good/ healthy' and 'bad/unhealthy' sex persisted, albeit recast as 'infantile' and 'mature' sexuality.

Meanwhile, the interplay between taken-for-granted, everyday knowledge, social power and scientific theory in Freud's work on female sexuality is unmistakable. As infants, Freud argued, both males and females believe that everyone has a penis. Girls take pleasure in their clitoris, assuming that it will eventually grow into a penis making them whole and complete human beings. At around the age of 5, children discover that this is not the case. Some people lack a penis. They (women) are 'castrated'. The boy child fears that he too will be castrated, and his anxiety is only resolved when he switches his affec-tions away from his mother (his primary love object) towards his father (the rival who may castrate him). The girl child is in a rather more unhappy situation. She sees herself as already 'castrated' and must somehow adjust to this mutilated condition. As Mitchell (1979: 96) puts it: 'Accepting castration means not only acknowledging the lack of the phallus, but, out of disappointment, abandoning the inferior clitoris as a source of sexual satisfaction.' Girls must come to focus on the vagina, rather than the clitoris, as the source of sexual pleasure. To achieve this transition Freud argued that girls had to transform their longing for a penis into longing for first their father, then their husband, to make a 'gift' of a baby, which is really a substitute penis.

Psychoanalytic theory thus posited the existence of two different types of female orgasm: the vaginal and the clitoral. The normal, non-neurotic, mature women might enjoy a little foreplay, but she would reach ecstacy only as a result of a penis moving in her vagina. The woman who sought or enjoyed 'clitoral orgasms' had failed to fully repress or transform her infantile 'penis envy'. This distinction between 'vaginal' and 'clitoral' orgasms entered popular consciousness through the medium of popular psychology, marriage and sex guides, women's magazines and so on – the term 'frigid' has its origin in the psycho-analytic concept of 'vaginal frigidity', that is, an inability to experience 'vaginal orgasms'. Where theologians censured masturbation, oral sex, anal sex and manual stimulation on moral grounds, psychoanalysts had scientific reasons for placing copulation at the top of the sexual hierarchy. The *normal* woman accepts the 'passive receptivity of the vagina' and only those 'frigid' women who fail to orgasm by dint of a quick poke by their husband desire such things. The misogyny which underpins this science is well illustrated in the following passage, written by two psychoanalysts in the 1950s:

> The neurotic woman, suffering from an inability to experience vaginal orgasm, finds a typical scapegoat: man. Ignorant of the fact that her own neurotic difficulty is responsible for her frigidity, she places the blame on the man's technique . . . [But] a healthy and experienced man is helpless when confronted with a frigid woman. The frigid woman's scapegoat theory is by no means harmless. It poisons a marriage, and frequently leads to extramarital affairs and divorce.
>
> (Bergler and Kroger 1954: 80)

Is it too cynical to point out that such ideas are remarkably convenient for men (who are absolved from the onerous task of discovering what their partner enjoys) and for psychoanalysts (who are assured a constant supply of fee-paying 'neurotic' women to treat)? Other sexologists certainly took issue with the Freudian distinction between clitoral and vaginal orgasms. In fact, as Bejin (1985a) points out, the orgasm became *the* central problem and concern of sexology from around the 1920s onwards. It was the female orgasm which provoked most dispute.

New sexology, traditional sexism

By the 1950s Alfred Kinsey, America's most famous sexologist, was able to dismiss the psychoanalytic view of female sexuality on the grounds that anatomic and clinical evidence showed that most of the interior of the vagina is without nerves and that the 'vaginal orgasm' is therefore an anatomical impossibility. Masters and Johnson's extremely detailed research into sexual physiognomy (the biological dynamics of sex) in the 1960s reinforced this position. They found the clitoris to be the centre of female sexual response and therefore the font of all erotic sensation. Orgasms experienced during penetrative sex, as much as those experienced as a result of masturbation, or manual or oral stimulation, were clitoral orgasms. There was no separate mechanism for attaining vaginal orgasm. Even today, a good thirty years after the debate between sexologists and psychoanalysts was most heated, its ghost still haunts the popular imagination. It is not uncommon to read letters to agony aunts bemoaning an inability to attain 'vaginal orgasm' and replies explaining that such an orgasm is biologically impossible. In the struggle of ideas between psychoanalysis and the more physiologically based sexology of scientists like Kinsey and Masters, it was the latter which won out. For this we must surely be grateful. Here, scientific enquiry produced empirical evidence which (like the discovery of the fact that women do not need to orgasm in order to conceive and the fact that venereal disease cannot be cured by coitus with an uninfected individual) can be used to promote greater equality.

This more biologically based variant of sexology certainly advanced our knowledge of the physiology of sexual response, but facts do not speak for themselves. They must be interpreted. This can only be done through reference to the researcher's theoretical, moral and political preconceptions, and many would argue that the new sexology was far from impartial in the way it interpreted the facts it uncovered. Both Kinsey and Masters and Johnson began with the theoretical assumption that males and females have very basic biological sex drives or sexual appetites which must be satisfied. Sex acts, whether heterosexual or homosexual intercourse, masturbation or bestiality, are all directed towards orgasm and so represent an 'outlet' for this drive. In their work, 'the orgasm is held up as a measure of good health, and therefore an essential component of 'happiness' (Bejin 1985b: 202). For this reason, critics have argued that the new sexology pushed us towards a world tyrannised by the orgasm. 'Good' sex became orgasmic sex and sex without orgasm became 'dysfunctional' sex which must be treated and cured by the 'sexperts'.

Certainly, these sexologists and those that followed them were practical and interventionist, they were pioneers in the field of sex therapy, and their researches informed and still inform explicit sex manuals which aim to help couples to have satisfying sexual relations (that is, to be proficient in obtaining and provoking orgasm). But while the new sexologists were permissive in many respects, one theme remained constant, that of the profound and incontravertible difference between male and female sexuality. Feminist critics like Jackson (1984, 1987) hold that it is here that the relationship between social research and social power is most visible. The gender inequalities which characterise and structure our lives in the public sphere of work, health, education and politics and which are maintained and reproduced in the private sphere of family and marriage have been reified in the research of sexologists. What is actually a social relationship of unequal power and advantage is constructed and presented as 'natural'. The domination of one group by another is disguised behind biological drives and imperatives.

Sexologists are members of society as well as scientists. As social and sexual beings, they themselves are part of the subject matter of their research, and they come to their work with beliefs and values learned from the society in which they grew up. They begin their research with the implicit assumption that (Western) male heterosexuality is 'normal' sexuality and they then measure women's sexuality against the yardstick of male normality. Freud's entire *ouevre* on female sexuality, for example, rests on the belief that to be fully human requires possession of a penis, and that the absence of this magnificent organ condemns one to a life of masochistic passivity (a belief which is hardly open to *scientific* investigation). The new sexologists, despite an emphasis on biology rather than psychic structures, were likewise convinced that to be normal is to be male and vice versa. Men were asserted to be 'naturally' more highly sexed, wanting sex more often, and achieving orgasm more quickly. Kinsey *et al.* (1953), for example, claimed that:

> For perhaps three quarters of all males, orgasm is reached within two minutes after the initiation of the sexual relation. Considering the many . . . females who are so *adversely conditioned* to sexual situations that they may require 10 to 15 minutes of the most careful stimulation to bring them to climax, and considering the fair number of females who never come to climax in their whole lives, it is of course demanding that the male be quite *abnormal* in his ability to prolong sexual activity without ejaculation if he is required to match the female partner.
>
> (Kinsey *et al.* 1953, emphasis added)

It is not 'adverse conditioning' that shapes the man's performance, of course, and if women were 'normally' conditioned (i.e., if they were like men) they too would be able to reach orgasm in two minutes flat. For men to prolong their sexual activity in order to match the female partner would require them to be 'abnormal'. For women to match the male partner by shortening their sexual activity is presumably 'normal'. Male sexuality (though Kinsey's model of the 'normal' male is highly eurocentric) is normal, anything that deviates from it is a problem. Many feminists argue that in this sense, the new sexology drew on and reinforced notions of male supremacy. The surgical procedure to reconstruct the vagina designed by Dr James Burt in the 1970s is perhaps the ultimate expression of this view of women's sexuality as sub-normal because different from men's sexuality. Dr Burt created the

'Mark II Vagina' by lengthening the pubococcygeal muscle so that the clitoris was 'more accessible to direct penile stimulation' – a 'medical response both to the "new" knowledge of the importance of the clitoris for women and the continued commitment to the pursuit of orgasms in the standard fashion most pleasing and convenient for men' (Bleier 1984: 173). Needless to say, surgery to refashion the penis in such a way as to make it more responsive to sexual activities preferred by women remains unthinkable.

By constructing male sexuality as 'normal' sexuality, science contributed to the maintenance of an ideology which legitimates male domination. Science drew the basic notion of a powerful male 'sex drive' from the stock of everyday, common-sense knowledge, elaborated it through reference to biology and fed it back into the well of popular thought where it could be used to explain and excuse various forms of sexual oppression. This idea of a 'sex drive' promotes the idea that men are 'victims' of their biology, living in a sexually repressive society but faced continually with overpowering sexual 'urges'. Sexual desire is presented in the same way as thirst and hunger, an appetite or physical need which must be satisfied, and Kinsey in particular was prone to explaining male sexual aggression as a consequence of 'sex starvartion'. While this kind of tolerance for male assaults is now less common amongst academics, it continues to inform much everyday thinking about sexual violence. Police officers, judges and jurists who would not dream of explaining housebreaking or armed robbery as an uncontrollable biological response to the sight of wealth still often understand and excuse rape as an irrepressible sexual urge brought about by the sight of a woman. Indeed, so 'natural' and 'understandable' are these male 'urges' that the honesty, sexuality and morality of the female victim of sexual assault is often interrogated far more closely than that of her attacker. In short, as Jackson argues, the sexologists' model of human sexuality 'not only reflects and legitimates the male supremacist myth that the male urge *must* be satisfied; it defines the very nature of "sex" in male terms' (1987: 73).

So far, then, we have seen that despite answering epistemological questions in a very different way to the moralists and theologians who went before, at the start of this century science had provided three approaches to studying human sexuality each of which, albeit for different reasons, managed to maintain the binary model so central to the Judaeo Christian tradition. Just as it did for the Christian moralists, this model of 'good/healthy' and 'bad/unhealthy' sex had a clear cut gender polarity as its corollary. Masculine and feminine roles were in explicit opposition. What was moral, natural, beneficial to the species, normal, healthy and mature sexual behaviour for the male was precisely the reverse when enacted by the female and vice versa (see Figure 1.1). And just as the pious wished to root out and prevent activities on the 'wrong' side of the moral dualism, so scientists, physicians and psychoanalysts prescribed ways of curbing, containing and curing deviance. The new generation of sexologists who still practice today are certainly more liberal and permissive than their predecessors in terms of the way in which they distribute particular sexual activities between the two poles of 'good' and 'bad' sex. Anything (or almost anything) that contributes to the ultimate goal – orgasmic copulation – is 'good'. Only that which fails to produce orgasms efficiently is 'bad'. But they still reproduce a polar model of sexuality and the implications of their approach for gender are not entirely progressive.

Consensual sex, penetrative sex and the radical feminist position

Two decades on from the 'sexual revolution' of the 1960s, feminist, gay and social constructionist thinkers have had an impact on such binary models and their associated assumptions about gender. Feminists have pointed out that research and thinking on human sexuality has invariably treated female sexuality as a negative subset of male sexuality; lesbian women and gay men have questioned the heterosexist bias implicit in sexology; social constructionists such as Weeks point out that sexology has proved a double-edged sword in the struggle for sexual 'liberation':

> Sexology has had important positive effects in extending our knowl-
> edge of sexual behaviours and I have no desire to denigrate its real
> achievements. Without it we would be enslaved to an even greater
> extent than we are to myths and nostrums. On the other hand, in its
> search for the 'true' meaning of sex, in its intense interrogation of
> sexual difference, and in its obsessive categorization of sexual
> perversities it has contributed to the codification of a 'sexual tradi-
> tion', a more or less coherent body of assumptions, beliefs,
> prejudices, rules, methods of investigation and forms of moral regu-
> lation, which still shape the way we live our sexualities.
>
> (Weeks 1986: 14)

Progressive thinkers today wish to reject this sexual tradition – to abandon the codified system which arranges sexual acts on a continuum from 'perverse' to 'normal' and talk instead of 'diversity'. Sexual acts have no intrinsic qualities and cannot be categorised as 'good' or 'bad'

	Epistemology (what will count as 'facts')	Dualisms	Man's essential nature	Woman's essential nature
Christian moralists	The scriptures and observations of the natural world	Moral/ Immoral Natural/ Unnatural	Active	Passive
Biological scientists	Rigorous and methodical observation of the animal kingdom	Natural/ Unnatural Beneficial/ Harmful to the survival of the species	Active	Passive
Medical scientists	Rigorous and methodical observation of the abnormal and perverse	Normal/ Pathological	Active	Passive
Psychoanalysts	Rigorous and methodical analysis of the unconscious mind	Mature/ Immature	Active	Passive
'New' sexologists	Rigorous observation of physiological responses, systematic surveys and case studies	Functional (orgasmic)/ Dysfunctional	Active	Passive

Figure 1.1 Sexual dualisms from the early Christian moralists to the 'new' sexologists

in themselves. Instead, acts have only those qualities that are attributed to them by the individuals concerned. The only remaining divide is between consensual and non-consensual sex acts. Such a position is, of course, highly problematic in relation to paedophilia (at what age is a person able to genuinely consent?), pornography and prostitution (if people are deprived of other opportunities for making a living, can we say that they are freely and genuinely consenting to selling their bodies?), also to extreme forms of sadomasochism such as mutilation and, of course, bestiality and necrophilia where the object of attention is, by definition, unable to either consent or dissent.

Many radical feminists problematise this whole notion of consent, arguing that in a patriarchal society, where male hegemony is omnipresent, it is virtually impossible to distinguish women's sexual consent from 'enforced submission' (Pateman 1988: 224; see also Dworkin 1987, Jeffreys 1990). But this position is equally troublesome. To insist that heterosexual intercourse is always and inevitably an expression of male domination denies the experience of those women who do desire, and obtain sexual gratification from, penetrative sex. If we accept the radical feminist line, we can only assume that such women are pathetic victims of false consciousness who mistake their pain for pleasure and/or betray their 'sisters' by colluding with the enemy. Equally, an insistence that penetration is synonomous with male violence and oppression makes the experience of those lesbian women and gay men who desire, and derive sexual pleasure from, fist fucking, 'artificial' penetrative sex or anal sex difficult to comprehend. Are these acts acceptable because they take place in the context of a different set of power relations? In that case, should we not also insist that the participants are 'equals' on non-gender hierarchies, such as age, class and 'racialised' identity, in case a middle-class man secures his 'class' domination by penetrating a working-class man or a white woman secures her 'racial' domination by penetrating a Black woman? Or is it that these lesbians and gay men are also duped by male hegemony into consenting to acts which bring them no real pleasure?

Few people would disagree with the radical feminists' condemnation of rape, sexual intimidation and child abuse, and they are also without doubt correct to note that power and powerlessness are eroticised in Western culture. But the radical feminist campaign against the power components of sexuality (violence and capitulation, domination and submission, control and humiliation) seems to carry with it a suggestion that the social structures which give rise to inequalities in power could be transformed if only individuals transformed their sexual desires and activities. This is too simplistic. The powerless are not made so because they are eroticised – they are eroticised because they are powerless (Segal 1993). Women's inequality in the spheres of work, family and politics is not a direct consequence of their *sexual* oppression (even though this sexual oppression may reinforce other forms of oppression). Moreover, if we move to the micro-level of individual men and women's actual sexual interaction, it seems clear that social expectations and/or explicit demands from partners that 'real' men be constantly ready with a huge, pulsating, rock hard cock does not actually make all men feel powerful, rather the reverse. As Segal observes, it seems likely that most men 'are *least* sure of their power over women, and *most* fearful of women's self-sufficiency and autonomy, precisely in their sexual encounters with them' (1993: 77). Without wishing to deny that in general, men have power relative to women, it is important to note that in (consensual) sexual life, power can sometimes be something of a chimera. Stoller (1991) notes that in sadomasochistic circles, a distinction is drawn not just between those who are 'tops' (acting out domination) and those who are 'bottoms' (acting out subjugation), but also between those who are 'pushy' (in control and making demands) and those who are 'submissive' (allowing the other person control and acquiescing to demands). It is not impossible, indeed it is quite common, to find 'pushy bottoms', that is, people who take control and make demands from their submissive position. It is not difficult to see how this can also be the case in 'normal' heterosexual intercourse.

After more than a century of scientific enquiry then, debates surrounding human sexuality remain complex, wide ranging and largely unresolved. Thus far, we have emphasised the intimate relationship between everyday, common-sense thinking and scientific research into human sexuality. The object of this exercise was to try to deconstruct the popular view of science as necessarily and always objective and detached from moral and political beliefs. But, as is argued in the following section, abandoning a blind faith in the inevitable neutrality of science should not lead us to reject all empirical research or all hope of advancing human knowledge.

EVERYDAY THINKING AND SCIENTIFIC KNOWLEDGE

This chapter began by asking about the relationship between common-sense and scientific knowledge. Different philosophical traditions would approach this issue in different ways and it is perhaps worth considering two diametrically opposed visions: positivism and relativism. Positivism is, at its most basic, a philosophical tradition which holds the methods of the natural sciences to be the best and most objective means of acquiring knowledge. It therefore draws a sharp distinction between scientific and common-sense thinking, asserting that only the former can reveal facts and truths about the natural and social world. Relativism, on the other hand, considers objective knowledge to be unattainable. Everyone views the world through the lens of their own culturally determined 'common sense', and the 'facts' produced by science are no more independent of culturally relative, taken-for-granted knowledge than the 'facts' produced by thirteenth-century theologians or by sooth sayers.

For positivists, everyday thinking has two main qualities. First, it is based on the uncritical acceptance of unsubstantiated beliefs or opinions about the world. It is received wisdom, often resting on ideas that have been passed down from generation to generation as articles of faith. Second, it is tainted by subjective perceptions, infused with personal values and laden with moral or political judgements. Scientific thinking, conversely, is based on rigorous, empirical observation and hypothesis testing. It is objective, it is value-free, it seeks to uncover 'facts' about the world and describe them neutrally. Take a simple example. Scientists do not rely on their own sensory perceptions to measure water temperature, because they know that subjective perceptions can be deceiving. When a person's hands are hot, water feels cool. When their hands are freezing cold the same water feels quite hot. The whole point of the scientific method is to eliminate the possibility of deception, or bias, that comes from the subjectivity of the scientist, by designing and employing neutral, passive instruments for observation or measurement (in this case, by using a thermometer).

The same approach is often recommended for the social sciences. Proper scientific procedures should be followed; hypotheses must be formulated, systematic and rigorous observations made, and, where possible, neutral measuring instruments used. Thus, psychologists, for example, do not have a little chat with a man and then assess whether or not he has homosexual tendencies on the basis of a set of subjective perceptions: 'He looked a bit effeminate to me' or 'He seemed dead sentimental about his mum.' Instead they design tests, like the Minnesota Multiphasic Personality Inventory, which is supposedly a neutral instrument for measuring aspects of the personality. The aim is to eliminate the bias that comes from the psychologist's subjectivity. Two psychologists testing the same man could not fail to produce the same result using this instrument, even if one started out with the impression that the subject was a rampant queen and the other took the man to be a roaring straight. Similarly, positivist sociologists emphasise the importance of neutral instruments, such as surveys, for observing, recording and measuring attitudes, behaviours and intentions. The idea is that where proper scientific procedures are followed, knowledge that is untainted by the subjective preconceptions, beliefs and values of the researcher is produced. Positivist sociologists thus have little regard for the common-sense, everyday knowledge that people have about the society they live in. It is not to be trusted. Scientific methods are necessary to clear aside common sense, so revealing underlying truths and allowing us to describe the external reality which exists independently of the individuals who perceive it.

The idea that the social scientist should follow the methods of the natural sciences, setting aside all preconceptions and popular opinions and observing the social world rigorously and methodically, sounds sensible enough, yet actually raises a number of rather thorny philosophical problems. To begin with, the idea that anyone, including both natural and social scientists, ever relies *solely* on their observations is doubtful. If you looked from your window now and saw in the sky what appeared to be a flying saucer, you would be unlikely to immediately abandon a firmly held conviction that extra-terrestrial beings do not exist. You would probably seek some alternative explanation – someone has slipped you a trip, your eyes are playing you up, you are suffering from overwork. People do not always accept what they observe, because they know that their senses can deceive them and because they know that some things do not exist or cannot happen.

Scientists behave in much the same way. They too are committed to certain core beliefs and theories, and are unwilling to discard them at the drop of a hat. If a young physicist observed something in the course of an experiment which disconfirmed Einstein's theory of relativity, for example, the rest of the scientific community will not simply say 'Oh yes, Einstein was wrong. Dr X. did an experiment last week that falsified the theory of relativity.' People are more likely to assume that Dr X. made a mistake, or that she misread her findings. Indeed, Dr X. might not even bother to report her findings because she herself may assume that she was mistaken. Even if finally, after numerous repetitions, the observation held good, scientists would not simply discard the entire theory but would invent sub-hypotheses to rescue it – 'The theory holds good in all circumstances other than those discovered by Dr X'. Likewise, social scientists have certain taken-for-granted beliefs about the world which observation alone will not cause them to abandon. Segal observes that psychological research designed to prove the 'fact' that everyone 'knows' – namely that there are innate and incontravertible *differences* between the two sexes – has continued unabated, despite the fact that 'the main finding of some 80 years research has been the massive psychological *similarity* between the sexes in terms of individual attributes' (Segal 1990: 63). Freud's seduction theory is another case in point.

When Freud first started practising, he was visited by many 'hysterics', who displayed symptoms such as a nervous tic or cough, depression, or suicidal feelings. Many of these people claimed that, in childhood, they had been sexually abused by their father, or another close male relative or family friend. Freud initially thought that these traumatic childhood experiences lay at the root of the adult hysteria. In 1896, he gave a lecture on the aetiology of hysteria, in which he argued that hysteria was directly linked to this earlier sexual assault. But his observations and ideas were not well received by the scientific community. The medical establishment complained that he was uncritically regurgitating the 'fantasies and invented tales' and the 'paranoid drivel' of 'hysterical' women. His seduction theory was even rejected by people from whom he had expected support. People simply did not want to be told that sexual abuse was common amongst well off, well educated, respectable families. By 1897, Freud had abandoned his seduction theory. He now saw his former willingness to accept the word of his patients at face value as 'naïve' and no longer accepted that sexual abuse was occurring on the scale he had thought. Though he did not deny that sexual abuse *ever* happened, he now thought it was a rarity and that in general, his female patients were not telling him about real experiences of sexual molestation, only describing to him their unconscious wishes and desires. Nothing actually happened, but the girls longed for it to happen. They then came to see their longing as unacceptable and had to repress it, and it was this repression, not a real experience of abuse, which lay at the heart of their neurosis. In other words, Freud reinterpreted his observations in the light of what the scientific community, and he himself, already *knew* to be 'true', namely that bourgeois fathers do not molest their children and that women are manipulative liars (see Masson 1984).

And just as pre-existing values and beliefs affect researchers' observations, so they infuse the measuring instruments they design. Using the Minnesota Multiphasic Personality Inventory, for example, may help to ensure that two psychologists come up with the same measurement of a man's homosexual tendencies. But given that it takes a man saying that he likes cooking, does not believe in heaven and hell and enjoyed reading *Alice in Wonderland* as indications of homosexual proclivities, it can hardly be described as a 'neutral' or 'value-free' implement for assessing the personality (see Ruse 1988).

Some philosophers look at this close relationship between the concepts science employs and the facts it reveals and the concepts and facts that are already part of our everyday knowledge and argue that it is impossible for scientists to uncover external, objective truths. In its extreme form, philosophical relativism asserts that there is no reality existing 'out there' independently of human consciousness, only sets of culturally relative meanings and classifications that people attach to the world. The philosopher of science, Feyerabend, for example, regards Western science as just one cultural tradition among many; just one way of imposing order on an unknowable world. There is no objective reality, for reality can only be constructed by a conceptual system, and different cultures and societies employ different conceptual systems:

> Not everybody lives in the same world. The events that surround a forest ranger differ from the events that surround a city dweller lost in a wood. . . . The Greek gods were a living presence; 'they were there'. Today they are nowhere to be found.
>
> (Feyerabend, cited in Trigg 1989)

What relativists are concerned with is the fact that we cannot check the picture of reality created by science against reality itself, in the way we might compare a photograph of a person against the person herself to see if it is a good likeness, because the only way we grasp reality is by using this self-same scientific conceptual schema – 'There is no way that we can somehow hold our concepts in suspense, while we compare them with reality' (Trigg 1989: 1). Human beings, rather than observing passively or recording events neutrally, are selective in their seeing. What they choose to observe, how they see and classify and interpret it all depends crucially on their pre-existing beliefs about the world which come either from their theoretical perspective, or from the stock of cultural knowledge and beliefs which shape the perceptions of members of that culture. Some philosophers thus arrive at a view of common-sense, taken-for-granted knowledge as something like a prism through which members of any given culture see the world.

What this means for social science research methods depends on how far along the relativist road you travel. Some would argue that the task of the social researcher is to submerge him or herself absolutely in other cultures (or subcultures or even the subjective worldviews of other individuals), in order to learn that stock of everyday knowledge which informs social action. The object of research would be to try to reconstruct reality through the lens of these other 'common senses'. But to the extreme relativist, this approach is as flawed as the positivism which tries to ignore common sense. To make the experience of another culture intelligible, for example, it is necessary to translate what is said and done into a form which the Western anthropologist can grasp. In so doing, the researcher may well distort its meaning, and most problematic of all, he or she would never be able to find out whether or how this had happened. A male anthropologist researching the sex lives of the Dyak people of Borneo, for instance, might try to understand why men insert two inch long rods of bone into a transverse orifice in their penises before coitus through reference to Western ideas about heightening the woman's pleasure (see Ellis 1987: 526). But he could not check this translation with a Dyak man, because the Dyak man would then have to translate Western notions of 'coitus' and 'woman's pleasure' back into Dyak notions before being able to answer, and in translating, more distortion may occur, and so on. Relativism ultimately leads us to abandon any hope of intersubjective agreement across cultures, or subcultures, perhaps even between two people. We are all hermetically sealed in the prison of our own common sense and our everyday thinking is not so much a lens through which to view the world as a set of blinkers which can never be removed.

But the idea that there is no reality separate from the conceptual systems employed by people to grasp it accords quite ludicrous powers to human thought (Trigg 1989). A tree that falls in a forest falls regardless of whether a person is there to witness and conceptualise the event, children in Somalia die of starvation regardless of whether the governments of the Western world believe that they are providing adequate aid. Many people in Britain and the United States fondly imagine that they live in a meritocratic, post-racist, post-sexist society, but this does not mean that a working-class child or a Black child or a female child is truly blessed with the same chances of obtaining wealth and social power as the middle-class, white, male child. Of course one person's freedom fighter is another person's terrorist. And of course you can never know with absolute certainty that another person understands what you say in *exactly* the same way that you understand it. And of course language, concepts and beliefs affect our *perception* of social reality. But this does not mean that there really is no solid world out there separate from human beings' concepts and beliefs. In practice, as King Canute is purported to have discovered, the object world has a nasty habit of intruding no matter what people may believe about it.

It is possible to accept that neither natural nor social scientists ever rely purely on observation and that their observations are never completely detached from their pre-conceived beliefs and theories about the world without having to argue that empirical observations are therefore useless, or that they are invariably disregarded by scientists, or that science is merely the subjective process by which scientists go about confirming their own prejudices. It is essential to recognise that empirical observations are not the be all and end all of scientific research, and that a commitment to natural science methods and procedures does not offer the final, ultimate, reliable and objective way to obtain knowledge, without abandoning all belief in reality or all hope of advancing human knowledge. Let us recast the problem and the argument.

Because social scientists are members of society, as well as scientists, they have knowledge of their subject matter which comes not just from their scientific investigations, but also from their own experience and socialisation. Decisions about what to observe and how to classify observations are powerfully shaped by this other knowledge, this 'common-sense' understanding of the social world. Sexologists can, for instance, do their utmost to set aside their personal beliefs about whether or not enjoying being urinated upon is a disgusting and immoral pleasure, but they cannot somehow forget or eradiacte the taken-for-granted knowledge about their culture which tells them this is a 'perverse' and 'deviant' form of sexual gratification. The society they live in has already provided them with a classification system ('normal'/'abberant') and a research agenda ('Why do some people do these abberant things instead of being normal like us?'). Social scientists initially draw on their knowledge as members of society, rather than as scientists, to decide what warrants investigation and how to categorise it.

Indeed, the idea of conducting social research without any reference to this everyday, common-sense knowledge is nonsensical. Try to imagine a martian scientist visiting planet earth to conduct research into, say, madness. Without an understanding of our common-sense thinking, how would it decide who and what to observe and study? What absolute, external criteria could it use to define madness? Unhappiness? Then all those who have recently been bereaved or suffered some other tragedy would be classified insane, along with countless others who live lives of quiet despair brought about by poverty, injustice, racism, war, famine and disease. Cruelty and brutality are not the exclusive property of mad people, but are regularly practised in many of our most cherished institutions; auditory and visual hallucinations are not considered untoward in the feverish, the religious fanatic, the psychic or the drug user; no therapeutic intervention has been designed to 'cure' the grandiose self-importance of statesmen, prelates and pop stars, and our political leaders' mendacity and ability to simultaneously maintain wholly inconsistent and contradictory positions is not taken as an indication that they are deranged.

If the martian used its own definition of madness, taking flower arranging and the wearing of air-cushioned trainers to be the prime manifestation of insanity and making detailed studies of the aetiology of these behaviours, its research findings would read to us as gobbledegook, even if they were presented in the most exquisite English prose. 'Madness' (like sexual 'perversity' and educational 'underachievement' and maternal 'deprivation' and political 'extremism' and all the other phenomena investigated by social science) cannot be identified and meaningfully researched except through reference to existing ideas and beliefs about the social world. Now although, as has been seen, social (and natural) scientists have conducted research which does nothing more than elaborate and codify such taken-for-granted knowledge, masking the moral and political values implicit in it behind a veil of 'neutral' pseudo-scientific terminology, the fact that social scientists are formed and informed by their subject matter (society) does not *force* them to uncritically regurgitate existing beliefs.

In fact, recognising 'the reflexive character of social research: that is, [recognising] that we are part of the social world we study' (Hammersley and Atkinson 1989: 14) is the first step towards escaping from the philosophical impasse between positivism and relativism. When social scientists observe, interview, survey and otherwise collect data, they do not have to uncritically accept the picture of social reality that is revealed to or by them. It is possible for them to compare their findings with those of other researchers, it is possible for them to take their findings to different groups of people and ask them how the picture of reality produced by the research fits with their lived experience, it is possible for them to reflect on their own findings to ask themselves questions about the relationship between their own political and moral values and the research findings they have produced. Because social scientists are human beings, like their subject matter, they are able to enter into dialogue with the people they study. They are not hermetically sealed in their own scientific worldview, unable to communicate, unable to hear when people refute their findings and interpretations, unable to comprehend that other researchers adopt different theoretical perspectives. Because intersubjective dialogue can take place, it is possible for social scientists to be wrong, and, at least potentially, proven so. Some facts can be established, even if this involves conceding that these facts will look slightly different according to the theoretical categories employed in the research process.

But establishing facts is not the end of the social scientific project. It is only the beginning. They then have to be explained, and this can only be done at the theoretical level. Facts underdetermine theories in the social sciences (Lukes 1978). The same set of facts can be compatible with a number of different theories. To discover unequivocally that in contemporary societies there is an extremely unequal division of domestic labour, for example, does not of itself prove whether this unequal situation is functional to society or to capitalism or an effect of patriarchy. Facts can never be enough to prove the validity of a given social theory, and debates between social theories cannot therefore be conducted without reference to political interests and moral values.

In short, social researchers draw on their everyday knowledge and on their political and moral values in the process of research; they use them to set the research agenda and to design classification systems; they use their social, as well as professional, skills to obtain information; they employ their knowledge as members of society and their political values to analyse and interpret their findings. But accepting this inevitable and indissoluble link between scientific and everyday thinking and between social theories and moral and political values does not make critical investigation impossible. As Geerz (1973: 30) comments in relation to ethnographic and anthropological work:

> I have never been impressed by the argument that, as complete objectivity is impossible . . . one might as well let one's sentiments run loose. As Robert Solow has remarked, that is like saying that as a perfectly aseptic environment is impossible, one might as well conduct surgery in a sewer.

Research that is rigorous and reflexive produces knowledge that is more objective than research which is sloppy and uncritical. Researchers who, as well as being technically competent, consider the impact of their own gender, 'racialised' and class identity upon the research process and who understand that research is itself a form of social interaction will produce a more reliable picture of the social world. In short, there are better and worse ways of conducting research. That is what the rest of this book is about.

Chapter 2

Dimensions of social research

The previous chapter argued that although there is an inevitable and indissoluble link between scientific and everyday thinking and between social theories and moral and political values, critical investigation is not impossible. There are better and worse ways of conducting research and good research produces knowledge that is more objective and reliable than bad research. However, within the social scientific community, there is little agreement as to what precisely constitutes good research practice. In fact, there are actually two key traditions within social science which recommend very different approaches to research, and this makes the whole question of ensuring that social scientific research produces reliable, objective knowledge extremely problematic. This chapter sets out to address some of these problems. It is therefore concerned with debates about two basic issues; the question of how social scientific research is to be distinguished from other ways of knowing about the world, and questions about bias and validity.

TWO RESEARCH TRADITIONS

The previous chapter gave a broad and general definition of positivism as a philosophy which holds that the methods of the natural sciences produce the most reliable and objective knowledge. Positivism, like all schools of philosophical, political and theoretical thought, comes in a number of different forms, but it is possible to identify a positivist tradition within social science. This tradition is comprised of thinkers who, though often in disagreement over details, share a common belief that in order to produce objective knowledge, the methodological principles of the natural sciences should be applied to the study of the social world. In general, they hold that social scientists should concern themselves with uncovering an external reality, not the inner, subjective world of human subjects, and believe that 'there is a fundamental distinction to be made between fact and value, science dealing with the former while the latter [belongs] to an entirely different order of discourse beyond the remit of science' (Hughes 1990: 20). In the nineteenth century, first Comte and then Durkheim set out their ideas on how sociology, as a discipline, should achieve its status as a distinct science through the application of empiricist, scientific methods and the early twentieth century 'saw the flowering of positivist philosophy as the orthodox philosophy underpinning empirical science' (Hughes 1990: 35).

For positivists, social scientific knowledge was distinguished from other ways of knowing about the social world by its basis in rigorous, natural science methodology. What this meant in practice was that many social researchers borrowed the language of the natural sciences (neutral observation, control of variables, causal relationships, correlations and so on) to describe their activities, and exhibited a strong preference for quantitative, numerical data which could be subjected to statistical analysis and expressed in tables, equations and mathematical formulae. For some methodologists, the very term 'empirical' came to mean not simply something drawn from experience, but something drawn from a very specific kind of experience – that of observations and experiments structured along natural science lines. The chapter on data preparation and analysis in a 1969 textbook entitled *Introduction to Empirical Sociology* (Mayntz *et al.* 1969), for example, *only* tells the reader how to perform quantitative data analysis, and makes no mention of any kind of empirical evidence that cannot be readily translated into numerical form.

But alongside, and in marked contrast to this positivist tradition, another way of knowing and describing the social world has developed. This second tradition, which falls under the heading of 'interpretative sociology' also incorporates a diverse range of ideas and approaches, but as Giddens (1982: 23) puts it, 'all are concerned, in some sense or another, with problems of language and meaning in relation to the "interpretative understanding" of human action'. Interpretative sociologists reject the idea that external truths about the social world can be revealed by following the methods of the natural sciences. They point to a key difference between the subject matter of the natural and the social sciences. People, unlike things in the natural world, are conscious, purposive actors. We have ideas about the world we live in, we attach meaning to events, institutions and actions, and we act on the basis of these ideas and meanings. This means that patterns or regularities observed in the social world are of a very different order to those observed in the natural world. The social scientist can observe a pattern of behaviour, for example, the way in which females typically undertake domestic labour while their male partners, fathers and sons typically do not. But since women are not drawn to the kitchen sink by some irresistible, physical force (they are not *compelled* to conform to this social convention in the same way that they would be compelled to obey the law of gravity if they jumped from a cliff), social scientists cannot hope to formulate general laws on the basis of observing this pattern. Instead, they have to ask questions about the beliefs people hold and the meanings they attach to action. They have to concern themselves with the inner world of their subjects in order to understand why they act as they do.

This concern has implications for methods. It is clearly impossible to find out about a person's motivations and intentions simply by watching their outward behaviour – the ideas people have about the society they live in and the machinations of their inner world cannot be directly observed. What people do has to be *interpreted* in the light of the meanings, motives and intentions behind their action. Women's tendency to shoulder an unfair proportion of domestic tasks, for instance, can be interpreted through reference to beliefs about biologically based sex differences, their gender socialisation, the sense of powerlessness that derives from a lack of opportunity for economic independence, the desire to avoid conflict, and so on. But what method or technique can be used to achieve this interpretative understanding? It is here that the notion of *verstehen*, brought to prominence by the German sociologist Max Weber, is important.

Verstehen essentially involves the attempt to understand social action through a kind of empathetic identification with the social actor. The researcher must try to see the world through the eyes of the research subject in order to grasp the meanings, motives and intentions behind their action. The idea is that through rigorous study, the researcher can build up a picture of how the world appears to others and of the choices and constraints that they perceive. Since the past can also be reconstructed in this way through careful examination of documents, the method of *verstehen* can also be applied in historical research. When interpretative understanding is achieved, the meaning of a given form of social action becomes clear.

An emphasis on *verstehen* affects the social research process in a number of ways. To begin with, a concern with the inner, subject world of human beings implies that the focus of research must be upon the individual social actor, rather than upon collectives of people, since, as

Weber put it: 'Action, in the sense of a subjectively understandable orientation of behaviour, exists only as the behaviour of one or more *individual* human beings' (1966: 101). Second, it implies a far greater concern with the researcher as a subjective being. After all, it would be difficult for a convinced atheist, for example, to empathetically identify with the worldview of religious zealots in order to attain a full interpretative understanding of the meanings and intentions behind their devotional acts. Indeed, the whole notion of interpretative understanding across cultures (perhaps even across gender and class) takes us back to the problem of *translating* beliefs and ideas into a form which the researcher can grasp (mentioned in the previous chapter in relation to certain Dyak sexual practices). Finally, the method of *verstehen* necessarily produces empirical data of a very different type to that generated by positivist research techniques. Talking to people, observing their interactions, analysing the language they use and the documents they produce in order to achieve empathetic identification and interpretative understanding yields qualitative data and evidence. Such data do not usually lend themselves to enumeration, tabulation and statistical analysis.

It is important to note that whilst there are those who would argue that *verstehen* is and should be the central method and goal of social research, Weber certainly did not see it as the be all and end all of sociological research. Indeed, Weber saw interpretation as but one step on the way to producing reliable knowledge about the social world. The process of *verstehen* might produce a convincing explanation for a piece of behaviour, but that did not mean it had provided a causally *valid* explanation. It merely constituted a plausible hypothesis. For Weber:

> the appropriate way to verify such a hypothesis is to establish statistical laws based on observation of what happens. In this way he arrives at the conception of a sociological law as a statistical regularity which corresponds to an intelligible intended meaning.
>
> (Winch 1980: 113)

The aim of this section has been to show that two very different traditions or approaches to social research are recognised within sociology (and some other social science disciplines). Although there are methodologists who adhere to extremes of either positivist or interpretative philosophy, there are also a great many who fall somewhere in the middle of this philosophical and methodological continuum, borrowing ideas from either end, attempting, with various degrees of success, to steer a course between the two poles. This lack of unanimous consensus over the appropriate methods for acquiring knowledge is another distinctive feature of social science. For as Kuhn observes, there tends to be far greater consensus in the natural sciences. He uses the term 'paradigm' to refer to this kind of general agreement over methods and procedures. This terms suggests:

> that some accepted examples of actual scientific practice – examples which include law, theory, application and instrumentation together – provide models from which spring coherent traditions of scientific research. . . . Men [sic] whose research is based on shared paradigms are committed to the same rules and standards for scientific practice. That commitment and the apparent consensus it produces are prerequisites for normal science, i.e., for the genesis and continuation of a particular research tradition.
>
> (Kuhn 1970: 10–11)

Adherence to this set of rules and standards is held to ensure that natural scientific research produces valid and reliable knowledge (an idea which has been severely criticised, most notably by Kuhn). Despite the lack of a single, clearly defined research paradigm, the social scientific community likewise attempts to apply a set of rules and standards to research in order to filter out biased or shoddy work. The idea is that even though social scientific knowledge cannot be distinguished from other forms of knowledge by its application of a single, unified research paradigm, the systematic application of these general rules and standards makes it a more reliable form of knowledge than, say, that produced by journalists or lay people. The following section looks at the relationship between methodology and the research community, asking whether the research community does or could help to reduce bias and increase the validity of research findings.

METHODOLOGY AND THE RESEARCH COMMUNITY

Chapter 1 argued that social research should begin from the premise that there is a world separate from our concepts and beliefs, despite the fact that researchers have preconceived ideas, values and beliefs which affect their view of the world. It suggested that it is possible to negotiate a course between the positivist view of social science as producing pure, objective knowledge unsullied by common sense and the relativist view of social scientists as permanently locked into a narrow vision of the world, determined completely by their prior common-sense or theoretical assumptions.

The relationship between methodology and the research community has been identified by some philosophers of science, in particular Popper (1963), as the best guarantor of reliable, unbiased scientific knowledge. As academic researchers know (though this may not be so apparent to students and some other consumers of social research), there is a kind of 'community' which operates behind the scenes, and exerts a great deal of control over what kind of research gets done and what kind of research gets published. Obtaining funding for a research project entails drawing up a detailed research proposal which is then closely examined either by colleagues in the same or another university or by members of a funding body (such as the Economic and Social Research Council), people who usually have been, or are involved in academic research. Articles and research reports that are sent to journals for publication will generally be sent out to two or three 'referees' (academics working in the same field) for approval, as well as being read by the editor and members of the editorial board. Even books are scrutinised by other researchers. Academic publishers send drafts out to readers for comment and criticism. Once published, and if the researcher is fortunate, research receives yet more critical, public appraisal from the research community in the form of reviews, comment and criticism – even praise if the researcher is more fortunate still. This kind of detailed, critical scrutiny certainly has an impact on methodology, though, as we argue below, it does not necessarily eliminate or even reduce all types of bias.

The methodological domain

It might be assumed that the term 'methodology' refers simply to the *techniques* employed to gather data and evidence in social research (surveys, interviews, observation, ethnography, textual analysis and so on). But in practice, these techniques should not be considered separately from the wider context of the community of researchers (and social scientists in general) who use them, and the methodological rules and procedures that govern their use. Take the survey, for example. We could describe it as a series of techniques that are used to acquire a comprehensive or general view of some social phenomenon, but when social researchers use these techniques, they use them in accordance with a set of methodological rules and procedures which are recognised as appropriate and reliable by the scientific community. There is a difference between, say, a teacher saying to a class of children, 'Let's do a bit of a survey, who here has any sort of a paid job?' or even asking them to fill out some kind of questionnaire, and a social researcher undertaking a survey into the extent and nature of child labour in a particular country or region. In order to obtain funding and to have his or her work recognised by the research community and published in an academic journal or book, the social researcher must follow certain rules and procedures, about, among other things, picking a sample, formulating questions, coding and analysing the data and so on. These rules and procedures, as well as particular research techniques and the findings of social scientific research, are the subject of public scrutiny and debate amongst the research community.

These three elements – the techniques, the research community and the methodological rules – together constitute a methodological *domain* through which all research must pass in order for it to achieve certain standards of integrity and validity. It acts as a mediator between the researcher's subjective beliefs and opinions and the data and evidence that he or she produces through research. If this domain is functioning properly, it acts as something like a filter which prevents bad research from passing through. It does not guarantee that research will produce universal or final truths or claims that cannot be changed in the light of further evidence or argument, but it does provide markers which allow us to make judgements about which research is better or more valid given the present state of knowledge on a particular topic or area.

However, it is important to stress that this methodological domain can only act as a safety net or filter out inferior research *if it is functioning properly*, and there are many things which can prevent this. Sometimes, standards are inadvertently breached. At other times, deliberate deception may take place, through the manipulation of results or even the outright fabrication of data. The eminent British educational psychologist, Sir Cyril Burt, for example, is now known to have invented not only much of his data, but also a number of co-authors for articles that he published in learned journals. There are also shades in between, where it is difficult to judge whether deception was intentional or inadvertent. Moreover, much of this methodological domain rests upon a consensus amongst the research community on appropriate standards and procedures, which is arrived at freely and through rational, public debate. These standards and procedures have the status of 'recommendations' by the research community. Unlike medical practitioners, social researchers cannot be 'struck off' some professional register or prevented from undertaking future research if they break such codes, although they may face difficulties obtaining funding, getting their work published or getting other posts if their work is thoroughly discredited.

Essentially though, researchers are required to exercise discretion over issues of judgement, effectively 'policing' themselves – guidelines are not, and cannot be, enforced on those researchers who do not happen to agree with them.

Indeed, some researchers believe that the consensus over standards, rules and procedures arrived at within the research community is itself invalid because it merely represents or reflects the interests of a particular group. Certain feminist writers believe that methods (and theories) in social analysis are saturated with male bias to the extent that they lack all credibility as a means of acquiring knowledge of women's lives and social position. Postmodernists have recently argued that all attempts at objectivity are inevitably flawed and they reject research claims which place the 'authority' of a 'scientific' observer or a research community above the local knowledge of research subjects (see Denzin 1990, Rosenau 1992). There are critical theorists who reject the research community's consensus as a bourgeois consensus, and hold that the only legitimate research is that which is geared towards the goal of emancipating oppressed groups. The research community also stands accused of white, eurocentric bias – as Asante (1990: 24) puts it, 'what often passes for objectivity is a sort of collective European subjectivity'.

Researchers are free to reject either the whole notion of a methodological domain and the standards which it reflects, or to selectively ignore those parts of it which are not congenial to their own purposes, and some do indeed attempt to side-step the influence of this domain. Stanley and Wise (1993), for example, argue that feminist researchers can and should reject the orthodox research community's standards of objectivity; 'We echo Adrienne Rich in insisting that 'objectivity' is the term that men have given to their own subjectivity' (1993: 59). Obviously, if some researchers or groups of researchers side-step this methodological domain, insisting on their right to develop an independent set of standards and procedures and separate criteria for assessing research, then that domain cannot be held accountable for standards of research across the board. Although we are sympathetic to much of the feminist, Black and radical *critique* of the orthodox social scientific community and its canons of research, we strongly oppose the idea of such separate methodological domains. If social science were to fragment into a number of intellectually isolated segments (feminist social science, Black social science, radical social science, orthodox social science and so on) each producing its own research and knowledge according to its own rules and standards, how could we hope to judge between the very different pictures of reality they would undoubtedly produce?

While recognising that the existing methodological domain does not always function properly, we believe that the only way it can ever consistently and effectively serve to maintain standards of research across the board is if *all* researchers (feminist, Africentric, post-modernist and critical researchers included) are fully involved in the dialogue about its rules, standards and procedures. A key problem here, of course, is that the social composition of the research community is ludicrously skewed towards white males. Kulis *et al.* (1986) found that in the USA in 1984, for example, only 5.7 per cent of the staff of all sociology faculties were Black academics. Furthermore, the research community does not welcome all contributions to the debate about methodology with equal enthusiasm. White and male researchers are over-represented in the upper echelons of the research community. To illustrate the point, though real efforts have been made in journals like *Sociology*, at the time of writing, over 90 per cent of the editorial board of a number of academic journals are white and male, and some even boast an exclusively male editorial board. Without wishing to deny the immensity of the political struggle it will take to change this situation, we would still argue that critics should devote their energies towards improving the existing methodological domain, rather than promoting a series of alter- native domains.

Methodological rules and procedures

It was noted above that, when functioning properly, the methodological domain (consisting of research techniques, the research community and its methodological rules and procedures) acts as a mediator between the social scientist's prior beliefs and assumptions on the one hand, and the evidence and data she or he produces on the other. Clearly, social analysis is, by its very nature, influenced by a number of opinions and assumptions that we, as researchers, bring with us to the research situation. Everyday, common-sense thinking as well as politics and values can affect the choice of topic and the way in which data is interpreted. Similarly, all observations are, to some extent, theory-laden – we have prior notions about the sort of explanation we are looking for – and shaped by the ultimate objectives of the research. If researchers begin with the assumption that homosexuality is a disease or a social problem, for example, they will produce different data and evidence to that produced by researchers who assume that it is merely a sexual preference. As Chapter 1 showed, such beliefs, preconceptions and moral and political values can potentially infiltrate the research process and bias or distort the findings. This is where the research community and methodological procedures enter the picture.

In order for research to be accredited by the community of scholars or other researchers (and this is a prerequisite for publication), it must be written and presented in a way which leaves it open to the critical scrutiny of others. Once published, it is open to an even wider audience for appraisal. This means that the methods used in the research and the sample of people or documents observed and consulted must be carefully described, and any deviations from standard practice must be noted. A study of homosexual masculinity, for example, must recognise that there is subcultural diversity among gay men when choosing participants for a study (Weeks 1986, Connell 1992). Some men who have sex with men enter, and define themselves as part of, a gay community. Others do not. The differences between 'straight' gays, 'leathermen' and 'drag queens' would likewise be important factors to be taken into account when selecting people for interviews. If the research report failed to describe the particular subculture or subcultures from which the sample was drawn, other scholars and researchers would be unable to assess whether or not its findings and conclusions were generalisable to the gay population as a whole, or valid only in relation to a very small subset of that population.

Researchers must also carefully define the events and activities that they analyse and do so in such a way that their work can be challenged by evidence and arguments provided by other researchers. For instance, in their study of racism among school children in predominantly white schools, Troyna and Hatcher (1992) distinguish between 'racist incidents' which are 'legitimated by and expressive of racism' (such as racist abuse) and 'racial' or 'inter-racial' incidents which involve conflicts between individuals or groups perceived to be 'racially' different. Such a distinction is pivotal to understanding the incidence and influence of racism in children's lives and to explaining why its prevalence has often been underestimated. But these kinds of key concepts and variables in a study must be defined rigorously, as they are in Troyna and Hatcher's study, so that other researchers can critically scrutinise them in relation to the findings in order to challenge or confirm them.

Because research funding bodies and the referees that act for academic journals and publishers encourage researchers to provide at least some details of their sample, variables, methods and techniques of data gathering and analysis, the bulk of social research is routinely (if sometimes superficially) monitored, and this helps to reduce the incidence of bad research slipping through into the published, public world. In this way, methodological rules and standards of procedure provide a common language and set of criteria for the evaluation of the conduct and findings of research and act as a filter for work that is, particularly in a technical sense, blatantly shoddy and ill-conceived. The methodological domain cannot, however, eliminate the impact of common-sense, political and/or theoretical assumptions on the choice of research topic. Moreover, the composition of the research community in terms of gender, class origin, 'racialised' identity and political allegiance has an effect on *which* types of bias get filtered out. It is quite possible for the research community to insist on, say, experimental laboratory research which is technically excellent in terms of controlling the bias that arises from certain theoretical preconceptions without noticing or bothering about the bias that comes from the fact that such research relies on a sample which is almost exclusively white and male.

The brief history of sex research provided in Chapter 1 testifies to the fact that research communities can remain oblivious to some forms of bias (in this case sexism) for long periods of time. Black feminist methodologists also show very clearly how and why the methodological domain, both historically and contemporaneously, fails to function as the guarantor of accurate, valid and generalisable research. Hill Collins observes that 'Afro-American female scholars are repeatedly struck by their own invisibility, both as full human subjects included in sociological facts and observations, and as practitioners in the discipline itself' (1991: 51). Sociological research and the concepts and theories it generates has been, and still often is, subjected to only a very partial form of critical scrutiny, then. Current interpretation of even key sociological concepts, such as 'work' and 'family', are revealed by Black feminist thought to be less than fully comprehensive:

> For example, labor theories that relegate Afro-American women's work experiences to the fringe of analysis miss the critical theme of the interlocking nature of Black women as female workers . . . and Black women as racially-oppressed workers. . . . Examining the extreme case offered by Afro-American women's unpaid and paid work experiences raises questions about the adequacy of generalizations about work itself.
>
> (Hill Collins 1991: 52)

Again, however, an awareness of the existing methodological domain's weaknesses and limitations should not lead us to condemn it as utterly worthless, or abandon a commitment to improving it. Because this domain allows researchers (not just academic researchers but also those who work for governments and other agencies) to subject their own research to the critical appraisal of the wider community of researchers, it does provide some kind of safeguard against bias and malpractice. Without it, there would be no hope of ever discovering and discrediting fraudulent research, no way of distinguishing between sloppy, self-serving studies and rigorous, well researched ones, no arena within which to discuss and challenge the sexism and racism implicit in much of this century's social research. To dismiss the methodological domain's actual and potential contribution to increasing the validity (the truthfulness and soundness) of research because of its imperfections is to throw the baby out with the bathwater. Rather than do this, critics need to unite and fight to expose and remedy those imperfections.

Since the research community itself plays a central role in defining the rules and procedures which govern research, and in ensuring that these are properly applied and adhered to, it should be a key focus of critical attention. Hammersley (1990: 62–3) argues that in order to maintain its authority and legitimacy as an arbiter of the validity of research, this community must do three things. First, it should assess all findings in terms of common agreements about validity and seek to resolve disputes in terms of these shared criteria. Second, researchers should be willing to change their views if the communal assessment has found them to be false, and third, anyone should be allowed to participate in the community, providing that they are willing to operate on the basis of the first two points. This formulation is fine, so far as it goes, but it is important to add a couple of points. To begin with, we should reiterate that the social identity of the members of this research community matters. So long as it remains predominantly white and male then its legitimacy will remain suspect, even if these men are reflexive and critical and committed to anti-sexist, anti-racist research. Furthermore, even if all of Hammersley's requirements and this last one were satisfied, the methodological domain would still remain a somewhat imperfect filter. This is because the research community does not and could not consistently enforce its rules, but relies on researchers not only to conform to them voluntarily but also to offer information about whether or not they have conformed. Given that a great many researchers do not provide very detailed accounts of their methodology, it is difficult for the research community to subject *all* research to an intensive validity check. (It is also worth noting that many members of the research community are not terribly well versed on what exactly the 'common agreements about validity' are. Researchers are not always methodologists and vice versa.)

If the existing methodological domain does not *guarantee* that all knowledge produced by social scientific research methods is sharply differentiated from common-sense thinking and prejudice, how can social research be distinguished from other ways of knowing about the world and how can researchers attempt to reduce bias? The following sections address these questions.

THE RESEARCH PROCESS: THEORY AND EVIDENCE

Lewins (1992) suggests that the central characteristic of sociology and social research is its attempt 'to provide an explanation which is based on the systematic use of evidence' (1992: 5). This distinguishes it from other types of knowledge and statements, for instance those based on prejudice or religious dogma, which either wholly lack systematic evidence to support them, or use evidence in a highly selective and self-serving way. The sociological research process is also one which connects the gathering of empirical evidence on a social phenomenon (say, crime, suicide, classroom behaviour) with the attempt to formulate theories which explain how and why they occur. Though this emphasis on theory does not guarantee that social scientific research is unbiased and value free, it does distinguish it from journalistic and other forms of investigation and evidence gathering. It is therefore worth examining the role of theory in social research more closely.

The range of theory–evidence linkages

Theories are forms of explanation. They give us some indication of the *nature* of a particular phenomenon (different sorts of crime or sexual activity, for example) and *why* it occurs. Theories are therefore explanations which indicate the sorts of conditions under which particular activities, events or forms of behaviour are likely to occur. As noted above, there is a connection between the gathering of evidence and data in the sociological research process and the attempt to formulate, develop, support or discredit theoretical explanations. But in practice, the relationship between theory and evidence in the research process varies a great deal.

The first thing to notice is that theories come in many shapes and sizes. They vary in terms of their level of abstraction and their scope and relevance. There are theories which are often referred to as 'general theories', which either attempt to explain large-scale and general features of society or offer fairly abstract explanations of recurrent and general features of social life, such as the nature of social activity or how social institutions are reproduced over time (Parsons 1951, Giddens 1984). The connection between these general theories and particular pieces of social research is often difficult to pin down, although they may form part of the broad framework of ideas which play a role in determining a given researcher's research agenda. Sometimes, however, researchers use different aspects of these theories to guide their research or to explain their research findings. Take Marxist theory, for example. A researcher would be hard pressed to set about systematically gathering evidence to demonstrate conclusively that the sum total of people's relations of production constitute 'the economic structure of society, the real foundation, upon which rises a legal and political superstructure and to which correspond definite forms of social consciousness' (Marx 1980: 181), even though this notion of a powerful relationship between economic base and legal and political superstructure might inform their choice of research topic and the way in which they interpret their findings. However, other aspects of Marxist theory do invite empirical investigation. Marx's writings on the capitalist labour process, for instance, have prompted numerous empirical studies of deskilling, managerial control and worker resistance (see Thompson 1983 for an excellent review of such studies).

More frequently in social research, theory refers to a rather narrower range of phenomena, for example, the relationship between two social variables, such as occupational group and suicide rate, or gender and mental health. In these examples, it is the exact relationship between the two variables that forms the substance of the theoretical explanation – why do some occupations have higher suicide rates, or why are women more likely to be classified as mentally ill? Social research often restricts itself to these narrower sorts of problems because it is generally easier to gather empirical evidence about topics of more limited scope and to be clear about what sort of evidence would disprove or falsify certain types of explanations (Popper 1963). Robert Merton (1967) called these 'theories of the middle range' because they lie between the minor working 'hunches' or 'insights' that characterise the beginning phases of research (and which abound in everyday life) and grander, more general theories. Merton also felt that because such theories could be more firmly anchored in empirical evidence, they were therefore less 'speculative' than theories which attempt to explain general and large-scale phenomena. His ideas have profoundly influenced the conduct of sociological research and their imprint is indelibly stamped on contemporary research (particularly of the theory-testing variety).

It is important to note, however, that while much social research is explicitly attached to the idea of theoretical explanation, there are some researchers (usually those who are committed to forms of observation that rely on close involvement with members of various social groups) who would deny that their interests are theoretical at all (Becker cited in Rock 1979). They see the purpose of research as *describing* the subjective worlds of particular groups and often feel that a preoccupation with abstract theoretical and 'scientific' concepts prevents researchers from fully grasping the lived experience of their research subjects (this view has much in common with postmodern methodology). Take drug use, for example. Many researchers have set out to study this phenomenon armed with theoretical concepts such as 'psychopathology', 'anomie', 'undersocialisation' and so on. But these 'scientific' concepts bear little relation to the meanings which the individuals being researched attach to their own behaviour. Marijuana smokers, for instance, do not typically explain their behaviour by saying 'What with being undersocialised and feeling pretty anomic, I just started on the weed.' Some researchers therefore argue that the application of abstract, theoretical concepts is actually a barrier to finding out about what people do and why they do it. They hold that an atheoretical approach, which focuses on the immediate, practical circumstances of people's lives and experiences, is more likely to yield an accurate description of the social world.

While there is room for this kind of research (and anyway, most research depends at some level on accurate descriptions), we see no reason to limit research in this way. Theory does not necessarily distort findings or act as a barrier to grasping the essence of people's lived experience and an *exclusively* descriptive approach cannot, by definition, provide any explanation of social phenomena. It is, however, entirely legitimate to gather new information and descriptive data which can, at some later date, be used as the empirical basis for theory construction or testing. This kind of approach is well illustrated by McKeganey *et al.*'s (1990) study of female street-working prostitutes and male rent boys in Glasgow in relation to risks of HIV infection and the practice of safer sex. The study simply aimed to fill gaps in knowledge about risk-taking practices. Indeed, there are many studies with a social policy orientation which content themselves, and rightly so, with providing information directly related to policy implications and intervention strategies (for example, the extent of needle sharing among intravenous drug users).

With the exception of these types of descriptive research, however, social research is essentially an attempt to relate a body of evidence to a set of theoretical assumptions. As will be seen below, an instructive way to view this relationship is to make a distinction between theory-testing and theory-constructing types of research (Rose 1982, Lewins 1992, Layder 1993), but to simultaneously recognise that though some examples of research clearly conform to one or the other of these types, a considerable number of studies fall somewhere between the two.

Theory-testing and theory-constructing research

In general, theory-testing research begins with a fairly well worked out set of theoretical assumptions, such as 'suicide rates vary with the degree to which people feel themselves to be integrated with their community' or 'women are more likely to be diagnosed as mentally ill than men presenting the same symptoms'. If these assumptions have not already been tested by confrontation with empirical evidence, then they constitute a hypothesis whose validity needs to be checked in relation to such evidence. If these assumptions have already been partly confirmed by previous empirical research, they can be further supported by similar research. Alternatively, assumptions can be further endorsed or else queried by research which checks whether they hold good with different groups or in different situations. Either way, the point of gathering empirical evidence here is to buttress, disconfirm or modify the initial assumptions or hypothesis. In short, as Glaser and Strauss (1967) have noted, this type of research has the *verification* of a prior set of assumptions (a theory or hypothesis) as its overriding goal.

Where verification is the goal of research, the researcher is confronted by a particular set of methodological issues. To gather data which will test out theoretical assumptions it is necessary to:

- Choose a sample (of people, activities, events, documents) to study. To reduce the risk of bias, this has to be *representative* of the wider social group or location or events under consideration;
- Choose a method or technique of investigation and data gathering (surveys, interviews, observation, interpretation of documents or statistics);
- Decide on and specify the main concepts, categories or variables to be examined.

Having decided on these, the researcher proceeds to collect empirical data. This is the fieldwork phase of the research. During this phase, other decisions have to be made about how to organise and store the data and what form the data should take. Many researchers who favour the theory-testing model of research also tend to prefer quantitative data. These researchers often feel that when the information gathered can be counted in some way (40 out of 100 teenagers interviewed regularly smoked marijuana) and so summarised in a numerical fashion, their results are more precise, scientific and authoritative. This stems from the positivist tradition which equates natural science methods with 'objectivity', as though being able to say that '40 per cent of the sample were drug users' makes us more sure of the validity of the findings. Not all theory-testing research is characterised by this passion for numerical data – some makes use of qualitative data and evidence, such as quotations from interviews, field notes or documents – but there are a significant number of researchers who feel that 'evidence is not evidence unless it can be quantified' (Lewins 1992: 42).

Once the data have been gathered, the researcher moves on to analyse them in relation to the initial assumptions. Are they straightforwardly confirmed by the findings? If so, no further modification of the theory or hypothesis is required for the time being. If the assumptions prove false in the light of the evidence, they may be abandoned altogether, providing that the scientific community feels certain that the research was properly conducted and without errors. But the results may also be inconclusive, providing neither enough evidence to support or deny the assumptions, or revealing something quite unexpected. Any of these outcomes will lead to the accumulation of theory and research in the particular area or topic in question. This applies even when assumptions are disconfirmed, since this will allow researchers to discount them in future research.

In contrast to the theory-testing approach, there are researchers who have theory clearly in mind in the long run, but who suggest that fieldwork is undertaken with little in the way of preconceived theoretical ideas (Glaser and Strauss 1967, Strauss and Corbin 1990). This is referred to as the theory-constructing (or generating) approach. It is, as we have already noted, neither possible nor necessary for researchers to divest themselves of all preconceptions. However, the researcher who takes the theory-generating approach does not decide in advance what kinds of evidence and explanations she or he will come up with. Instead, the theory emerges directly from the evidence gathered during the research, and this ensures a closer fit between the two. According to Glaser and Strauss, this is preferable to theory-testing research, which seeks primarily to verify existing theory, and hence tends to seek only specific and particular kinds of evidence. The aim of verification or disconfirmation leads to a narrow focus for theory and ultimately blocks its development.

Glaser and Strauss's case against theory-testing research is perhaps over-stated. We believe that there is some room for the development and accumulation of theory through theory-testing research and that the difference between the two types of research is one of emphasis. Most research actually involves elements of both testing and construction, and the point of distinguishing between the two types is not to advocate the use of one rather than the other, but to allow a better understanding of the scope and objectives of particular pieces of research which, in turn, facilitates critical evaluation. It is important to stress, however, that the theory-constructing approach is directed more towards the development of new theory than toward the evaluation of existing bodies of knowledge.

The idea of theory-constructing research is to begin to gather data and empirical evidence on a particular area (say nursing care, or sado-masochistic sexual activities, or drug use) by observing and talking to those people who are involved in such practices or activities. Initially, very general questions will drive the researcher: What is going on? Who is involved? What problems do they face? How do these people relate to each other? As data and evidence are gathered and the researcher becomes more familiar with the practices of the group, he or she will begin to refine or alter these questions. Ideas which begin to explain the behaviour of those being studied will start to emerge.

Unlike the theory-testing approach, then, the theory-constructing approach begins by collecting and analysing data and attempts to generate explanations from these. But despite this difference, theory-constructing research must still grapple with those methodological issues that confront the theory-testing researcher. A sample of people, events, documents and so on, has to be selected and must be representative of the group being studied. A method or technique for gathering data has to be chosen (observation, interviews, documentary analysis and so forth). Finally, the main analytic categories and concepts need to be identified and related to the empirical materials. However, though these elements are similar to those involved in theory-testing research in the formal sense, there are a number of differences in application and emphasis. To start with, it may not be possible or desirable to decide on the exact size and characteristics of the sample in advance of the research. The 'emergent' nature means that priorities may change as the research unfolds and the researcher begins to generate theory. Sampling must therefore be kept as flexible as possible to take account of the changing priorities of the research.

Second, because the aim of such research is to discover evidence and theory rather than to tinker with already established knowledge, it is often necessary to use methods and techniques of data gathering which do not presuppose too much about the area in question. A survey questionnaire or interview schedule, for example, can only be constructed if the researcher already knows enough about the relevant issues to be able to decide in advance which questions to ask. Theory-constructing research therefore employs more open-ended methods, such as various forms of involved observation or in-depth interviews, techniques which do not impose a set of issues and priorities in advance of the research. In short, there is a preference for qualitative data such as quotations from interviews or field notes which convey a sense of how research subjects experience, perceive and respond to their social worlds. Again, it is important to recognise that this is not a hard and fast rule. Although there are purists who would insist on qualitative data (just as there are those who appear to believe that only quantitative data is scientifically respectable), many researchers use combinations of the two.

The same considerations apply to the main categories and concepts used in the research. Where the emphasis is on theory-construction, there is a tendency to hold off deciding on what is relevant until the researcher has had time to really assess the evidence. Obviously, it is important to do this as soon as possible, otherwise analysis of the data would be so confusing as to be almost impossible, but again, the main point is to allow categories and concepts to *emerge* from the evidence itself. In theory-constructing research the fieldwork phase of research thus often merges with, and proceeds alongside, the process of sampling and of assessing the analytic categories, concepts and variables. As more and more evidence is gathered the researcher becomes clearer about the sort of sample that is needed and more able to identify the key analytic categories.

At this point, the distinction between theory-testing and theory-constructing begins to blur. An emerging theory needs to be continually tested against the evidence as the research unfolds. This is obviously a different process from that involved in starting research with a preconceived theory, but it is a form of theory-testing none the less. In other words, almost all research will involve elements of both theory-testing and theory-construction, and a good deal of excellent social research therefore falls somewhere between these two pure models of the research process. However, by examining the elements of these two models in their purest form, it is possible to discern their influence in particular pieces of research that are based on different combinations of them. Quantitative and qualitative methods, for example, are frequently used together in research but combined in different ways and to different ends. Also, different elements of sampling and mixtures of data gathering techniques (methods) can be variously related to both theory-testing and theory-constructing. This section concludes with a few examples of these 'mixed' types.

Goffman's (1961) classic study of a mental hospital and the inmates' culture demonstrates how research can both construct and 'test' a theory at the same time. Goffman was attempting to illustrate the usefulness of the concept of the 'total institution' by presenting evidence on the lives of inmates in mental asylums. Manning (1992) points out that Goffman's main priority was to develop a set of ideas around this concept which could be applied to the experiences of *any* group of people (not just mental patients) whose lives are closely controlled by the constant monitoring of time and space (for example, those in monasteries, military establishments, religious cults and so on). As a result, Goffman's analysis switches between his own observations and analyses of the hospital and the findings of other researchers in other settings.

Despite the fact that subsequent researchers have found Goffman's formulations a little vague (see Manning 1992: 114–15), his study helped to clarify the characteristics of total institutions. In this sense, his work can be understood as testing out the usefulness of a theoretical concept. But in another sense, Goffman's study can be viewed as a theory-constructing enterprise. His observations of some of the behaviour of inmates, such as fantasising, hunger strikes, dirty protests and so on, led him to develop ideas about how people typically deal with the pressures of living within a total institution. Goffman presents an analysis of different types of 'adaptation strategies' used by the patients to cope with stress and the ways of 'playing the system' which were adopted in order to sustain a sense of their own identities. In so doing, Goffman is clearly constructing a theory (concepts and forms of explanation) from his own observations and conversations conducted in the hospital.

In a very different study, Hochschild (1983) also combines different elements and approaches. Her central concern was with the 'emotional labour' provided by women in a number of different jobs. Her research on flight attendants, for example, showed how economic competition between airlines led companies to seek ways of extracting more and more emotional labour from women employees, and thus highlighted an extremely subtle and complex form of exploitation. The research made use of both quantitative and qualitative data and used a number of different samples (of students in her own survey, of census statistics, of company documents, of flight attendants, trainers and company officials), as well as a number of techniques of data gathering (participant observation, interviews, interpretation of documents). Although she began with the concept of 'emotional labour' as a theoretical guide, her research qualified, amended and extended its application to a number of different areas (such as emotional burn-out produced by the constant management of emotional displays). Furthermore, Hochschild weaves back and forth between the micro level (smiling at and dealing with passengers) and the macro level (economic competition between airlines, company control over employees) in her analysis. She thus draws upon a range of theoretical resources to explain and interpret her findings and her study serves to emphasise the fact that some of the most productive and illuminating research combines elements of both theory-testing and theory-construction. It is the innovative mixture of styles in relation to the particular problems studied and particular research objectives that produces robust explanations, firmly anchored in empirical evidence.

TOWARDS BETTER RESEARCH AND RESEARCH PRACTICE

So far, we have discussed the relationship between social research and the research community, and that between theory and evidence. This section briefly considers some of the issues which seem to us to be central both to doing better research and evaluating the research of others. Since the goal of research is to produce valid knowledge about the social world and as reliable a picture of social reality as possible, the issue of bias is clearly critical to any discussion of methods. Some methodologists tend to think of this as an essentially technical issue. Positivist textbooks on survey design, for example, provide readers with guidelines on how to avoid bias from sampling techniques, interviewers and question wording. The implication is that, providing the correct measuring instruments are used in the proper fashion, undistorted truths will be produced. Others imagine that scrutiny by the academic research community somehow guarantees good practice and objectivity. But there are methodologists who see bias in less simplistic terms. Central to the feminist critique of orthodox social science methods, for example, is the idea that social scientific research has a strong and general masculine bias and therefore produces a specifically male view of social reality. It is not simply that sociologists have picked unrepresentative samples or asked loaded questions – this kind of bias is not reducible to technical issues. Feminists point out that the concepts most researchers have started out with reflect men's and not women's experience. The concept of 'work', for instance, has typically been used to refer to 'paid work' and has excluded women's domestic labour. Even within the sociology of work, it is *men's* paid work that has received most research attention. There are innumerable studies of heavy manufacturing industries but very few of retailing or clerical work where more women are employed. Since there is a powerful link between empirical evidence and theory, the fact that empirical data has typically consisted of evidence about men means that theories generated from it often explain men's rather than women's experience.

Some feminist methodologists take this critique further, arguing that the very methods and techniques employed in orthodox social research are imbued with masculine values to such a degree that they can only produce male-biased knowledge. As will be seen in later chapters, they hold that the controlling and hierarchical style adopted by positivist researchers is a peculiarly masculine approach. There are even those who claim that the application of theoretical concepts to material gathered in the course of research is an example of male 'conceptual imperialism', since 'theoretical language' is not based upon and does not reflect women's experience (see Stanley and Wise 1993). The critique of orthodox social science as androcentric (centred on men's experience and world views) leads a number of feminist writers to make the case for a specifically feminist methodology. There is, as yet, little agreement on what precisely such a methodology would consist of, but such writers tend to emphasise the importance of non-exploitative, non-hierarchical approaches to research subjects (Oakley 1981, Rama-zanoglu 1992, Stanley and Wise 1993), to argue that emotion as well as reason can, does and should play a role in acquiring knowledge (Jaggar 1989), and to see the *description* of women's experiences as offering insights into the social world that are of equal value to those obtained through more rigorous methodological analysis.

We discuss the value and limitations of feminist methodologies in more detail in later chapters, but for the moment it is important to note that some feminist methodologists have themselves been faced with charges of bias. Hill Collins identifies a problem with much of the literature in the area by noting that 'when white feminists produce generalizations about "women", Black feminists routinely ask "which women do you mean?"' (1991: 51), while Narayan observes that 'some of the themes of feminist epistemology are problematic for nonwestern feminists in ways that they are not problematic for western feminists' (1989: 258). Feminist research does not necessarily or automatically produce a rounder and more accurate picture of social reality. White eurocentric bias can be, and often is, a feature of feminist research as well as of orthodox, masculinist social research, and for the same kinds of reason. Though there are notable exceptions (for example in the work of Phizacklea 1983 and Segal 1990), white feminist researchers often begin with an agenda that is informed by their experience of and concern with just one kind of oppression (gender) and may not be particularly attuned to other forms of oppression ('racialisation' or class). These preoccupations then impact on the methods they employ and the evidence that is produced. Cannon *et al.* (1991) observe that feminist research often relies heavily on qualitative methods, employing volunteer and other non-random sampling techniques. But samples drawn in this way tend to over-represent middle-class white women, and as a result 'although qualitative research on women has accumulated useful data in many substantive areas, too often the emergent body of knowledge excludes women of color and working-class women' (1991: 107).

The problem that is being addressed here is that which was emphasised in Chapter 1, namely, social researchers are members of society as well as scientists. They are formed and informed by the very thing which they study. As members of society, they come to their research with a particular social identity (which is gendered, 'racialised' and affected by social class), a particular set of moral and political values, and a particular set of theoretical preconceptions or preoccupations. These inevitably exert an influence on the questions they ask, the methods they employ and the way in which they analyse the data they produce. But this does not mean that social researchers are necessarily or inevitably *blind* to any picture of social reality other than that which mirrors their own preconceived vision. As human beings, they are capable of recognising and understanding not only that different conceptual categories and meanings can be attached to the same things (that one person's freedom fighter is another person's terrorist, for instance) but also that they themselves view the world through a particular lens. Our position is that these human qualities of empathy, reason and self-consciousness can and should be used in the research process, and that when they are used properly, better research which produces a more accurate picture of social reality will result. We therefore recommend that *all* researchers take a *reflexive* approach to their research and, as far as possible, make use of what is known as *triangulation*.

Reflexivity

Orthodox sociology has often failed to recognise the fact that a white middle-class male view of the world is actually only a partial view. This unquestioning confidence in the universality of their vision is probably partly a result of the fact that in their day-to-day experience, unlike women and people belonging to groups that have been 'racialised', white middle-class men are rarely told that there are things they cannot see, do or be, simply because of the socially constructed categories into which they fall. Many white male sociologists therefore react to Black and feminist critiques in rather the same way that the English respond to Americans telling them 'I love your accent', that is, with surprise, saying 'But I haven't got an accent.' This perhaps accounts for the number of recent textbooks which devote no more than a couple of pages or paragraphs to questions of male and ethnocentric bias in social research. Indeed, some methods textbooks still get by without dealing with issues of gender or 'racialisation' in connection with the research process at all. This reflects the orthodox view that social scientists are capable of producing value-free knowledge – a view promulgated by many advocates of more qualitative methods, like Max Weber, as well as by advocates of straightforwardly positivist methods. The idea is that while the selection of a research topic may be informed by a particular set of values, researchers can and do go on to gather facts about that topic in a neutral, value-free way (see Nagel 1961). In other words, many methodologists assume that the decision to investigate something can be sharply demarcated from the actual process of investigating it. The values and identity of the researcher may influence the former, but need not and should not affect the latter.

It was a reaction against precisely this kind of reasoning which led Scholte (1972) to argue for the practice of reflexivity in anthropology. The case he makes is pertinent to other social scientific disciplines. Rather than imagining that the anthropologist can go to another society or culture and act as a sort of human tape recorder, neutrally describing 'facts' and 'reality', the anthropologist should reflect on his or her own part in *constructing* a view of reality through the interpersonal relations of fieldwork and also reflect more generally on 'the discipline itself, questioning the conditions and modes of producing knowledge about other cultures' (Callaway 1992: 32). In the same way, we would argue that sociologists and other social researchers should continually reflect upon the ways in which their own social identity and values affect the data they are gathering and the picture of social reality they are producing. If researchers are reflexive in this way, there is the potential to pre-empt or reduce bias and distortion. It may be possible to adjust or modify the design of the research, and examples of research which fail to even address issues of gender, 'racialisation' or class until fieldwork is completed (tagging on comments like 'Although this was not a deliberate sampling strategy, all respondents were Caucasian' (Hertz 1986, cited in Cannon *et al.* 1991)) would be less common. Researchers should also reflect upon the conditions under which they are producing knowledge, thinking, for example, about the ways in which their desire to win praise from the academic community or to comply with funding bodies is shaping the picture of social reality that they are painting through the research. An awareness of these issues is central not just to producing better research, but also to critically evaluating the research of others.

It may seem that there is a danger of reflexivity leading to a form of relativism, that we are asking researchers to be so hypersensitive to their own role in constructing the data that they would lack all confidence in their findings. How can even the most reflexive white male researcher, for example, ever be sure that the picture of social reality produced by his research is generally valid and not a biased or partial portrait? It is here that triangulation can play an important role in increasing our confidence in research.

Triangulation as a validity check

Denzin's (1970) comments on triangulation as a form of cross-checking research findings have become a widely accepted means of ensuring validity. Essentially, triangulation involves looking at the research topic or problem from a number of different vantage points in order to check whether similar pictures are produced. If not, the validity of findings and their interpretation are questionable. The most common form of triangulation entails the use of multiple data sources and techniques of data gathering. For example, the results of a survey on sexual attitudes might be supplemented by in-depth interviews with a smaller sample of participants. If the in-depth interviews confirm the survey findings, we can be more confident of those original results. If the interviews are at odds with the survey results, however, we might want to question them and gather further data and evidence, perhaps using other techniques such as documentary analysis or participant observation. The more sources and types of data we can gather and compare, the surer we can be of the validity of our overall findings and interpretations.

Hochschild's (1983) study of airline flight attendants and the kinds of 'emotional labour' that is required of them (particularly the women), provides a good example of the use of multiple strategies of research and data sources. Hochschild began with questionnaire survey data on a sample of students to see how emotional management (the display and control of emotions) varies by gender and class. This was supplemented by further quantitative material derived from census data on the distribution of men and women in the occupational structure according to the demand for emotional labour. Women, she found, were concentrated in those occupations, such as teaching, nursing, flight attendants, which demanded the highest levels of emotional display and commitment. She then focused on the flight attendant's world by using qualitative methods and data. She observed training classes for flight attendants and conducted in-depth interviews with them. She also talked with trainers, sat in on recruitment interviews and studied company documents. The different vantage points and kinds of evidence that she gathered allowed Hochschild to be confident of her more detailed analysis of the ways in which flight attendants are constrained to manage their own, and passengers emotions in the course of the job.

Denzin (1970) noted that there are a number of other forms of triangulation that could be useful for checking the validity of findings. These include the use of different investigators on the same research project and the use of different theories as a means of understanding and interpreting the data. This usually means trying out different and fairly narrowly defined explanations of the same data, but can involve the application of a number of more general theories or approaches. Hochschild, for example, moves between interactionist theories of emotion and Marxian theories of political economy in interpreting her data. In this way she manages to bring together micro analyses of face-to-face conduct with macro analyses of power and economic and social organisation (see also Layder 1993). Triangulation thus not only allows the researcher to look at a given topic or social phenomenon from a number of different vantage points, but also to explore it at a number of different levels. The subjective, day-to-day experience of, say, women flight attendants can be considered at the level of the individual woman, and looked at in relation to the whole company's employment policies and organisational structure, and examined in relation to women's position in the economy as a whole.

Again, this represents a way of checking the validity of a study, because to rely solely on the individual research subject's view of their own position may be misleading. Oddly enough, given Denzin's very convincing arguments in favour of triangulation, in his later writing as a postmodernist, Denzin (1990) appears to make the case for simply accepting the subjective worldview of research subjects as the only or the most reliable vantage point, rather than considering a topic from as many vantage points as possible in order to develop a more reliable overview. He now suggests that researchers should give priority to the 'local knowledge', feelings and emotions of the research subjects. One has only to imagine conducting research with battered women who blame themselves for their husband's brutality to see that a method which precludes questioning the subject's version of reality is extremely limited. People's subjective perceptions should not be ignored or dismissed (they are interesting and warrant investigation in their own right), but if postmodern research involves nothing more than simply accepting these subjective worldviews at face value and describing them, it seems a fairly pointless exercise. Why not cut out the middle-person and just let people tell their own stories?

For those of us who are not postmodernists, the purpose of social research is to try to produce a better picture and understanding of social reality, to add to the sum of human knowledge. Of course, we cannot claim that our 'scientific' findings are automatically valid, anymore than we can claim that people's 'local knowledge' is necessarily a faithful and valid description of social reality. We need a way of checking the validity of various and competing 'facts' and interpretations. Triangulation is a means of doing so. When used in conjunction with the practice of reflexivity, it is perhaps possible to surmount some of the methodological and philosophical problems which arise from the fact that there are different versions of the truth, and that social researchers do not and cannot observe neutrally.

The question of ethics

Finally, it is necessary to turn to the question of ethics in social research. Ethics concern the conduct of researchers and their responsibilities and obligations to those involved in the research, including sponsors, the general public and most importantly, the subjects of the research. In this sense, ethics refer to an abstract set of standards and principles which social researchers can refer to in order to decide what is appropriate and acceptable conduct. Although various professional research associations in the UK and the USA have adopted written codes of conduct which set out standards and responsibilities, these are essentially guidelines, rather than mandatory or enforceable rules.

In practice, the question of ethics in social research is complex and a subject of heated debate. It overlaps with questions about reflexivity and the political responsibilities of researchers, and it is also central to some feminist critiques of orthodox methods. Oakley (1981), for example, sees orthodox survey techniques as exploitative and morally indefensible. Part of the difficulty comes from uncertainty as to whether we could ever define a set of universally applicable ethical principles, or whether the particular circumstances of a research project need to be taken into account in order to decide what is, and what is not, ethical. Should a feminist researcher be constrained by the same code of conduct when interviewing both rapists and the victims of rape, for example? If each individual project requires or permits a different code, then the researcher is left with a good deal of discretion as to how to interpret ethical guidelines.

Ethical guidelines generally attempt to embrace a number of issues. First, there is the question of how to ensure that academic research is independent. Researchers need to consider the degree to which their funded research projects are controlled by the sponsor. As Homan (1991), among others, has noted, there is a trend towards increasingly tight control by statutory sponsors, who are able to influence not just the research agenda and methodology by making awards on the basis of certain criteria, but are also able to limit the freedom of the researcher by imposing controls on what is published and when. Homan observes that:

> The ethical implications of these constraints are clear. Social scientists are morally committed to the pursuit of truth and the advancement of knowledge. The right of approval asserted by government departments allow for manipulation and massage so that the truth and knowledge derived from the project will either be withheld from public access or else will be distorted. Further, it is critical to the integrity of social researchers that they should not, whether wittingly or unconsciously, be committed to the pursuit of specified conclusions.
>
> (Homan 1991: 30)

For a researcher to allow a funding body to push them to produce research which contributes to the more effective exploitation of already vulnerable groups, or which merely strengthens the resource base of a powerful vested interest group, is ethically unsound. To cite Homan again, 'information is expensive and therefore not universally available, but it is often the basis of the retention of power, especially if its publication can be controlled' and social researchers should therefore be extremely cautious about collecting data from powerless individuals and 'delivering them to be held and used by powerful institutions' (1991: 176).

The ethical issues raised by the power dimension of social research also underpin ethical guidelines about 'informed consent'. The principle of informed consent suggests that researchers should inform potential research subjects about the nature and purpose of the study, should obtain their permission to be a subject of the research and assure them confidentiality. In medical research, the reasoning behind this principle is obvious. People have a right to be made fully aware of all the potentially harmful effects that could result from participating in the research. The same could be said of some social research, and, as will be seen in Chapter 6, Milgram's classic social psychology experiment, famed for its blatant abuse of research subjects, would not have been possible had he been committed to the principle of informed consent.

The need for informed consent is also said to be particularly important in research which involves relatively powerless groups, such as children or the mentally ill, in order to prevent their exploitation. But it is not always clear when or whether such consent has been obtained, as Denscombe and Aubrook (1992) notes in relation to the administering of questionnaires to schoolchildren in their classrooms. Although they may have been told by their teachers and/or by the researchers that they are free to choose not to participate, it is unclear whether the children feel constrained to fill out questionnaires because they are in the classroom situation wherein control relations are implicitly operating. There are also times when a researcher will only obtain information if he or she breaches the principle of fully informed consent. Cases where researchers are economical with the truth in order to obtain subjects' co-operation slide into the domain of debates about whether researchers are ever justified in deceiving subjects by lying or using 'covert' methods (that is, disguising their identity in order to gain access to a group or information about it).

Even deception can take many forms in social research. Researchers sometimes decide to lie to subjects in order to maintain confidentiality or to protect friends and other informants (Burgess 1984: 201). Covert methods are sometimes the only way that certain information can be collected. Humphreys' (1975) study of homosexual encounters in public toilets and Rosenhan's (1973) study of a psychiatric hospital (both of which are discussed in Chapter 7) are two examples of research which produced data that could not have been obtained except through the use of covert methods. But the ethics of the two studies tend to be judged differently because of differences between the relative power of the groups they deceived. Humphreys' study involved the deception of a relatively powerless group, and critics point to the potentially damaging consequences of such research that could result from breaches in confidentiality and the dissemination of findings in various forms of publication. Rosenhan's study involved the deception of members of the medical profession – a relatively powerful group. The use of overt methods would have required permission for the study from the higher echelons of the medical profession, permission that was unlikely to be forthcoming. The question here is whether the wider public has a right to know about the practices of various powerful groups (lawyers, managers, politicians, doctors) who may use their power to block access or simply refuse permission for research. Is the social researcher's commitment to the pursuit of truth and the advancement of knowledge about such powerful groups a more important ethical principle than that which condemns the use of deception and covert methods?

Issues surrounding the use of covert methods overlap with those surrounding the invasion of the privacy of subjects. Generally speaking, ethical guidelines suggest that privacy should be respected. Again, this is especially the case with vulnerable individuals and groups. On the other hand, it can be argued that in order to support such groups politically and socially, it is necessary to acquire information about their needs and practices, and that this can only be obtained through research, sometimes only through research which invades their privacy. Humphreys used this argument to justify his study of male homosexuals. In other cases, when the subjects are powerful people or public figures (politicians, civil servants, directors of large corporations), the need to publicly account for the consequences of their actions and decisions can be held to override their right to privacy (Hammersley 1990: 133).

In general, researchers need to be aware of the potentially damaging consequences that their research may have for the subjects of that research. This needs to be considered in relation to the power and control of the individuals and groups concerned, as well as the purposes of the research and whether it serves the interests of the wider community. This, of course, brings us straight into the terrain of politics. Socialists and right-wingers, feminists and patriarchs, gay rights activitists and moral conservatives, for instance, will make rather different judgements as to what is in the interests of the wider community. The specific circumstances of a research project and the moral and political values of the researcher will inevitably have a powerful effect on the ethical stance which is taken. This does not mean that general guidelines and principles are useless or pointless, however. They may not always be applicable, but they do at least provide a set of standards which can inform and educate researchers when confronted by conflicting ideals (Homan 1991: 40).

CONCLUSION

This chapter has focused on two issues; the question of how social scientific research is to be distinguished from other ways of knowing about the world, and the question of bias. We began by looking at two very different philosophical traditions which inform research in the social sciences, and pointed out that the absence of a single, universally accepted research paradigm is one of the things that differentiates the social from the natural sciences. The question of *what* methods can be used to produce reliable and objective knowledge about the social world has not been fully or finally answered, but remains a subject of debate even amongst those working in social science disciplines. Some academics seem to assume that despite this problem, a methodological domain exists which can and does function as a safeguard, sieving out biased and defective research. They would thus insist that social scientific knowledge differs from prejudiced or common-sense knowledge because it is produced in a more rigorous fashion and subjected to the searching scrutiny of a critical audience. Against such a view, we have argued that the composition of the academic research community (in terms of gender, 'racialised' identity and political allegiance), combined with the fact that many researchers do not describe their methodology in detail and that many members of the academic community are not experts on methodological issues, means that the existing methodological domain is a far from perfect filter. It is, of course, feminist, Black, Africentric and radical writers who are largely responsible for revealing and critically analysing these imperfections, and there is little doubt that such scholars need independent, sometimes even separatist, forums within which to debate and develop ideas. However, we believe that it is also vital for these scholars to unite in a struggle to improve the quality of this filter, rather than accepting or even promoting a form of methodological Balkanisation. If the academic community fragments in pursuit of a number of separate methodological domains, the contributions, knowledge and insights of already marginalised groups will only be further marginalised.

We then argued that social scientific knowledge is distinguished by its attempt to formulate explanations and theories that are grounded in some form of empirical evidence, but that in collecting such evidence, researchers should do a number of things. They should be reflexive, they should attempt to improve the validity of their findings by looking at the research problem or topic from as many different vantage points as possible, they should consider the ethics of their research practice. As the rest of this book shows, these issues are also relevant to the evaluation of research conducted by others. The next six chapters are designed to give the reader an overview of the main sources, methods and techniques that can be used in social research. We hope that the arguments advanced in this chapter and the preceding one will encourage readers to view these methods and the knowledge that derives from them critically, yet also retain a belief that, used properly, such methods have the potential to advance human knowledge and contribute to struggles against inequality.

Chapter 3

Official statistics and social research

When social researchers want a general overview of some social phenomenon (say, how many people in Britain are unemployed, or how many
people are patients in psychiatric hospitals, or how many women are
raped each year), they often begin by consulting the government's
official statistics. The Oxford Dictionary defines statistics as 'numerical
facts systematically collected on the subject', and social statistics have
been compiled in Western European countries for several hundred
years. In nineteenth-century Britain, the state's growing involvement in
industrial, economic and social affairs triggered the rapid expansion of
the state's statistical services. From the 1880s onwards, the state monitored and measured more and more aspects of social life more and more
closely, and in 1941 the Government Statistical Service (GSS) was set
up as a distinct section of the Civil Service. It expanded steadily until the
1970s, after which growth levelled off (Government Statisticians'
Collective 1993: 147). Today, governments in all economically
developed countries produce official statistics which describe population trends, employment patterns, mortality rates, trends in crime and
sentencing, levels of economic activity, and much, much more, and
these statistics are a source of information which can be used by social
researchers. The way in which such statistics are produced has been
summarised as follows:

> The most crucial documents in the whole process of producing
> statistics are the *forms*, or *returns*, sent out by the government depart-
> ment (not necessarily by the statisticians) to the organizations from
> which information is needed: for example, to the offices of business
> firms, local tax offices, police stations, employment exchanges and
> local authority social services departments. The unfortunate people
> given the job of filling in these forms collect (or sometimes invent)

and record the requisite information with varying degrees of accuracy and comprehensibility. . . . The completed forms are typically posted, or ferried by van, to a data processing and computer centre in a provincial town. . . . It is the statisticians' job to order, analyse and interpret computer output so as to meet the requirements of the departmental administrators for information, and to compile statistical volumes and reports.

(Government Statisticians' Collective 1993: 149)

The production of official statistics thus involves thousands of people and millions of hours of work. The state alone has the finances and power to produce social statistics on such a scale, and these figures feed directly into the daily lives of every member of society through their impact upon administrative, policy making and planning processes. Since it is the state which organises and finances the production of official statistics, it is those people with power within the state who set the research agenda and decide which social phenomena will, and which will not, be monitored and measured numerically. Furthermore, 'the methods and concepts developed and used for official statistics are shaped by the sorts of policies powerful people in the state wish to consider and by the concerns which preoccupy them' (Government Statisticians' Collective 1993: 153).

This is perhaps the first problem to confront sociologists who wish to make use of official statistics for research purposes, for their interests and preoccupations will not necessarily coincide with those of powerful people in the state. Take official statistics on mental health. Statistics based on admissions to hospitals are routinely collected and provide information about the sex, age, social class and diagnosis of each psychiatric patient admission. This information may be adequate to satisfy the concerns of policy makers and local health authority officials, but it does not provide full answers to the kinds of questions that sociologists might wish to ask. For instance:

Although hospital statistics include diagnoses, they do not tell us about the severity of the condition, nor whether the decision to admit someone to hospital was influenced by their social or other circumstances in addition to the severity of their condition.

(Macfarlane, 1990: 56)

Sociologists working in this field also find that while recent official health statistics adequately describe the decrease in the number of people admitted to long-stay psychiatric hospitals that has resulted from the government's policy of replacing institutional care with community care, there is a lack of 'adequate data to monitor the extent to which people are able to obtain the help and facilities they need to enable them to live outside long-stay institutions' (Macfarlane 1990: 56). The sociologist who is concerned with the treatment of psychiatric patients faces even greater problems. It might be expected, for instance, that the use of an extremely controversial treatment such as electroconvulsive therapy (ECT) would be closely monitored and that health authorities would collect and publish details of who received it, how often and why. But as Samson (1993) discovered, it is actually extremely difficult to use official documentation to answer even the most basic questions about the use of ECT. To glean some indication of the extent of ECT usage in just two psychiatric hospitals, Samson had to collect separate information on admissions and on courses of ECT treatment from five different sources, then use the two sets of figures to calculate a rate of ECT usage per admission. This was a valuable undertaking, for it suggested that 'contrary to popular belief, ECT has not become marginalized as a treatment procedure despite the widespread public unease over its use' (Samson 1993: 10), but the statistics could not be used to address other vitally important issues. They revealed nothing about the social class, gender or 'racialised' identity of the patients receiving the treatment, and clearly, if obtaining figures for but two hospitals is this difficult, establishing the rate of ECT usage in the country as a whole would be a Herculean task.

Sociologists will also often find difficulties with the conceptual categories and theoretical assumptions employed by official statisticians. As Nichols (1979) shows, this is particularly clear in relation to the issue of social class. The state collects a vast array of official statistics which are related to social class, yet these figures cannot be uncritically used by sociologists since official, sociological and Marxist concepts of social class are very different. Official statisticians analyse data either in terms of the Registrar General's five social classes (I. Professional Occupations; II. Intermediate Occupations; IIIn. Skilled Non-Manual Occupations and IIIm. Skilled Manual Occupations; IV. Partly Skilled Occupations; V. Unskilled Occupations) or in terms of the Registrar General's 16 socio-economic groups, also classified on the basis of occupation. However, these are 'essentially descriptive categories that relate to *status*' (Nichols 1979: 152), and are of limited use to the Marxist sociologist who defines class in relation to ownership and control of the means of production. Because the Registrar General conceives of class as an occupational hierarchy, there are no specific categories to cover the ownership classes, that is, landowners and those whose income derives from investing capital rather than from a wage:

> In *Classifications of Occupations 1951*, for instance, the 'capitalist', the 'business speculator', the 'fundholder' and the 'landowner' were lumped together into the same residual category as the 'expert (undefined)' and the 'lunatic (trade not stated)'. A rather pleasing coincidence perhaps, but one which serves to remind us that in the 'five social classes' of the Census the owners of capital are lost to sight.
>
> (Nichols 1979: 159)

The classification of occupations upon which the Registrar General's categories are based has also been much criticised. Occupations which require vastly different skill levels and qualifications are placed in the same category for no very clear reason, and since the official classification of jobs is reviewed only once every ten years, many commentators doubt that the official classification system actually keeps 'up-to-date with the changing status of many jobs and occupational groups, especially that greyest of boundaries between skilled manual workers and the lower middle-class' (Slattery 1986: 50). Any sociologist who wishes to know about women as well as men will also find working with official statistics frustrating. Although the Registrar General defines social class in relation to occupational groupings, the state has traditionally displayed a tendency to gather only information about men's occupations. For example, it was not until 1986 that birth registrars were required to record the occupation of a baby's mother as well as its father (unless a woman was registering a birth outside marriage and without the father), and only after 1982 that the mother's occupation started to be recorded at the death registration of a child under the age of 16. Even where information on women's occupations is gathered, published tabulations and analyses of the data typically places married women living with their husbands in 'socio-economic groups derived from their husband's occupations' (Macfarlane 1990: 25).

A further problem to confront the social researcher using official statistics is that whilst some data are collected from individuals for the specific purpose of measuring the social world (for example, the Census, the Family Expenditure Survey, the Labour Force Survey), other statistics:

> are produced as by-products of administrative systems existing mainly for other purposes . . . [for example] unemployment statistics [are] based on the records kept by employment exchanges . . .

homelessness statistics [are] based on the records kept by local authorities on those who apply to them for help.

(Government Statisticians' Collective 1993: 154)

Such statistics are generally measuring the activities of employment exchanges, local authorities and other state agencies rather than measuring the social phenomenon to which they relate. British unemployment statistics, for example, classify only those who are eligible for means-tested benefits as unemployed and therefore measure the number of claimants arriving at any one employment exchange, not the actual number of unemployed people living in a given district. Again, this systematically obscures information about women, since many unemployed married women are ineligible for benefits because of their husband's earnings. Likewise, homelessness statistics are of limited use to sociologists or, indeed, to policy makers, since they tell us nothing about those homeless people who are ineligible for local authority help (and this includes the majority of single people) and who are therefore generally discouraged from making formal applications for help.

Essentially, then, official statistics are secondary data (i.e., data produced elsewhere for other purposes) and this creates certain problems for sociologists who work with them. But despite these problems, they still represent a very cheap, comprehensive and relatively high quality data source, providing information on a scale which would be impossible for any individual academic researcher, or indeed team of researchers, to match. For this reason, official statistics have long been exploited by social scientists. Sometimes, these statistics are used uncritically and simply taken to be objective, numerical descriptions of the social world. This 'empiricist' approach to official statistics has been challenged by writers from a number of different traditions. Some critics hold that because of their socially constructed nature, official statistics are of little or no value to social researchers, but there are others who believe that where official statistics are used critically and in conjunction with other types of data, they can play a role 'both in developing critical theory and analysis, and in political struggle' (Griffiths *et al.* 1979: 366). The remainder of this chapter reviews these debates by looking at the now classic critique of Durkheim's use of official statistics in his study of suicide, then moving on to consider the limitations and value of official statistics on sex crimes to researchers.

DURKHEIM, SUICIDE AND OFFICIAL STATISTICS

The natural sciences investigate facts about the natural world through systematic observation and rigorous testing, and Durkheim held that, as a science, sociology should adopt similar methods. He therefore insisted that sociologists should concern themselves with observable social phenomena (collective behaviours and institutions, which he called 'social facts') rather than with individual subjective feelings, perceptions and beliefs, which are not open to observation. In this sense, Durkheim's methodology falls into a school of positivism which can be termed empiricist. It assumes that only those things which are immediately accessible to the senses can properly be said to exist, and that the only way to test scientific claims is to ask 'whether or not they are consistent with the empirical *data*, with the body of facts that is established via the senses' (Keat 1979: 77). Suicide may therefore seem an unlikely candidate for sociological investigation. It is an intensely personal act and since it appears to be the outcome of the individual suicide's internal, subjective world of emotions and beliefs, it is hard to see how it could be understood through empirical methods alone. But Durkheim (1952) [1897] argued that explanations of suicide rates which focused solely upon the inner, emotional experiences of the individual suicide were inadequate. He pointed out that suicide rates remain fairly stable in any given society from year to year and from this he concluded that these suicide *rates* had an existence external to, and independent of, any one individual suicide. It was therefore possible to think of suicide rates as 'social facts' which needed to be explained in terms of other social facts. Durkheim's aim was to explore the type of social conditions which could be expected to generate high rates of suicide.

In his *Rules of Sociological Method* (1964) [1895] Durkheim had stressed the importance of the initial definition of social phenomena by the scientist. He held that the common-sense definitions used by ordinary lay persons are of no use to the scientist, for they not only embody a set of preconceptions and value judgements, but further 'words in everyday language, like the concepts they express, are always ambiguous' (cited in Thompson 1991: 93). Before embarking on his study of suicide, he therefore drew up the following precise, scientific definition of suicide: 'Suicide is applied to every case of death which results directly or indirectly from a positive or negative act, carried out by the victim himself, knowing that it will produce this result' (cited in Thompson 1991: 95).

Having defined suicide thus, Durkheim went on to use official statistics from various different European countries in order to study the phenomenon. These statistics confirmed the existence of marked and stable differences between European countries. Year after year, the suicide rate for England was twice as high as that in Italy, while the suicide rate in Denmark was four times as high as the English rate. Suicide rates were lowest in Catholic and highest in Protestant countries. Where populations were mixed, suicide rates were in the middle of these extremes. Durkheim pointed out that since suicide was condemned as sin by both Catholic and Protestant churches, these different rates could not be explained through reference to religious teachings, and he went on to elaborate a theory about the link between the level of social solidarity (which he believed was higher in Catholic communities) and suicide rates. He expanded upon this by considering the impact of other forms of social integration on suicide rates and found, among other things, that suicide was less common amongst the wed than the unwed, and less common amongst members of large family units than small ones (see Giddens 1978: 44–8).

But Durkheim's *Suicide* has been criticised on a number of counts. To begin with, he based his work upon three different types of statistics (unpublished French official records, published compilations of official statistics and secondary sources, themselves based upon published and unpublished official statistics) but was uncritical so far as the quality of these data went. The figures he used may have contained straight-forward errors and inaccuracies. Relatives or police may have failed to discover evidence that would have pointed to suicide, or may have failed to make such evidence available to coroners. Doctors may have inaccurately diagnosed the physical causes of death (Scott 1990: 49–51). Furthermore, Durkheim did not have complete sets of data for each of the countries he studied and as Scott points out:

> In so far as he was concerned with the general issue of suicide, we must ask whether the countries for which data were available comprised an adequate sample of all the societies to which he expected his theory to apply. . . . In fact, the bulk of his statistics came from France and the German states, and this may not warrant his large-scale generalisations.
>
> (1990: 51)

Even if he had been able to obtain figures from a representative sample of European societies, we would still be left with doubts about how comparable such data are. It is very unlikely that, in the 1890s, suicide statistics were collected in a standard way across the whole of Europe. If official statistics are to be used in comparative studies, researchers must look in detail at how statistics are produced in each different country before making claims on the basis of such figures. For a death to appear as a suicide statistic, it has to be classified as such, and even today, official classification systems in different countries are not all the same. In some countries, for example, deaths can only be classified as suicide by a coroner if a note has been left by the victim, whilst in others, circumstantial evidence will suffice. The issue of comparability does not only arise in relation to suicide statistics. A contemporary researcher interested in European unemployment rates, crime rates or homelessness would face similar difficulties. Without matching data sets, researchers must be extremely cautious about making generalised comparisons on the basis of different countries' official statistics.

There are other, even more fundamental problems with Durkheim's use of suicide statistics. Durkheim wanted to treat social facts as 'things', because only 'things' are open to scientific, empirical observation. He was therefore careful to avoid any reference to people's (unobservable) intentions and motives when defining suicide, commenting:

> How do we know what the agent's motive was and whether, when he took his decision it was death he desired and not some other aim? Intention is too intimate a thing to be understood from outside other than by gross approximation.
>
> (Durkheim in Thompson 1991: 93–4)

Suicide, according to Durkheim, was the result of actions which the victim *knew would* (rather than intended to) lead to death. Eliminating all consideration of people's intentions leads to some rather bizarre classifications however. Durkheim classified soldiers who go onto the field of battle against overwhelming odds, as well as people who lose their lives by entering burning buildings to try to save others, knowing their actions are likely to result in their own death, as suicides (even though he distinguished such deaths from other suicides by referring to them as 'altruistic suicides'). Using his definition today, any smoker who died of lung cancer would also be a 'suicide'. After all, people who smoke generally *know* the possible consequences. This highlights the problem with Durkheim's definition. In practice, the distinction between doing something knowing that a particular consequence is likely to follow, or may be unavoidable, and doing something *intending* that such a consequence should follow is crucial to understanding social action (Giddens 1978). Smokers do not typically light up with the intention of contracting a terminal illness, and to fail to distinguish this act from, say, taking an overdose is unlikely to help further our understanding of the phenomenon of suicide.

If social researchers want to make use of official statistics, they must consider the relationship between their own definition of a given phenomenon (whether that be 'suicide', 'crime', 'poverty', 'unemployment' or whatever) and official definitions and categories. Durkheim did not do this. Durkheim's 'expert', 'scientific' definition of suicide bore little relation to official and everyday definitions, and this rendered his research highly problematic. For having developed his rather extraordinary definition of suicide, he went on to make use of official statistics that were produced by ordinary people, who used the term 'suicide' in an ordinary way, i.e., to refer to *intentional* acts of self destruction. As Atkinson observes:

> The fact that official statistics have been so widely used in studies of suicide implies that sociologists have decided that the death registration category 'suicide' is defined in a similar way to their own theoretical concept of suicide, and is, therefore, an acceptable indicator.
>
> (1971: 88)

In none of the countries that Durkheim studied would the official death registration category have included soldiers who went knowingly to their death or 'altruistic suicides'. Official statistics did not, therefore, measure Durkheim's theoretical concept of suicide. But problems would have remained even if Durkheim had stuck to the official or common-sense definition. A researcher would only be justified in taking official statistics as a true measure of suicide rates if she or he could be certain 'that officials apply [an] official definition consistently, so that all, or at least most eligible deaths are included in the category "suicide", while all ineligible deaths are excluded' (Atkinson 1971: 88). For a death to be recorded as 'suicide' actually requires a whole series of people (relatives, doctors, police, coroners) to make inferences about the individual suicide's intentions and motivations. Unless the victim leaves a note, these social actors will have to try to reconstruct his or her mental state prior to death, they will have to make judgements about what will and will not count as evidence of a suicidal frame of mind. Did all the different social actors in all the different societies studied by Durkheim consistently make these judgements in the same way? It seems highly improbable that the relatives, doctor, police and coroner in a rural town in southern Italy would have reacted in exactly the same way as the relatives, doctor, police and coroner in London to finding say, the body of an unknown woman on a railroad track. If these social actors did not consistently ask the same questions, consistently make the same judgements based on the evidence, and consistently apply the same definition of suicide, then the 'social fact' which Durkheim studied was not the actual numbers of suicides, but the rates *constructed* by a series of social actors in different European countries.

More problematic still, there may have been systematic differences in the ways in which these social actors constructed these rates. It could be, for example, that the social solidarity Durkheim referred to in different communities did not affect the number of suicides so much as the way in which deaths were recorded. If suicide was seen as more of a dishonour in communities with a high degree of social integration, families may have attempted to conceal the true cause of death and coroners may have been more reluctant to record a verdict of suicide. In this way, the subjective ideas, beliefs and values of the individuals involved in discovering, investigating, classifying and recording deaths affect the statistics, making them a less than objective measure of the actual number of suicides in any given country. It is also worth noting that official figures on suicide refer only to successful acts of suicide and give no indication of how many unsuccessful attempts have been made. They therefore provide only a partial measure of the number of suicidal *actions* in any given country (see Wilkins 1967 and Atkinson 1971).

Durkheim's *Suicide* thus highlights two interconnected problems surrounding the use of official statistics in social research. On the one hand, it raises questions about whether it is possible to investigate social phenomena without reference to unobservable phenomena like intention and meaning. On the other, it raises questions about the relationships that exist between social power, official conceptual schema and the picture of the social world painted by official statistics. These two sets of issues are central to the critiques of official statistics that have been advanced by phenomenologists, Marxists and feminists.

THE PHENOMENOLOGICAL CRITIQUE OF OFFICIAL STATISTICS

Positivists hold that providing researchers limit themselves to the scientific study of observable phenomena like behaviour, rather than trying to understand people's intentions and motives, 'facts' about the world can be uncovered that are not distorted by the subjective perceptions or values of either researcher or researched. Phenomenologists, conversely, reject the idea that patterns or regularities in the social world can be thought of as 'facts' which exist independently of the individual actions that constitute them. Although it is not possible to talk about phenomenology as a single, unified philosophical position, broadly speaking phenomenologists are concerned with "'the study or description of phenomena"; and a "phenomenon" is simply anything that appears or presents itself to someone. . . . Thus phenomenology involves the description of things as one experiences them' (Hammond *et al.* 1991: 1). Phenomenologists argue that human beings make sense of their experiences by imposing meanings and classifications upon them, and that it is these classifications and meanings which make up social reality. There is no way of observing reality, experiences or 'facts' without reference to the meanings people attach to them. Phenomenology thus forms part of the broad tradition of interpretative philosophy which was mentioned in Chapter 2.

In the 1960s, such ideas were employed to develop a critique of official statistics, particularly suicide and crime statistics. So far as suicide was concerned, phenomenological writers pointed out that 'a suicide is not simply a dead body . . . to *describe* a death as a "suicide" is not simply a matter of observation' (Keat 1979: 82). While we can observe that different deaths have different physical causes (poison, internal injuries, blood loss), we cannot divide suicides from murders or accidental deaths on the basis of such observations. To classify a death that results from someone crashing their car into a tree, for example, we draw upon ideas of intention rather than upon observations of the physical world. We try to reconstruct the dead person's experience. Did he or she *intend* to drive into the tree or was it accidental? This in turn draws us further into the world of ideas. Had the victim recently undergone some experience (bankruptcy, bereavement or some other tragedy) that would enable us to impose meaning upon, and therefore explain, a suicidal frame of mind? Though death itself is a fact, 'suicide' is a human idea, and the meanings we attach to different deaths, how they are classified and recorded, is an expression of the internal, subject world of human beings. For phenomenologists, official suicide statistics are not objective measures of a 'true' suicide rate, but socially constructed descriptions of the meanings that a series of people have attached to certain deaths.

Official crime statistics provided an equally easy target for attack by phenomenology. As soon as attention is focused on the social actors who are involved in the production of an official crime statistic, it becomes apparent that whatever these statistics do measure, it is not the absolute level of criminal activity in society. Instead, as Kitsuse and

Cicourel's now classic argument goes, '*rates of deviant behaviour* are produced by *the actions taken by persons in the social system* which define, classify and record certain behaviours as deviant' (1963: 135, original emphasis). There is a systematic bias in both the type of crimes and the type of criminals that receive attention from the police (Cicourel 1976). People are not randomly observed, stopped or searched by the police. Instead their age, social class, skin colour, sex, accent and style of dress all affect their chances of attracting attention from the police in the first place and subsequently affect whether or not the police will classify, record and prosecute their actions as 'criminal'. For phenomenologists, official crime statistics provide a record of how a selection of events have been *interpreted* by a series of social actors rather than an accurate numerical description of all criminal events. Applying such ideas to official rape statistics usefully illustrates both the value and the limitation of this approach.

A phenomenological approach to rape statistics

One thing that can be said with certainty about official rape statistics is that they tell us very little indeed about the actual incidence of acts of sexual violence. Whether or not an act of sexual aggression is transformed into a rape statistic is powerfully affected by the values, perceptions and beliefs of the police and judiciary. For an act of sexual violence to appear as an official rape statistic, the police officers dealing with the case must first decide to classify and record that act as 'rape'. In Britain, a number of different categories of sexual offences exist, for example, 'rape' which refers only to those acts of sexual violence wherein penetration by the penis into the vagina has taken place; 'indecent assault on a female', which includes those acts of sexual violence wherein the victim has been penetrated by an object other than a penis; 'indecent assault on a male' which includes virtually any act of sexual violence against a male victim; as well as 'unlawful sexual intercourse with a girl under 13', 'incest', 'gross indecency with a child' and so on. The police have to decide on the appropriate category for the particular offence, and clearly this decision is not based upon observation, but results from the social processes of interviewing and interrogation.

Although police forces across England and Wales are issued with standard rules of guidance as to how to make such decisions, there is still room for discretion on the part of individual officers. If the suspect has been apprehended, he too will be interrogated and as with all crimes, his age, appearance and manner, and above all his social class and whether or not he belongs to a 'racialised' group will powerfully affect what the police decide to record. The victim is normally questioned closely and asked to provide details of his or her ordeal as well as being medically examined, and again, the police officer's perceptions and assumptions about the victim will affect how, and indeed whether, an offence is recorded. The hostile and disbelieving way in which rape victims have historically been interviewed by the police is well known. In the USA, Medea and Thompson (1974: 117) observe that as well as facing disbelief and suspicion, 'many women . . . reported . . . that they were questioned by police officers who appeared to be getting voyeuristic kicks by demanding graphic answers to questions which were basically irrelevant to the investigation' (1974: 117). In Britain, the police attitude towards rape victims was well illustrated by the 1982 'Glasgow razor rape' case, in which the authorities refused to prosecute though the woman herself later successfully undertook a private prosecution (Soothill and Walby 1991: 10).

For an attack to be recorded as 'rape', the police officer involved must believe that the woman did not consent to sexual intercourse. Many women find it hard to convince the police of this, even where weapons have been used and injuries sustained. This is partly because

> in the same way that the police have a shorthand, or series of signs and symbols that they look for in order to make sense of crime and criminal offenders, they also share certain common assumptions about the 'typical' rape complainant.
>
> (Edwards 1981: 119)

In the misogynistic world of many police officers, even a short skirt or high heeled shoes can be read as a 'sign' that the victim was really 'asking for' sex. Western societies abound with myths about rape and about women's sexuality which serve to justify sexual violence (see Scully 1990), and many so-called 'experts' on the subject have busily promulgated these ideas. In 1971, John Macdonald, a professor of psychiatry wrote:

> Some women invite rape. By their seductive behaviour in dress, bodily movements or suggestive remarks, they convey to men the impression that they are eager or at least willing to indulge in an illicit sexual relationship. . . . Failure to indicate disapproval of suggestive sexual comments encourages sexual advances which may take the form of forcible rape.
>
> (1971: 78)

The term 'victim-precipitated rape' is used by such 'experts' to refer to situations where the raped woman does not conform to cultural stereotypes about the 'blameless victim'. Macdonald provides two examples of such rapes. In one case, a woman answered her front door to find three unknown men standing there, who then forced their way into her apartment and gang raped her, one striking her face and cutting open her chin. We are told that the victim 'precipitated' these brutal attacks by having had a drink that evening and opening the door wearing only a sweater. In another example, an 18-year-old girl had a gun held to her head while she was gang raped in a car. We are asked to believe that the men would not have behaved thus had she not 'precipitated' the attack by talking to one of the men (whom she had mistaken for a friend), agreeing to go to a drive-in with them, and laughing when one of the men first made an explicitly sexual proposition to her (see Macdonald 1971: 78–9). It seems highly probable that many police officers, like many 'experts', attach different meanings to different rapes, and are less willing to classify the rape of a 'seductively dressed' or inebriated woman as rape, preferring to blame the victim even for the most extreme instances of male aggression.

The reluctance of the police to record or prosecute rape complaints appears to be matched by the reluctance of judges to convict and sentence men accused of rape, particularly when those men are known to or related to the victim. In 1987, only 18 per cent of rape complaints in Britain resulted in the conviction of a rapist (Soothill and Walby 1991: 1). A 1986 North American survey with a randomly selected sample of women found that out of 66 rape or attempted rapes reported to the police, only six cases resulted in convictions, whilst out of 187 cases of incestuous abuse, only one had led to a conviction and this was a case which 'involved an apparently psychotic and very violent biological father – a Latino ex-convict who knocked his daughter unconscious and who may even have been caught in the act of attempting to penetrate her' (Russell 1986: 91). Again, the stereotypes, values and beliefs of judges and members of the jury exert a powerful influence over whether or not a given act of sexual violence ever becomes a rape statistic.

For these reasons alone, we can argue that rape statistics are social constructions rather than a neutral, objective measure of the number of rapes that are actually committed in any given country. If the victim herself (a social actor who has tended to receive less attention in phenomenological treatments of crime statistics – see Edwards 1981: 118) is considered, there is even more reason to suppose that official rape statistics reveal only the tip of the iceberg. For a crime to appear as a criminal statistic, it must first be either discovered by the police themselves or reported to the police by the victim or a member of the general public. The percentage of rapes discovered by the police and reported by members of the public is very small. As a general rule, rapes are brought to the attention of the police by either the victim or a close friend or relative of the victim. To assess whether the number of reported rapes can be taken as a measure of the actual number of rapes, we need to ask whether rapes are likely to be consistently reported to the police. Again, a phenomenological approach would lead us to consider the meanings people attach to events, and the relationship between subjective ideas and action. All violent crime is humiliating and terrifying for the victim, but because of the ideologies surrounding sexuality in most cultures, this is even more true of rape. There is a great deal of evidence to suggest that sexual offences are amongst the most under-reported crimes. It is, of course, impossible to know precisely how many victims fail to report their ordeals. However, evidence from the 1988 British Crime Survey (which asked a large random sample of the population about offences they had experienced the previous year) suggests that in 1987 at best, only 77 per cent of sexual offences ever came to be recorded by the police, and at worst, the recorded figures may represent only 17 per cent of the actual number of sexual assaults (see Mayhew *et al.*, 1989: 70). In the States a similar picture emerges from survey research. Some commentators suggest that only one rape in ten is reported, and the report rate for incestuous rape is far lower (see Russell 1986).

Given prevailing attitudes towards rape victims, the widespread existence of myths which hold that 'nice girls don't get raped', that rape is 'every woman's unconscious fantasy' and so on, and given that most women are well aware of the humiliation that rape complainants often face at the hands of the police and judiciary, the unwillingness of rape victims to report such attacks is unsurprising. Evidence is beginning to emerge that suggests male victims of rape are equally reluctant to go to the police. In Britain, as well as suffering the same sense of fear, shock and humiliation experienced by female victims, male rape victims may be deterred by the legal system:

> Male rape does not exist as a criminal offence under British law; the assaults are recorded as non-consensual buggery. Convicted rapists can be imprisoned for life, whereas buggery carries a maximum sentence of 10 years. Men also run the risk of having their names published during court cases, unlike women, who are guaranteed anonymity.
>
> (Bennetto 1992; see also Mezey and King 1992)

The real point is that, as Edwards comments

> the process that begins with the commission of a crime and ends with an individual law-breaker being sentenced or acquitted is negotiable and is at each stage informed by ideas and assumptions, discourses and theories external to the legal process itself.
>
> (1981: 151)

Considered phenomenologically, we can see that official rape statistics do not provide 'numerical facts' on the subject of rape. They are not an objective measure of the incidence of rape, but rather reflect a series of interpretations and actions by different social actors (the rapist, the victim, the victim's friends and relatives, the police surgeon, police officers, solicitors, barristers, judges and jurists), which are critically shaped by those social actor's ideas, values and beliefs. Should we therefore dismiss these statistics as worthless to the social scientist? The following section considers the case for the radical use of official statistics.

MARXIST AND FEMINIST CRITIQUES OF OFFICIAL STATISTICS

Though the phenomenological critique of official statistics provides some valuable insights into their socially constructed nature, many commentators argue that it is a limited and partial critique. Because phenomenologists are primarily concerned with the subjective meanings attached to events by individuals, there is a tendency to overlook the role of structural factors in shaping official 'facts' about the social world. Though the more sophisticated phenomenological accounts, such as that provided by Cicourel, point to the role of organisational processes in shaping official statistics, showing, for example, how the judgements made by individual police officers are powerfully affected by 'ideologies within, and pressures upon, the police force' (Miles and Irvine 1979: 118):

> Phenomenologists . . . often seem to treat society as a given environment in which individuals are free to create their own social realities and practices; it would be easy to conclude that they have replaced the [empiricist] view of statistics as a neutral snapshot of reality with one that treats them as no more than a patchwork aggregation of the impressionistic sketches of individuals.
>
> (Miles and Irvine 1979: 117)

In this sense, the phenomenological approach highlights one of the more general problems of the interpretative tradition, namely, its focus on the individual social actor tends to downplay the importance of structural constraints and influences. Marxist and feminist writers tend to agree that official statistics 'are not *collected*, but *produced*' and that 'research results are not *findings*, but *creations*' (Irvine *et al.* 1979: 3), but go on to argue that such data are not randomly produced and created. Official statistics are not simply the sum projection of a mass of individual, subjective consciousnesses, rather 'individual "subjective" experiences and group interests alike take place through systems of meaning and social institutions which have been formed as part of a wider structure of power, that of class [and gender] relationships' (Miles and Irvine 1979: 118–19).

Take official rape statistics. The social processes that mediate between an act of sexual aggression and the creation of an official rape statistic are not determined solely by the attitudes and beliefs of the *individual* woman, police officer, doctor, solicitor, judge and jurist who happen to be involved. The meanings attached to this act of violence are not a matter of 'pot luck', with one victim feeling too degraded and humiliated to tell a soul and another burning to share this outrage with anyone and everyone, or one police officer happening to ask a lot of questions about the victim's actions/dress/demeanour prior to the rape and another treating the attack in the same way as a report of any other sort of violence would be treated.

Instead, the victim and all the other social actors involved in the process of producing (or failing to produce) an official rape statistic draw on systems of meanings that form part of a broader ideology about relations between the sexes. This ideology both reflects and helps to reproduce a particular set of power relations. Ideas about rape, which have been critically shaped by the legal and medical professions, are a case in point. Nineteenth-century medical science provided a new basis for patriarchy by claiming to offer 'scientific' evidence to support existing sexist assumptions about female sexuality, and the law not only assimilated these ideas and constructs, but 'supported the discriminatory ideologies in its very institutional practices' (Edwards 1981: 173). The police officers, doctors, judges, jurists and so on involved in each rape case do not individually invent the stereotypes and constructs which impose meaning on sexual violence in our society, but draw on those produced by medical science and psychoanalytic theory ('hysterical' women, 'nymphomaniac' women, 'masochistic' women) as well as more general popular ideas about women's sexuality. The subjective perceptions of all the social actors involved in the production of an official rape statistic are all filtered through the lens of this intensely sexist ideology, a lens which *systematically*, not randomly, shapes the meanings that are attached to events.

Likewise, the techniques and concepts which underpin the production of official data are not created afresh by each individual actor. In a now classic text on official statistics, Hindess argues that 'official statistics are produced by a conjunction of "conceptual" and "technical" instruments of production' (1973: 44). Hindess uses the term 'technical' to refer to instruments of production such as the social survey, while the 'conceptual' instruments refer to 'the system of concepts and categories governing the assignment of cases into classes'. Rape statistics are not, of course, collected through the use of survey methods but rather rest on returns provided by the police. Yet there are still technical issues surrounding their production. For the reasons noted above, rape is under-reported and under-recorded so that the figures provided by the police are not effective in terms of measuring what they set out to measure. But even if we could somehow be absolutely certain that all rape victims reported the crime to the police, and that the police dealt with each rape allegation in the same way regardless of their assumptions about the victim, the official rape statistics could not be treated as unproblematic 'facts' about sexual violence. This is because the conceptual categories that are used to classify sexual violence are not straightforward observational categories. Sexual attacks, like everything else in the social world that official statistics attempt to measure, cannot be classified without reference to pre-existing theoretical ideas. The boundaries between all the different acts of sexual hostility that women suffer – 'wolf whistling', bottom pinching, 'goosing', workplace harassment, sexual assaults with and without actual penetration, and so on – are conceptual and theoretical boundaries. They are drawn in relation to ideas about what is and is not proper and/or acceptable for men to do to women. Thus, in Britain until 1991 if a man happened to be married to the woman he attacked, his act of sexual violence would not be classified as 'rape' since the marriage licence effectively made the woman's body his property. Still today, if a man rapes another man, it will not be classified as such, because only women can be 'raped'.

The same points can be made in relation to all official statistics. These figures are produced using technical and conceptual instruments which together assign particular cases into particular categories (for example, the married man who is looking for work and receiving benefit will be assigned to the category 'unemployed', the married woman who is looking for work but not entitled to benefit will not). As Hindess (1973) argues, though some official statistics are more technically reliable than others, the evaluation of such statistics cannot be 'reduced to the identification or estimation of errors resulting from the technical inadequacy of the agency with respect to its tasks' (1973: 42). Instead, evaluating such statistics 'is always and necessarily a theoretical exercise and, further . . . different theoretical problems must produce different and sometimes contradictory evaluations of any given set of statistics' (Hindess 1973: 47). For both technical and theoretical reasons, official rape statistics are of very little value in determining the absolute number of rapes that occur in any given country, yet, as will be seen in the next section, if different questions are addressed, the same statistics can be of use to the sociologist.

USING OFFICIAL STATISTICS CRITICALLY

This chapter has attempted to show that the naïve empiricist view of official statistics as 'numerical facts' which measure the social world objectively and dispassionately is highly problematic. But it has also argued that these statistics cannot be dismissed as simply the sum of individual, subjective ideas and impressions. Official statistics should not be uncritically accepted or cited by sociologists, but at the same time, they can be important to social researchers both as an object of study in their own right and as a data source. How can official statistics be used critically? The short answer is simply that the social researcher must be aware of their limitations, and therefore cautious about making generalisations on the basis of such data. If the researcher approaches these statistics as social products rather than incontrovertible 'facts' and thinks carefully about how the process of production may have shaped the final product, then there are ways of using official data for sociological purposes. Griffiths et al. (1979) outline three ways in which this data can be radically re-used: 'undermining the validity of dominant ideologies; developing radical theory; and applying these theories in political struggle' (1979: 366).

Official data can be 'used to call into question theories or viewpoints that are used to promote conservative, or to oppose radical, theory and practice' (Griffiths et al. 1979: 366). This strategy basically involves the detailed study and analysis of official data to discover and emphasise those 'facts' which the government, media and other bodies prefer to ignore. Likewise, feminist writers who are concerned with rape can make use of the Home Office's crime survey to support their claim that rape is an under-reported crime and therefore a more extensive and urgent problem than is often assumed. Official statistics can also be used to help develop alternative forms of theoretical analysis. Griffiths *et al.* argue that:

> Radicals should be able . . . to provide alternative theoretical explana-
> tions of the causes of unemployment and lack of housing, and to relate
> these to the statistics – drawing on data such as the numbers of un-
> employed construction workers and unoccupied houses. Like conser-
> vatives and liberals, they need data to support, and indeed to improve,
> their theories and arguments, which are otherwise liable to remain
> unconvincing, inadequate or trapped at the level of pure abstraction.
>
> (Griffiths *et al.* 1979: 367)

Thus feminists can also use official statistics to develop general theories about rape and ideology, and to buttress particular arguments, such as those about the attitudes of the police and courts towards raped women. Soothill and Walby (1991), for example, point out that although the number of women reporting rape to the police in Britain increased dramatically in the ten years between 1977 and 1987, the rate of con-viction actually declined:

> In 1977 32 per cent of rape complaints were concluded by conviction of
> the rapist, while in 1987 only 18 per cent were similarly convicted. The
> rate of increase of convicted rapist is 39 per cent as against an increase
> in rape reports of 143 per cent. [If the increase in the rate of reporting
> indicates a large increase in the level of rape] . . . this would mean that
> not only are more men raping, but also the judiciary is increasingly
> allowing them to get away with it. [If the increase in the rate of reporting
> indicates that more women are reporting the crime] . . . then we are
> seeing a constant rate of rape over the last decade but where women are
> more willing to make legal complaints . . . the police and courts [are] not
> willing to convict other than a very small increase in the number. . . .
> Whichever way we look at the figures . . . the decreasing conviction rate
> indicates that the state has not effectively responded to demands that sex
> crimes be treated more seriously.
>
> Soothill and Walby (1991: 2)

Edwards (1981) also makes critical use of official rape statistics to support her theories about the way in which unequal power relations between the sexes are institutionalised within the legal process and about the social control of female sexuality. Angela Davis (1982) mean-while, draws on statistical data to show how the myth of the Black rapist played a central role in the shaping of post-slavery racism in the USA. A variety of official and non-official sources suggest that in the 30 years following the Civil War, more than 10,000 African-American men were murdered by lynch mobs. It was the rape charge which proved most effective in mobilising such mobs and justifying the lynching of Black men. As Davis observes, 'the institution of lynching, in turn, complemented by the continued rape of Black women, became an essential ingredient of the post-war strategy of racist terror' (1982: 185). The persistence of the myth is demonstrated by the fact that 'of the 455 men executed between 1930 and 1967 on the basis of rape convictions, 405 of them were Black' (Davis 1982: 172). Again, such work draws attention to the structural inequalities which systematically shape the meanings which are attached to events and so affect the picture of the world painted by official statistics.

Official statistics can also serve as a stimulus for research questions. For instance, Home Office research into changes in rape offences and sentencing between 1973 and 1985 (Lloyd and Walmsley 1989) found that most of the increase in rape convictions between these years was accounted for by a rise in convictions for rape by 'intimates', that is, relatives, friends and ex-partners. Where intimates accounted for only 14 per cent of convicted rapists in 1973, in 1985 this had risen to 30 per cent. Lloyd and Walmsley note that:

> The greatest increases are of rapes by friends and ex-partners. Perhaps such groups more often committed rape in 1985 than in 1973 – a study of convicted cases can provide no evidence to support or refute such a possibility – but it may also be that the increases reflect a greater willingness of victims to report such cases, of the police to investigate them and prosecute, and of the courts to convict.
>
> (1989: 11)

Though the number of convictions is, for reasons outlined above, a very poor indicator of the actual number of rapes committed, such figures provide some valuable information about the practices of the police and courts, information which could not be readily found through survey or qualitative methods alone. This information is not the be all and end all of social research, but it can help the sociologist to identify areas which require further investigation. The Lloyd and Walmsley study, for example, might prompt a social researcher to design research that would explore the attitudes of the police and/or judiciary towards rape by intimates. Finally, official data can often be re-analysed by sociologists working in the field. Arber's (1990) work on women's health provides an excellent example of this type of secondary analysis. She shows how the General Household Survey (GHS) can be re-analysed to reveal 'gender differences in sickness absence, gender and care of elderly disabled people, and inequalities in women's health' (1990: 63), and how the 'secondary analyst of the GHS need not be constrained to operate within the same set of conceptual assumptions as those held by the original designers' (1990: 65).

One of the aims of this book is to challenge the naïve positivist desire to limit social scientific investigation to the study of observable social phenomena. This chapter has argued that official statistics cannot be treated as neutral descriptions of social reality. Quantifying a given social phenomenon requires the enumerator to fit particular cases into certain classificatory categories and since there are no neutral observational categories, only conceptual categories based upon particular theoretical and political assumptions, then all numerical descriptions of the social world are theory impregnated. But an awareness of the limitations and socially constructed nature of official statistics does not render them useless to the social researcher. Used carefully (and often in conjunction with other types of data) official statistics can not only provide some basic or preliminary data against which theories can be developed or assessed but can also be wielded as part of an attack on dominant ideologies and popular beliefs about the social world.

Chapter 4

The survey method

Surveys are perhaps the most familiar method of social research, and for many people, they are the most 'scientific' form of investigation. They produce numerical descriptions of the social world (eight out of ten cats prefer Whiskas, 20 per cent of the population believe x, 50 per cent have never done y) and surveys often receive such wide publicity that their findings become part of people's daily knowledge about the world. Surveys on sexual behaviour are no exception. Readers of this book will probably have heard it said, for example, that on average young men think about sex once every eight minutes, and that the average erect penis is six inches long. It is the survey method which produces this type of numerical 'fact', for the survey method generates a very particular sort of data. Where other research methods produce unstructured data (perhaps in the form of field notes written by the researcher, or in the form of taped conversations) the survey method produces a structured or systematic set of data which de Vaus (1991) calls a 'variable by case data matrix'. The researcher begins by listing the variables with which she or he is concerned, and then systematically collects information about each of these variables.

A researcher conducting a survey on the sexual behaviour of young people, for example, might be interested in numerous different variables – age at which the respondent reached puberty, first dated, first had sexual intercourse and so on – as well as background variables such as age, education, social class and area in which the respondent was brought up. Information about every variable would then be collected from each respondent (case), to produce a data matrix along the lines of the one shown in Figure 4.1.

Although surveys are typically associated with the use of question-naires to gather information, in practice, a range of techniques for collecting information can be employed; questionnaires, structured

Variables	Case 1	Case 2	Case 3	Case 4
Age				
Social class (Registrar General's classification)				
Address (town/area)				
Age at first experience of sexual intercourse				

Figure 4.1 Example of a variable by case data matrix

interviews, in-depth and semi-structured interviews, document searches and so on. Likewise, though the 'cases' may be individual respondents, they can equally well be countries, years, towns, or institutions such as schools or firms. The Workplace Industrial Relations Survey, for example, records the attributes of firms (rather than those of individual workers) on a number of different variables in order to produce the rectangular set of data which is a defining characteristic of surveys.

Surveys are distinguished not only by the form of data they produce, but also the way in which this data is analysed (see Marsh 1982). Because survey data takes this matrix form, it can be analysed in a number of ways. First, and most simply, straight frequency counts can be conducted. By totting up the responses in each row researchers can summarise the information they have collected.

Frequency counts thus allow the researcher to describe the sample numerically; the mean age of the respondents was x, 45 per cent were from social classes I and II, half lost their virginity at the age of 16, and so on. But more than this, because surveys produce data in this matrix form, it is possible to *compare* cases. The data can be analysed in search of systematic links between characteristics. Using the above example, the researcher can ask whether the age at which respondents first

Variable	Case 1	Case 2	Case 3	Case 4	Total
Age at first experience of sexual intercourse	15	16	17	16	15-year-old = 1 (25%) 16-year-old = 2 (50%) 17-year-old = 1 (25%)

Figure 4.2 Example of a frequency count

experienced sexual intercourse is systematically linked to their social class, the area in which they live, and so on. In short, the aim of this type of analysis is to explore relationships between two or more variables.

If a survey produced the results shown in Figure 4.3, it would suggest that there was a relationship between social class and the age at which respondents first experienced sexual intercourse. Respondents from social classes I, II and III appear to be sexually active at an earlier age than respondents from social classes IV and V. However, such results would not demonstrate a direct causal relationship. We could not conclude that being in social class V *causes* people to refrain from sexual

	Social class I & II	Social class III	Social class IV	Social class V
First experience of sexual intercourse at age 16	20	15	0	0
First experience of sexual intercourse at age 17	0	0	15	20

Figure 4.3 Relationships between variables (social class and age of first experience of sexual intercourse)

activity until the age of 17. All that the researcher could infer from such data would be that some association between social class and sexual habits existed, and this would then prompt further questions about the nature of that association and the investigation of other variables.

In summary then, the survey method is designed to compare cases systematically and search for relationships and links between variables. Part of its appeal as a method is that because it produces a structured data set, it makes it possible to collect, process and analyse vast quantities of information. If a researcher conducts unstructured interviews with 200 people, allowing the respondent to set the agenda rather than systematically seeking their views on a predetermined range of variables, he or she will be left with perhaps two or three hundred hours of transcribed tapes, and the problem of how to impose some kind of order upon this mass of information. Because the survey method produces a systematic, structured matrix of data, information from 200 or even 2000 people can simply be fed into a computer, and a statistical program can be used to produce frequency counts and cross tabulations, as well as to show whether there are statistical relationships between variables. A number of statistical programs have been designed for use in the social sciences, SPSS and Minitab being the most commonly used for analysing survey data (see Ryan *et al.* 1985, Bryman and Cramer 1990).

Survey data is thus perhaps the most manageable form of data, and this is one reason for its popularity. Furthermore, the survey method produces a numerical 'snapshot' of the social world, and journalists as well as funding bodies tend to like this type of 'hard' data which can be easily summarised and quoted. The method may therefore also be attractive to social researchers because they often assume that this general admiration of 'hard' data will readily be translated into offers of 'hard' cash to fund their work. However, like all social research methods, surveys have limitations as well as advantages. To understand these limitations, it is necessary to look more closely at what is involved in designing and conducting a social survey; namely, sample design, nonresponse, questionnaire design and coding. In the following section, the problems associated with each of these processes are illustrated through reference to a classic piece of North American research into sexual behaviour conducted by Alfred Kinsey.

SEX RESEARCH AND SURVEY METHODS

Orthodox methods textbooks often argue that one of the advantages of the survey method is that it forces 'the researcher to formalise on paper for all to see certain phases of the research process that other designs are likely to skip over' (Hessler 1992). This is certainly not true of Kinsey's work, which developed in a somewhat *ad hoc* fashion and spanned a period of almost twenty years. For this reason, it might seem strange to devote so much attention to Kinsey's work in a chapter on survey methods. But since Kinsey was committed to producing data in a variable by case data matrix form and searching for systematic links between variables, he can be thought of as a survey researcher and because his work does not conform to textbook guidelines on how to design and conduct a survey, it can be used to highlight some of the traps that can ensnare the unwary social researcher.

Alfred Kinsey was a biologist who began research into human sexual behaviour in 1938 and continued until his death in 1956. He founded the Institute for Sex Research at Indiana University, which continued to publish books and articles on human sexual behaviour long after his death. His two main books, *Sexual Behavior in the Human Male* (1948) and *Sexual Behavior in the Human Female* (1953), received such wide publicity that Kinsey was virtually a household name in North America in the 1950s and 60s. His admirers claimed that 'the Kinsey Report has done for sex what Columbus did for geography. It makes a successful scientific voyage to explore an unknown world . . . the sex life of human beings' (Morris and Loth 1948, cited in Pomeroy 1972). What did Kinsey find on this voyage? In essence, his research revealed that people were not only far more sexually active than had ever been imagined in terms of frequency, but also in terms of *what* they did. The decent and God fearing American public found it distressing to be told, for example, that 24 per cent of males under 15 years of age, and 52 per cent of 16-year-old boys were sexually active; that 5.9 per cent of boys under 15 years had had sexual contacts with animals; that 28 per cent of married men aged between 31 and 35 had had extra-marital intercourse; that 38.7 per cent of single males aged between 36 and 40 have at some point engaged in homosexual activity to the point of orgasm; that 15-year-old boys masturbate on average 23 times per week. This list goes on. Kinsey's two volumes on human sexual behaviour provide statistics on the incidence of a wide range of sexual activities, broken down by class, age, educational level and 'racialized identity'. Those seeking titillation will be disappointed by these books however, for they make intensely dull reading. Each volume consists of around 700 pages of dreary figures and tables of statistics and dry commentary upon them.

Kinsey claimed not to be interested in moral or cultural issues. As a disinterested, impartial scientist, he simply wanted to gather together the

'plain facts' of human sexual behaviour. Such an ambition has implications for methods. Kinsey wanted to quantify sexual behaviour and
systematically explore links between variables so that he could describe
the sex lives of North Americans numerically. To do this required a
variable by case data matrix. But Kinsey did not simply sit down and
plan a survey in the traditional way. Instead, his research evolved from
his teaching on the biology of sex for a marriage course which was set
up in 1938 at Indiana University. According to Pomeroy (1972),
Kinsey's lectures prompted a number of students to seek him out for
advice about their sexual problems. Kinsey took the opportunity to
obtain what he called 'histories' of the students who came to confide in
him. He would grill them about the age at which they had first had
intercourse, about the frequency of their sexual activity, the number of
partners they had had, and so on. His appetite whetted by these early
counselling sessions, Kinsey went on to appeal for student volunteers to
provide him with yet more 'histories'. After only one year, Kinsey had
collected 350 'histories' in this way and decided to embark on really
large-scale research into human sexual behaviour. Being a somewhat
obsessive personality type who had always had a fondness for collecting
things (stamps, specimens of insects, classical recordings, even drinks
recipes), Kinsey decided that he would acquire 100,000 'histories'.

Getting hold of 100,000 people who are prepared to answer questions
about the most intimate aspects of their sexual lives (for example, 'Have
you had sexual contact with an animal or masturbated an animal?'), is
clearly no easy task. In the end, Kinsey did not realise his ambition, but
he and his associates did manage to collect around 18,000 'histories'
(Pomeroy 1972: 4). Where and how did they find 18,000 people willing
to participate in this research, and how representative of the American
population as a whole were these people? Much of the criticism of
Kinsey's work centres on precisely these questions. To understand these
criticisms, it is necessary to outline the principles of sample design.

THE PRINCIPLES OF SAMPLE DESIGN

Selecting a sample is a problem that is common to all research, regardless of the methods being employed. However, survey methods tend to
be associated with a rather more rigorous approach to sample design,
and for this reason, the issue is dealt with in some depth here. It would
be impossible for a researcher who was interested in British women's
sexual behaviour to ask every single woman in Britain to take part in the
study. Even in the unlikely event that resources in terms of time, money

and researchers, were available, the logistics of tracking down and talking to 100 per cent of the female population would doom the project to failure. The researcher must therefore find a group of women small enough to study. But if the researcher wants to be able to generalise about the behaviour and attitudes of all British women, this group must be a microcosm of the wider population. Selecting 100 nuns, or 100 street prostitutes in King's Cross would clearly be inappropriate. 'Sampling' is the term for choosing a group that is small enough to study, but which is still representative of the wider population being studied. A number of different techniques for selecting a sample can be employed, but broadly speaking they fall into two types: random and non-random sampling.

Probability or random sampling

The object of this type of sampling method is to eliminate or reduce possible bias from the researcher. If researchers simply chose who to include and who not to include in their study, they could bias the research either by selecting people who are more likely to support their hypothesis or by excluding certain groups of people from the sample. Probability sampling is a method of selecting a sample *for* the researcher, so that their subjective preconceptions and values cannot intrude upon the selection process. Random sampling gives each individual in the population an equal chance of being selected, rather than leaving this to the researcher's discretion.

Simple random sampling and systematic sampling

This is perhaps the purest form of random sampling. The researcher begins by obtaining a sampling frame (a pre-existing list of names, such as an electoral register, postal addresses, doctor's lists or list of firms, schools, agencies depending on whether it is individuals or institutions which are to be surveyed). A number is then assigned to every name on this list and a Quantum Random Number Generator is used to produce a list of numbers that are systematically related to nothing at all. Lists of such numbers are also available in table form, and de Vaus (1991: 62–4) provides a clear guide to using them. The sample will include those individuals who have been allocated numbers which correspond with the randomly generated numbers. A simpler and more common technique is known as a 'systematic sampling'. As with simple random sampling, the researcher begins with a sampling frame which includes, let us say, 10,000 names. If the researcher wanted a sample of 1,000 people, instead of using randomly generated numbers to pick each individual member of the sample, he or she would pick a number between 1 and 9 at random, begin there and take every tenth name after that.

Both simple random sampling and systematic sampling techniques present certain problems, however. To begin with, obtaining a complete sampling frame is not always easy, and an incomplete frame may lead to 'systematic error'. Take the British electoral register, for example. It excludes people under the age of 18 and non-British nationals. There have always been people who are eligible to vote, but do not for one reason or another, register to do so. Relying on the electoral register as a sampling frame therefore means that certain groups either will not appear, or are less likely to appear in the sample. The views of young people, poor people, students, migrants, as well as groups who are disaffected with the British electoral system will be under-represented in the research. Systematic sampling can also lead to bias if there is what is known as 'periodicity' in the sampling frame. For instance, if a list of married couples was used which had been compiled as husband, wife, husband, wife, and so on, and the researcher decided to include every tenth name in the sample, no men would appear in the study. Before taking a systematic sample, then, it is necessary to think carefully about whether the sampling frame covers everyone in the target population, and whether there is any periodicity in the list that could affect the research.

Can we safely assume that providing the sampling frame covers everyone in the target population and there is no periodicity in the list that systematic sampling will produce a representative sample? Unfortunately, random samples do not actually *guarantee* representativeness. Random errors can occur, which are down to simple bad luck. Imagine a woman has been awarded a large grant to research attitudes towards abortion. She systematically draws a sample of 100 people from a perfectly good sampling frame, and finds to her dismay that 50 of them are religious fundamentalists. The probability of this happening is extremely low, but it can happen. Faced with this misfortune, the researcher cannot simply discard some of these fundamentalists and go back to the sampling frame to replace them with other names, for this would destroy the whole point of random sampling. If she did so, she would be exercising her subjective judgement over the sample selection by deciding whether or not a sample comprising 50 per cent of religious fundamentalists was representative of the population as a whole, and if not, how many fundamentalists should be included. She cannot reject subjects once they have been randomly selected, but if she continues with her survey using this sample, the findings will be seriously biased. Bearing in mind issues of funding and professional reputation, social researchers cannot afford to use a method which carries a risk of this kind of odd quirk of fate. They must therefore find ways of avoiding such random errors. This can be done in one of two ways. First, the researcher can take a bigger sample. The larger the sample, the less likely it is that random error will bias the findings. If our researcher increased her sample to 1,000 people, it is extremely unlikely that many more religious fundamentalists would be randomly selected, and the existing 50 fundamentalists would come to represent only 5 per cent as opposed to 50 per cent of her final sample. This should reduce bias. But the larger the sample, the more expensive the survey is in terms of time and money. Most researchers therefore prefer to use a technique called 'stratification' to try to prevent random errors from interfering with the representativeness of their samples.

Stratified sampling techniques

When researchers want to use random sampling methods, but still ensure that the number of males and females in the sample exactly mirror the proportion of males and females in the country as a whole, they use sex as a stratifying factor. The sampling frame is rearranged as two lists, one of males and one of females, and 51 per cent of the sample is systematically selected from the list of females, 49 per cent from the list of males (a technique known as 'proportionate stratified sampling'). The same principle can be applied to any stratifying factor, whether it be age, social class, religion, trades union membership or whatever. The researcher is still randomly selecting subjects but the risk of random errors distorting the final results is minimised.

The decision to stratify by any given factor rests on whether the researcher believes there is some kind of relationship between the stratifying factor and the perimeter (the thing) they are attempting to measure. In the case of a survey into attitudes towards abortion, for example, religion is likely to have a significant effect upon attitudes. It would therefore be desirable to stratify in terms of religious belief. However, it seems unlikely that there is a relationship between people's shoe sizes and their attitudes towards abortion, and it would not therefore be worth stratifying to ensure the proportion of people with size 5 feet in the sample matched the proportion of people with size 5 feet in the population as a whole. Researchers draw on pre-existing knowledge (from official statistics, or previous research or from their basic 'common-sense' knowledge) to decide whether or not it is worth using a particular stratifying factor. But no matter how much a researcher might want, ideally, to stratify by certain factors, however, it is not always feasible. A stratified sample can only be taken if the researcher has the necessary background information about the way in which members of the target population as a whole are distributed between strata. Though fairly reliable information on sex and age can be obtained from census data, to rely on official statistics for background information of the population in terms of, say, social class or ethnicity is problematic for reasons discussed in the previous chapter. To stratify by religion, meanwhile, would require reliable knowledge about the number of atheists, Muslims, Catholics, Hindus, and so on in the population as a whole, which would be extremely hard to get hold of. As de Vaus (1991: 67) observes, 'information on the stratifying variable is often unavailable', and even where it is, the researcher further has to be able to locate members of different strata, which again can be very difficult.

When the attitudes or behaviour of a fairly small population or group, say, employees in one or two particular firms or children in one particular school, are being measured, stratifying a sample is reasonably straightforward because it is usually possible to get hold of background information and to locate the members of different strata. But when researchers are interested in the entire country's population, simple stratified sampling is more problematic. To get around these problems and avoid expense, a technique known as 'multistage cluster sampling is often used.

Multistage cluster sampling

Instead of trying to draw one random sample from the entire country, multistage cluster sampling puts a grid over the country and divides it into areas. A manageable number of areas are randomly picked, and then further subdivided into smaller districts, and a number of these districts are randomly selected. The principles of random sampling are still intact, for, 'since everyone lives in a district, everyone has an equal chance of being selected in the final sample' (de Vaus 1991: 67), but this is far cheaper and easier to administer than any other method of random sampling. An interview headquarters can be set up in each district, and it is possible to manage without a pre-existing sampling frame if the districts are broken down still further. Street directories for each of the chosen districts can be found and used to randomly select streets;

households in the chosen streets can be identified and listed, particular households can then be randomly selected from this list of households. Russell (1986) used this type of technique to obtain a random sample of women for a survey concerned with incest. The survey was undertaken in San Francisco, and 'key addresses' were randomly selected from the telephone directory:

> Each address served as a starting point for obtaining a cluster of household listings. Enumerators used these key addresses as a starting point for listing all the addresses on the entire side of that block. . . . A 'Dear Resident' letter . . . was mailed to each address drawn in the sample. . . . An interviewer followed up the letter with a visit to the address. Her first task was to obtain a list of household members, their ages, relationships with each other, and their marital and employment status. If there was more than one woman eighteen years or over in a given household, a random procedure was applied to select one of them.
>
> (Russell 1986: 26)

Cluster sampling makes research financially possible, but it can increase error. For example, if three retirement resorts in the south of England were selected as the initial clusters to be further subdivided, the researcher would probably find that the final sample over-represented the wealthy and the elderly and under-represented England's working-class and African-Caribbean and Asian population (since people of different age and social class are not evenly geographically distributed, nor is the white, African-Caribbean and Asian population randomly dispersed across England). The way to get around this problem is to take as many initial clusters as possible, so that as much variety as possible is introduced into the sample. To further minimise sampling error, the researcher can use stratification techniques to try to ensure that the final sample is as much like a microcosm of the entire population as it possibly can be.

Even the most carefully designed sample may not fully achieve this, however. Indeed, one criticism of the most recent survey of sexual behaviour in Britain by Wellings *et al.* (1994) – published as this book was going to press – centres on this issue. Using the country's postcode address system to achieve a well geographically spread sample, this survey produced far lower figures for homosexuality than would have been predicted on the basis of previous research. But it is highly unlikely that the homosexual population is evenly geographically dispersed across Britain. For a number of reasons, not least a very real fear of discrimination, abuse and assault, lesbians and gay men often prefer to live in cities where there is an existing gay community. As activists have pointed out, given the extremely high concentration of lesbians and gay men in urban areas, the sampling techniques used by Wellings *et al.* were unlikely to accurately reflect the level of homosexuality in Britain today (see *The Pink Paper* 1994).

Non-random sampling techniques

It should be clear from the above that random selection is a time-consuming and therefore a costly process. For this reason it is not always a practical option for survey researchers. One cheaper alternative, which is widely used by market researchers and opinion pollsters, is known as 'quota sampling'. This is basically 'a method of stratified sampling in which the selection within strata is non-random' (Moser and Kalton 1979: 127). The researcher begins by deciding how the sample should be stratified in order to correspond to the target population; that is, how many men and how many women, and how many people from each age group and each social class should be included in the sample. Rather than using a sampling frame to randomly select individuals from each of these stratum, however, interviewers are simply told to go out and find them. They may be instructed, for example, to find a quota of 20 male and 5 female professionals, 50 male and 20 female manual workers and so on.

The problem with this method is that it increases the possibility of bias. Although the quotas have been decided in advance, it is up to the interviewers to decide exactly who to ask to take part in the survey. An interviewer might be standing in a crowded shopping centre trying to fill a quota of 20 females aged 65 plus. If random techniques were being used, every woman over 65 years of age would stand an equal chance of being selected for study. The same is not true of quota sampling. Faced with a choice between stopping a sprightly, smartly dressed woman in her mid-60s and a bag lady who is stopping to investigate the contents of every rubbish bin, the interviewer will probably prefer to approach the first. Interviewers have a job to do, and will wish to conduct the interviews as quickly and easily as possible. Their judgements and preconceptions will inevitably colour the selection process and a sample culled in this way is unlikely to cover the full range of characteristics within any one stratum. (For a fuller discussion of the limitations of quota sampling techniques, see Moser and Kalton 1979.) Though cheap and simple to administer, quota sampling is less likely than random techniques to produce a sample which is representative of the target population.

Sometimes, random sampling is inappropriate because of the nature of the planned research. Imagine a researcher wanted to conduct a survey to discover the impact of Aids awareness campaigns on the attitudes and behaviour of male homosexuals. If the researcher drew a random sample of men from the entire population, it would be unlikely to include enough male homosexuals to make the study worthwhile, and there is no pre-existing list of *all* homosexual men in the population which could be used as a sampling frame. In such circumstances, researchers generally turn to either 'volunteer' or 'snowballing' sampling techniques, or some combination of the two. Volunteer sampling has been widely used in experimental research (see Chapter 6), but it is also often used when the subject of the research is seen as particularly sensitive. A number of recent North American studies of prostitutes and homosexual men have adopted this approach. For example, Levine and Siegel (1992) were concerned with gay men's participation in unprotected sex. They obtained a sample of 150 men as follows:

> Respondents for the study were recruited through flyers distributed and posted at a variety of gay service, political and social organizations (including the large Lesbian and Gay Community Centre, which serves the organized gay community in New York). In addition, recruiting announcements were run as advertisements in gay newspapers and as public service announcements on gay cable television, announced at various gay organizational meetings, published in a range of gay newspapers, and distributed through a constantly growing recruitment network.
>
> (Levine and Siegel 1992: 51)

Snowballing is a method which involves the researcher starting out with one or two individuals from the target population and asking them to put him or her in touch with others. It is widely used to obtain a sample from 'deviant' populations, such as drug users or criminals, who are imagined to have contact with other 'like minded' individuals, and who could not be recruited in sufficient numbers through random techniques. Where random sampling techniques represent an attempt to find a group that is small enough to study but which is still representative of the wider population, snowballing is a way of selecting enough respondents from a group with very particular characteristics to make a worthwhile study. The use of this technique in qualitative research is discussed in more detail in Chapter 7.

Here it is important to note that survey researchers who use non-random samples run the risk of biasing their findings. Every member of the target population does not stand an equal chance of being selected for study, which means that the sample is less likely to be truly representative of the wider population. For survey researchers this is a problem. It means that bias can be introduced by the interviewers who choose who will fill the quota, or the volunteers who select themselves to participate in the research, or the contacts who recruit friends or associates to take part in the study. Though a technique like snowballing is perfectly legitimate when the research objective is not to make large-scale generalisations about the population as a whole, the findings of *survey* research which relies on non-random samples are less reliable than those based on surveys which employed random sampling techniques.

KINSEY'S SAMPLING TECHNIQUES

Despite his background as a natural scientist, Kinsey is said to have had a deep mistrust of random probability sampling 'on the grounds that not only did it not guarantee a representative sample, but it led people to be content with inadequate small samples' (Gebhard and Johnson 1979: 25). He further argued that rigorous random sampling techniques were in-appropriate for a study of sexual behaviour, noting that it is not feasible:

> to stand on a street corner, tap every tenth individual on the shoulder and command him to contribute a full and frankly honest sex history. . . . Theoretically less satisfactory but more practical means of sampling human material must be accepted as the best that can be done.
>
> (Kinsey *et al.* 1948: 93)

In the early years of the project, Kinsey used straightforward volunteer methods. Students, colleagues, prison inmates, members of Parent Teacher Associations and all manner of other groups were invited to come forward and were reassured that 'we have seen so much of the personal lives of our students that we are surprised at nothing, make no moral evaluations and are interested primarily in the scientifically objective fact' (Pomeroy 1972: 55). Alongside this, snowballing techniques were employed. Whenever Kinsey interviewed someone, he would press them to persuade their friends to come and give 'histories'. When he turned his attention to homosexuals, he would locate gay 'taverns and clubs' and ask men to take part in the study and to put him in touch with other homosexuals they knew. At this point his aim was to get as many 'histories' with as much variety as possible. In a letter to a friend he wrote:

Am waiting right now for the arrival of a taxi driver whose amazing experience of seventeen years is already half in my history. . . . He learned through a friend that I was collecting data, came around to volunteer (gratis) all he knew. If there is anyone who knows about variety and organized erotics, he is the one who knows it.

(cited in Pomeroy 1972: 63)

As the research grew, Kinsey took on a number of researcher assistants. He also became increasingly aware of critics who argued that his sampling techniques were far from scientific (Eisenbud and Mead 1948, Wickware 1948). The most damning criticism that could be levelled against him was simply that his volunteer and snowball samples were self-selecting. Using non-random techniques, Kinsey was getting information about the sex lives of the sort of people who would willingly volunteer to supply details of their sex lives to a complete stranger. Were such people representative of the American population as a whole? Perhaps he was only talking to members of a sub-group of especially exhibitionist people, whose sexual behaviour, like their willingness to discuss it, was completely unlike the general population's. Kinsey's sample is made even more suspect by the fact that he actually paid some respondents, termed 'contact men', to find him new volunteers. The contact men knew that Kinsey was doing sex research, and that they were being paid to find him subjects. It is highly probable that they assumed that in order to secure further payments, they should find subjects who would provide Kinsey with really colourful histories and that they therefore biased the sample further. As Kinsey himself noted:

It was difficult at first for [the contact men] to understand that the forty minute history of an inexperienced teen-ager is as important as the two- or three-hour history of an older person who has been involved in every conceivable sort of sexual activity.

(1948: 103)

Kinsey's response to criticisms of volunteer and snowballing methods was to adopt a form of sampling which he termed '100 per cent samples'. To his mind, this was similar to multistage cluster sampling. The idea was to take cases from a number of geographical locations (like taking clusters from the country as a whole) then break these clusters down further into smaller and smaller areas. Finally, the areas were broken down into what he termed 'cells'. Each cell was supposed to contain a particular stratum of the population. For example, to get a cross-section of age groups, he would take a high school as one cell, a college as another, an old people's home as another, and so on. He then attempted to get every single member of that cell to participate in the study. Kinsey explains the principle as follows:

> Since it is impossible to secure a strictly randomized sample, the best substitute is to secure one hundred percent of the social unit from which the sample is drawn. One hundred percent of the members of a family group, all the persons living in a particular apartment house, all the members of a college sorority or fraternity, all the persons in some service club, all the members of some Sunday School class or some other church organization, all the persons in a city block, all the persons in a rural township, all the inmates of some penal or other institution, all the persons in some other unit, provided that unit has not been brought together by a common sexual interest.
>
> (1948: 93)

The idea was thus to take clusters which were microcosms of the population of the USA as a whole, consider the main lines along which these clusters were stratified (age, social class and religion) and find social units from each stratum. In this way, Kinsey held that he could secure a sample that was representative of the population as a whole, and he clearly had confidence in his sample's representativeness since he used his data to make general claims about the population as a whole. Was his confidence justified? To answer this, it is necessary to look at how he selected his sample in a little more detail.

The whole idea of multistaged cluster sampling is that it ensures that each individual stands an equal chance of being selected even where no sampling frame is available, for each individual lives in a district or block, and the districts and blocks are randomly selected not hand picked by the researcher. Bias from the researcher or elsewhere is thus kept to a minimum. But each individual in the US population did not stand an equal chance of being selected by Kinsey, who was opportunistic in his selection of cells. Neither the original clusters nor any of the cells he used were randomly selected, instead Kinsey targeted certain institutions or 'social units' because they offered ease of access. Take the data upon which the Male volume is based. The 100 per cent cells he refers to actually consisted of a number of colleges, some groups of (unspecified) professionals, some groups of conscientious objectors, some high school classes, some speech clinic groups, some groups of people living in rooming houses, groups taken from prisons, borstals and mental hospitals and he even claimed to have interviewed 100 per cent of hitch hikers in each geographical area over a three year period. Taken all together, did his cells add up to a representative cross-section of the US population? A fairly high percentage of this sample was drawn from penal or other total institutions; more than half were college students or professionals; and the remainder was a motley collection of hitch hikers, high school students, speech clinic attendees, conscientious objectors and so on. At the very least, the class composition was completely skewed, with virtually no working-class people in the sample at all except those in total institutions or rooming houses.

Given Kinsey's admiration for all things scientific, he should have been more careful and systematic in his selection of these cells. To use multistaging effectively, researchers need a lot of pre-existing knowledge about the population as a whole. This enables them to check whether their sample has gone astray by comparing its composition in terms of social class, sex, ethnicity, age and so on, against existing information. Russell (1986) for example, used multistaging, but then checked certain demographic characteristics of her sample against census information on San Francisco as a whole to ensure that she had achieved a similar distribution. Kinsey did not trouble with this sort of detail. Indeed, it would have been impossible for him to do so given the cells he had chosen to use. There is no information available about the total population of hitch hikers, for example, so there is no way of knowing whether Kinsey really interviewed 100 per cent of hitch hikers, nor of telling how many hitch hikers should be included in a sample to make it representative of a given geographical cluster. Equally problematic is the fact that his 100 per cent cells were not mutually exclusive. It is quite possible for individuals to be at the same time a student, a hitch hiker and a speech clinic attendee, or at the same time a prisoner and a conscientious objector. If the cells or districts or areas used in a multistaged cluster sample are not mutually exclusive, there is a danger that only a very small and completely unrepresentative sub-group of the population will be sampled.

It is also surprising to discover that Kinsey did not even keep accurate records of who had been interviewed or where he had recruited them. Gebhard and Johnson (1979) observe that 'One might have expected that a taxonomist such as Kinsey would have formulated some clearly-defined system and detailed recording of sources; but, a combination of opportunism, overwork, and the inherent complexity of humanity joined to defeat taxonomy' (1979: 27). Kinsey believed that providing his cells were diverse enough (and he went on to use wildly different groups such as Parent Teacher Associations and Communist Party groups, YMCAs and the staff of museums, in his search to cover different groups) and his sample was big enough, there would be no problem of bias. As Gebhard and Johnson observe, 'To Kinsey, the solution to sampling problems was to increase the size and diversity of the sample, and he felt that all biases and other problems would average out and nullify one another as the sample grew and proliferated' (1979: 25). But simply being diverse is not enough to produce a sample that is representative of the population as a whole.

Though Kinsey's 100 per cent sampling technique was probably an improvement on straight volunteer and snowball sampling, it was not an adequate substitute for random sampling methods. In any case, out of the 18,000 histories on which Kinsey's research and writings were based, only around a quarter came from these 100 per cent cells. The bulk of his sample was recruited from volunteers, or through snowballing and the use of paid contact men. Now when he compared the results from the two different types of sampling, he found that the samples culled through the volunteer and snowballing techniques were more sexually active than samples drawn through the 100 per cent cells method. Yet Kinsey did not take this discrepancy as an indication that his findings from volunteer samples might be seriously over-exaggerating the level of sexual activity in the population as a whole. Instead, he rationalised things the other way about, and argued that the 100 per cent cell samples were biased in such a way as to make the population appear *less* sexually active than they really were. He said that the student cells contained too high a proportion of Jewish males, whom Kinsey asserted to be less sexually active than gentiles. He argued that people drawn from the 100 per cent cells were more likely to 'cover up' the truth, especially about socially taboo items such as animal contacts, because they did not contribute as willingly as volunteers. Finally he claimed that since the sample culled from 100 per cent cells were smaller numerically, they were therefore less reliable than his volunteer and snowball samples which numbered around 13,500 histories.

Kinsey of all people should have borne in mind that maxim dear to so many men – 'technique is more important than size'. Just because the volunteer samples were bigger numerically does not mean that they produced more reliable data. Bigger samples help to eliminate random error. They only reduce the impact of quirks of fate like getting the Marquis de Sade or certain politicans in a sample. If the researcher is not using random sampling techniques, then expanding the size of the sample will do nothing at all to improve reliability. Getting information from 10,000 people who actively wanted to talk about their sexual experiences to a complete stranger is no more likely to produce accurate information about the population as a whole than getting information from 100 such people. The problem of bias from volunteer samples and opportunistic 100 per cent samples was compounded by the fact that these sampling techniques prevented Kinsey from knowing anything at all about his response rate. As will be seen, survey researchers must concern themselves with the question of non-response in order to assess how representative their sample is, and how reliable their results are.

THE PROBLEM OF NON-RESPONSE

The term 'response rate' basically refers to the percentage of the sample that agrees to participate in the survey. Social researchers cannot force their human subjects to comply with the research process, but the response rate is vitally important to the reliability of survey findings, since non-response can lead to bias. Returning to the example of a survey into attitudes towards abortion, let us say that an excellent sampling frame was found and a simple random sample was successfully drawn, but only 60 per cent of the sample responded to the questionnaire. Of these respondents, the majority firmly supported the notion of the woman's right to choose. Can the researcher be sure that the results from this 60 per cent are representative of the attitudes of the entire sample? What if the women who did respond to the questionnaire were qualitatively different from those who refused to participate? Could it be that the 40 per cent who did not respond were fiercely anti-abortion? The problem is that the researcher does not know the answer to these questions. She has no information about the non-respondents, and therefore cannot tell whether it is valid to conclude that a majority of women are in favour of liberal abortion laws, even if more than half of the people who answered her questionnaire expressed these views.

Moser and Kalton (1979) note that there are a number of different types of non-response. The researcher may find that people who have been randomly selected to take part in the survey have moved house, or are out at the time she or he calls to interview them. This problem can sometimes be solved through the use of call backs, but financial constraints impose limits on how many return calls can be made. This type of non-response can lead to bias, depending upon what exactly the survey is investigating. It is important to ask whether people who do not move house or flat often, and are generally at home at the time the interviewers call (whether that be day time or evening), are likely to differ significantly from the people who are unavailable. Next, the researcher may find that people have been randomly selected to take part in the survey who are 'unsuitable for interview', perhaps because they are ill or disabled in some way which prevents them from being interviewed or completing a questionnaire in the conventional way. People who are unfamiliar with the English language may also have been selected and unless multi-lingual interviewers are employed on the project, they are unlikely to participate in the survey. Again, depending upon what is being studied, this type of non-response can lead to bias. For example, in Britain, migrant women workers are over-represented in low paid, insecure work. Any survey concerned with low waged employment such as home working should ideally ensure that questionnaires and/or interviews are available in Punjabi, Urdu and Bengali, otherwise the survey will only fully reveal the attitudes and experiences of English speaking home workers, who are probably the least exploited of this highly vulnerable group of workers. Similarly, if a survey is being conducted in a town or city with a very mixed population in terms of first languages, the response rate may fall if the research is conducted in English only. Clearly, to employ bilingual interviewers would add considerably to the cost of a survey, and is therefore, in many cases, out of the question. Russell's (1989) research into incest was based in San Francisco, and though for financial reasons the interviews had to be conducted in English, she attempted to minimise non-response by making sure that the initial letter asking people to participate in the study was written in English, Spanish and/or Cantonese, depending on the ethnic makeup of the block in which they lived.

It has been argued that the response rate is also affected by whether the survey seeks to elicit information through a self-administered questionnaire or through face-to-face interviews. Mailed questionnaires are widely believed to result in a lower response rate (people find it easier to throw a questionnaire away than to say 'No' to an interviewer) and to 'result in an upward bias in social class composition and educational level' (Moser and Kalton 1979: 268). However, de Vaus argues that the difference between mailed questionnaires and face-to-face interviews is no longer so pronounced; 'The response rate obtained in a particular study will be due to the combined effect of the topic, the nature of the sample, the length of the questionnaire, the care taken in implementing the survey and other related factors' (1991: 107).

Non-response also arises when individuals who have been randomly selected for study simply refuse to co-operate with the research. Refusal rates vary a good deal, and may have to do with the subject matter of the survey (Russell notes that 19 per cent of her sample refused to participate when they found out that study was about sexual abuse), or with the agency involved in conducting it (private market research firms commissioned by management to undertake research into employee attitudes often get more refusals than independent academic researchers). Where refusal rates are high, it is vital to consider who refused and why. The researcher needs to ask whether the people who refused to respond form a distinct sub-group of the sample as a whole, since if this is the case, the findings may be seriously biased. For example, if a large percentage of manual workers refused to participate in a survey of employee attitudes, the views of managerial and clerical employees would be exaggerated and the results would not accurately describe attitudes within the organisation as a whole. It is also worth noting that people who have been randomly selected to take part in the survey may be forbidden from so doing by another person. Just as employers act as 'gate keepers' to employees, husbands can sometimes prevent access to their wives, parents often act as gate keepers to their children, and children can act as gate keepers to elderly or infirm parents. In other words, researchers can be denied access to certain powerless individuals, and again, this can bias the survey by under-representing their views. If non-respondents all come from a distinct sub-group of the sample population, and have significantly different attributes and characteristics to those of the respondents, the survey findings will not present an accurate description of the population as a whole.

KINSEY'S RESPONSE RATE

There is simply no way of knowing what kind of response rate Kinsey's research enjoyed, because where volunteer and snowball sampling techniques are employed it is impossible to gauge non-response. Kinsey had no idea how many people had been approached by previous volunteers and had refused to participate, he had no idea how many people had seen advertisements or listened to his calls for volunteers and had failed to respond. Furthermore, it was also impossible for him to find out what kind of people these non-respondents were. He had plenty of information about those who responded, but knew nothing about those who did not. Were they qualitatively different from the group of individuals who did volunteer? Were they less sexually active, or less exhibitionist than his volunteers? Was there a whole segment of the population with very different sexual histories about whom Kinsey knew nothing? If random sampling is used, researchers at least know what the response rate is. They know that if 90 per cent of the sample co-operated with the research, the findings are more reliable than if only 10 per cent co-operated. Because Kinsey was using non-random sampling methods, he had none of this information, and therefore no way of assessing how reliable his results were.

What about the portion of his sample that was drawn through the 100 per cent cell method? Here at least, it should have been possible to monitor non-response. If he asked 100 per cent of a college sorority to take part in the study, for example, he would know how many refused the invitation. Oddly, Kinsey made little attempt to measure the refusal rate, and certainly does not highlight what he did know of it in his books. His associates, Gebhard and Johnson (1979) comment that:

> The major reason for not routinely recording rates was simply the complexity of such a task. . . . Despite the complexity, there were many instances wherein we should have and could have calculated refusal rates. In our later work in prisons and hospitals, we did keep records of refusals . . . and published these. Such refusal rates were quite low since the respondents in those institutions were literally captive and bored. I have tried to recollect past field trips to re-construct, even roughly, some idea of refusal rates outside of closed institutions. I have failed because the responses were so diverse. . . . I clearly remember my refusal rate among Manhattan longshoremen was 100 per cent.
>
> (Gebhard and Johnson 1979: 31–2)

Besides, while it would theoretically be possible to obtain a list of members of cells such as PTA groups or church organisations, it would be quite impossible to gain a list of members of 'more nebulous sources such as groups of friends or a homosexual community' (Gebhard and Johnson 1979: 28) or indeed hitch hikers, and therefore many of the 'cells' Kinsey chose to use precluded the possibility of measuring non-response.

Kinsey was not blind to the problem of non-response. In fact, one of his reasons for rejecting rigorous random sampling techniques was that they would 'result in an intolerably high refusal rate' in a study of sexual behaviour (Gebhard and Johnson 1979: 25). What he seems to have overlooked is the fact that non-response could compound the bias from non-random sampling methods. If only a small portion of the population, rather than a representative cross-section, were asked to participate in the research, and if of those, a fairly large proportion declined, those who actually made their way into the study may well have been doubly atypical.

There is no way of determining the precise extent to which Kinsey's results were biased by his sampling techniques and the problem of non-response, since no parallel research using a random sample was conducted in the USA at that time. Michael Schofield (1968) conducted a survey which investigated the sexual behaviour of young people in Britain in 1965, however, and though the two studies cannot be directly compared, as they took place in different countries at different points in time using different interview schedules and techniques, Schofield's work does raise some interesting questions about Kinsey's studies. Schofield's sample was numerically far smaller than Kinsey's, only 1,837 people were surveyed, but the teenagers who participated in Schofield's research were randomly selected from reasonably good sampling frames. Each person who was selected to take part in the study was sent a letter which explained the nature of the research, and an interviewer then called on them to ask to arrange an interview. There was no substitution. Once a person had been randomly selected as part of the sample, the interviewer would do his or her best to persuade them to co-operate with the research, but if the teenager ultimately refused, they were not replaced by anyone else from the list but were counted as a non-respondent. As it was, only 14.9 per cent refused to be interviewed (Schofield 1968: 34–5) which is a fairly respectable response rate for any survey, let alone for this type of research. What is worth noting here is that, unlike Kinsey, Schofield not only knew exactly what the refusal rate was, he also had some information about non-respondents. Those teenagers who were unwilling to co-operate fully were asked to answer some basic background questions about themselves, and because Schofield took this precaution, he was better able to see whether this 14.9 per cent who refused were qualitatively different from those who agreed to participate.

Using random methods, Schofield's study revealed far *less* sexual activity amongst teenagers in Britain than Kinsey had found in the USA, and this is interesting given that the two countries are not so very different in terms of cultural mores about sexual behaviour, and that, if anything, we might expect teenagers to have been more rather than less likely to be sexually active in the 1960s than in previous decades when Kinsey conducted his research. Of course, Schofield's findings cannot be used to refute Kinsey's, but they do suggest that the upward bias from using predominantly a volunteer sample may be quite pronounced.

Sample design and non-response are two important issues in survey research. Equally important for most survey research is the design of the questionnaire or interview schedule and the process of coding which are considered in the following section.

ISSUES OF CODING AND QUESTIONNAIRE DESIGN

Although survey data can be collected in other ways, questionnaires are the most commonly used technique for gathering information (de Vaus 1991: 80). A questionnaire is simply the list of questions which will be put to each respondent. Sometimes respondents fill this out themselves, sometimes an interviewer puts the questions to the respondent and marks down their responses for them. In either event, there are a number of problems associated with questionnaire design which need to be addressed by the researcher. At the most basic, practical level, researchers must bear in mind that there is a limit to how much time respondents will be willing to devote to the research and must try to keep questionnaires as short as possible. Some surveys do need respondents to expend a great deal of time and effort. The government's Family Expenditure Survey calls on respondents to keep a fortnightly diary outlining their spending on food, clothing, drink, heating and so on, whilst some medical research relies on subjects monitoring aspects of their health. For example, a Bristol based study asked almost 2,000 people to 'keep strict records of how many times they went to the loo during the week, as well as the shape and size of their stools' (Smith 1993: 122). Even if you volunteered to participate in such research, your commitment to furthering scientific knowledge might begin to wane after a few days of inspecting your own faeces and ticking off whether it was 'like a sausage or snake but with cracks on its surface' or 'fluffy with ragged edges' and so on, on a questionnaire. In general, the more effort that the researcher demands of the respondent, the less consistent and reliable the results. People may forget to fill in a diary at the proper time and invent answers later, or just dash through a long questionnaire, ticking off items in an arbitrary way to get it over and done with.

The researcher may also find that people are reluctant to give information on certain background variables such as age, voting intentions, or 'ethnic origin' or to answer questions on particular topics. It is often best to leave potentially sensitive questions until the end of the questionnaire, rather than risking a refusal by asking them straight away. The respondent has by then already invested time and thought in completing the questionnaire and is more likely to respond, and if he or she does not, the researcher has obtained at least some information.

The actual content of questions is generally determined by the survey researcher's empirical or theoretical agenda. As well as including questions on those background variables which will be relevant to the analysis, such as age, sex, occupation, and so on, the researcher considers what he or she needs to know about the respondent's views or behaviour in order to answer the basic hypothesis. So far as deciding upon the type of questions to be asked and the question wording, survey researchers need to keep future analysis in mind. If they wanted to examine views on premarital sex, for example, an open question could be asked; 'Please state your views on premarital sex'. Respondents could then outline their views in the space provided. But open questions of this type generate an enormous amount of work later on. Respondents may all give very different replies and the researcher would have to code every one of these into a numerical form in order to analyse the data. For this reason, researchers often prefer closed or forced choice questions, which present the respondent with a predetermined set of responses (such as agree, neither agree nor disagree, disagree) and ask respondents which of these responses most closely matches their own to a statement such as 'I do not approve of premarital sex'. Forced choice questions are quick to answer and simple to code, but against this it should be noted that they also run the risk of obscuring nuances in people's views. Respondents cannot qualify their answers (for instance, 'I approve of premarital sex but only in the context of a committed and loving relationship'). De Vaus observes that a category called 'Other, please specify' can be used 'to allow for unanticipated responses' (1991: 87), but this of course leads to the coding problems associated with open questions.

Question wording also needs careful attention. Ideally, questions should be short, clearly and unambiguously phrased using simple, jargon-free language. The following chapter on interviewing considers the problems associated with question wording in more detail, but here it is worth noting a few key points. First, the way in which questions are phrased can encourage or discourage certain responses. A person might feel more reluctant to answer 'yes' to the question 'Have you ever engaged in unnatural and perverted sex acts such as fellatio?' than to answer 'yes' to a question which simply said 'Have you ever engaged in fellatio?' Second, researchers should be aware of the fact that the same words can hold different meanings for different people. It would be better, for instance, to ask people to state how frequently they desire sexual intercourse than to ask them whether they are 'high', 'medium' or 'low sexed'. One person's nymphomaniac may be another person's sexual abstinent. Third, it is possible, but not very useful, to get people to answer questions that they do not understand, or to express opinions about things they know nothing about. It would not be worth asking respondents whether they had engaged in fellatio without checking that they knew what the term meant. Finally, researchers should consider the fact that it is possible to artificially construct attitudes. As de Vaus notes:

> On certain issues people will have no opinion. You should therefore offer people the option of responding 'don't know' or 'no opinion'. This can lead to some people giving these responses to most questions, which can create its own problems, but not including them will produce highly unreliable and therefore useless responses.
>
> (1991: 85)

Potential problems with question wording can often be identified through the use of a 'pilot test' (trying the questionnaire out upon a number of individuals first) after which questions can be modified as necessary. A more detailed discussion of question construction can be found in de Vaus (1991). Before concluding this section, however, it is important to reiterate the close relationship between questionnaire construction and the process of coding. Coding is the penultimate stage of survey research. Having collected information from the sample on a number of variables, the researcher has to code it up into a numerical form before it can be analysed. Coding can be very straightforward. If respondents have been asked to reply 'yes', 'no' or 'don't know' to a series of questions, then these three replies can be given codes 1, 2, and 3 respectively. If the respondent answered 'yes' to questions 1 and 2, 'no' to questions 3 and 4, and 'don't know' to question 5, the coded responses would look like Figure 4.4 below.

If the range of possible responses to each question is more extensive, or if each question includes a number of sub-questions, coding becomes

Question	Respondent 1
1	1
2	1
3	2
4	2
5	3

Figure 4.4 Example of simple coding

more complicated and time consuming. When open ended questions are used, coding can be quite laborious. The fact that social research itself is a social process, and that research is often designed (and published) by relatively senior academics, but carried out by their juniors or non-academic staff, also has an effect upon the design of questionnaires and coding frameworks. Coding up hundreds of questionnaires is a monotonous job, and if a researcher wishes to avoid this donkey work, he or she will attempt to ensure that the questionnaire is designed in such a way as to simplify coding. The easier the coding framework is to use, the easier it is to pass the coding on to untrained staff, postgraduate students or whatever source of cheap labour is most readily available. Once again, practical as well as theoretical or technical concerns can influence research design.

KINSEY'S QUESTION SCHEDULE AND CODING SYSTEM

It was noted above that survey research is typically associated with a researcher identifying a clear empirical or theoretical agenda, and consciously designing a programme of questions which address a basic hypothesis. Kinsey, however, advocated an 'atheoretical approach' to sex research in the early stages 'feeling that one must accumulate a large body of data before one could construct useful hypotheses or theories' (Gebhard and Johnson 1979: 11). When Kinsey first started his research in 1938, he therefore devised a series of questions which were intended to uncover the basic, 'plain facts' about human sexual behaviour; what people did and did not do, how often, at what age, and with whom (or what). Since he was, at this time, taking histories from students, the interview was designed very much 'with college students in mind and, in addition, bore the imprint of Kinsey's own social milieu and generation' (Gebhard and Johnson 1979: 12). Yet this same basic interview continued to be used over a twenty year period, and with people of different ages and social backgrounds. Kinsey was disinclined to change the interview, adding only a few new questions reluctantly. This was because he was committed to producing data in a variable by case form. If new questions (variables) were added, then the people who had been interviewed in the early stages of the research would not have answered them, and data from earlier interviews would not be strictly comparable with data from the later research. His associates, Gebhard and Johnson, comment that:

> [T]he most serious criticism that can justly be labelled at the interviewing instrument [is that] Kinsey allowed it to fossilize at an early

stage and remedial actions were more afterthought appendages . . .
than basic integral parts. The instrument should have been regarded
as provisional and subject to substantial modification as our knowledge increased.

(1979: 12)

This is one of the limitations of the survey method. Once underway, the
researcher is committed to a given set of questions, for they must
discover the attributes of each 'case' on each 'variable' or else end up
with an incomplete data matrix, which in turn will mean that systematic
comparison of cases at the analysis stage is impossible. As de Vaus
notes, 'it is difficult to go back to people to collect additional information we might later discover we need. Therefore it is crucial to think
ahead and anticipate what information will be needed to ensure that the
relevant questions are asked' (1992: 80). This is all very well if the
researcher is working towards a clear theoretical and empirical agenda
and therefore *knows* in advance what information will be needed. If the
researcher is investigating a relatively uncharted area, however, it may
be a tall order. A researcher cannot plan to include a question about a
sexual practice that she or he has never heard of, for example. Employing survey methods means that if, half way through the research, the
researcher stumbles upon this novel act, it cannot easily be included in
all subsequent interviews. Likewise, if the researcher discovers or
decides during the course of research that a particular question is fruit-
less, it is difficult to abandon it. Kinsey's associates observe that:

Questions of dubious worth were caught in the fossilization process
. . . and never extirpated. Thus we continued to ask males which testis
hung lower than the other and whether the scrotum was on the left or
right side of the central seam of the pants. Both of these matters
would have better dealt with by a urologist and a tailor.

(Gebhard and Johnson 1979: 14)

In this sense, the survey method is not the most flexible of research
techniques. In theory, providing that the question schedule is designed
with proper reference to existing research in the field, and providing a
proper pilot test is conducted, such problems should not arise. In practice things are not so simple, and a method which relies so heavily on the
researcher anticipating what information will be needed in advance of
doing the actual research imposes limits upon what can be successfully
investigated. De Vaus notes that survey methods have also been criticised for the inflexibility that arises from the use of highly structured

questionnaires which artificially limit the data that can be collected. He contends, however, that 'this criticism is based on too narrow an understanding of what techniques can be used in surveys' (1991: 8). So far as Kinsey's research goes, a variable by case data matrix was produced without the use of a tightly structured questionnaire. His interviews were loosely based around a number of subject categories, and were modified to accommodate individual differences. Gebhard and Johnson explain that:

> The basic interview . . . consisted of roughly 300 questions. I say roughly because of all the possible questions in our repertoire, only those which proved relevant in each individual case were asked. Thus, if a person were an only child, one did not inquire as to the gender and age of siblings and if the person were a virgin, one did not ask the multitude of questions concerning coitus and reproductive history.
>
> (1979: 13)

Another of Kinsey's associates, Pomeroy (1972), stresses the flexibility of their approach by noting that 'whenever there was any indication of sexual activity beyond what the questions covered, we would go as far beyond the basic interview as we thought necessary to get the additional material' (1972: 111). Thus, Kinsey did not use a standard, questionnaire format, indeed, he never even wrote out a full question schedule. The interview was, according to his associates, very much Kinsey's brainchild and it seems he did his utmost to retain personal control over it. Learning the interview questions and the coding techniques used by Kinsey sounds, from the descriptions of his associates, rather like initiation into some secret sect. Everything had to be committed to memory. Since a full 'history' required information on 521 items, each of which could elicit a number of different responses, this meant that researchers had to memorise over 500 different questions and codes. Possibilities for human error clearly abounded, though Gebhard and Johnson insist that their 'recording method was extremely compact and efficient'. But training interviewers was a 'monumental task', so that the system was 'suitable only for persons who could devote years to interviewing' (Gebhard and Johnson 1979: 17–18). It is interesting to note that, with regard to the interview, just as with his sample design, Kinsey appears to have displayed an odd blend of respect and contempt for 'scientific' methods. Though he refused to modify the interview for fear of losing comparability:

> he would on occasion scandalously hurry through or omit some of the duller routine questions in order to devote more attention to those

portions of greater interest. This was truer in the later years of his life when fatigue and boredom combined to make the dogged pursuit of routine items intolerable.

(Gebhard and Johnson 1979: 15)

Furthermore, whilst the interview was a fairly flexible instrument and interviewers did not stick rigidly to pre-set questions, the survey method still imposed serious limits upon what use could be made of data gathered in this way. People were routinely asked questions that were intended to uncover the presence of sexual predilections such as paedophilia and sadomasochism, but because Kinsey had initially considered such phenomena to be uncommon, he had not designed a list of questions to probe them more deeply. The interviewers were therefore simply instructed to get 'the essentials', and since these phenomena were not covered by the original interview schedule, there were no codes to record responses. This meant that information was simply recorded in the form of notes. Gebhard and Johnson comment:

> Retrieval and use of these data will be worthwhile but difficult, since they are not in neat quantifiable categories but in brief almost narrative form. Such 'soft' data are not to be despised since they gave us valuable insights. Thus, listings of why children were preferable to adults as sexual partners are of no small significance even though only a few paedophiles volunteered this information. Indeed, the case histories are replete with esoteric data which have not and perhaps cannot be transmuted into holes in a punched card and stored on tape [the method of preparing data for analysis prior to introduction of modern computers].
>
> (Gebhard and Johnson 1979: 15)

This is a revealing passage. It basically shows that information which Kinsey did not know was important *in advance*, and which was not therefore routinely sought through the established interview schedule, was effectively lost. It did not fit into the pre-determined variable by case data matrix, and therefore could not be easily recorded or analysed alongside the rest of the data. The interview may have been flexible and adjusted to individual cases, but the 'soft' data which this flexibility yielded was made redundant by the method of analysis. It also illustrates how the researcher's preconceptions can influence research findings. If Kinsey had been expecting to find a reasonably high incidence of paedophilia, for instance, but little evidence of animal contacts, his interview would have included a standard set of questions relating to paedophilia but none to probe into the extent and nature of bestiality.

Indeed, the absence of routine questions relating to paedophilia reflects the way that the research agenda is shaped by social attitudes and concerns of the time (a researcher today could hardly ignore child sex abuse in a survey of this nature) as well as the researcher's own personal values and preconceptions. Kinsey was generally unwilling to deal with incest and child sexual abuse (see Herman 1981 and Russell 1986) and dismissed reports of abuse by victims as 'hysterical'.

SOME CONCLUSIONS

There are two rather different sets of criticisms that can be levelled at Kinsey. First, we can make technical criticisms of the design of his research. The sampling methods, the inability to measure non-response, the absence of a pilot study, the over-long interview and the refusal to modify the questions, and the ludicrously complex coding system all break with textbook advice on survey design. These flaws make his findings questionable. But even if Kinsey's research had been better in these very practical senses, we might still question the findings on the grounds that his pre-existing theoretical and moral values led him to ignore certain questions and investigate others and thus to produce a very partial picture of human sexual behaviour. Kinsey claimed his research agenda was 'atheoretical' – a simple search for the 'plain facts' about human sexual behaviour uncontaminated by normative or moral values or by pre-existing theories. But in reality, his own pre-conceived beliefs about what people did and did not do played an important part in shaping the questions he asked. Furthermore, the very idea that it is possible to investigate sexual behaviour without considering the meanings people attach to it is, in itself, a theoretical assumption. Because Kinsey ignored these meanings and simply counted up the incidence of various types of sexual activities or 'outlets' (which he believed to be the expression of a basic biological drive), he overlooked the enormous problems inherent in classifying sexual behaviours. It is impossible to count how often something occurs until it has been classified and this is highly problematic when the meaning actors attach to their sexual behaviour are considered. When a prostitute performs the same sex act with a client and with a dearly loved partner, do the acts count as the same, or should they be classified under different headings? If a wife has dull and non-orgasmic sex with her husband out of a sense of obligation, is this an 'outlet' for her sexual urges? If a man has quick and furtive coitus with a prostitute twice a week, is he as sexually active as the man who has long and rapturous sexual adventures with the woman of his dreams twice a week? Can rape be counted as an 'outlet' for a man's sexual drive? If all these acts are counted as the same because in all cases penetration occurs, then what do figures about the frequency of sexual activity contribute to our understanding of human sexual life? Sexual acts do not take place in a social and cultural vacuum as Kinsey seems to assume. In British and North American society, they take place in the context of extremely unequal power relations between men and women and between adults and children. They also take place in the context of a set of cultural ideas about the proper nature, limits and purpose of sexual pleasure. Without some consideration of meanings, motives, and power, even reliable facts about how often penetration (or anything else) occurs do not bring us much closer to understanding human sexual behaviour. All this leads to some more general conclusions about the survey method.

The survey method is not the be all and end all of social research, merely one method amongst many. Like all methods, surveys have their limitations. Surveys cannot establish definite causal relationships between variables, and they are limited by the fact that many social phenomena are simply not open to this type of investigation (de Vaus 1991: 8). No survey could test Marx's contention that class struggle is the motor of history. No survey could either establish or disprove feminist theories about how power, inequality and oppression function along socially constructed gender lines. If sociologists relied solely upon survey methods, they would impose limits both upon what they could study and how it could be theorised. But these limitations do not render the survey method worthless. It can be used to acquire valuable knowledge. For example, it was noted in Chapter 3 that official health statistics do not provide reliable or comprehensive information about the extent of electro-convulsive therapy usage in British psychiatric hospitals. By conducting a survey, Rogers *et al.* were able to ask a sample of users of mental health services whether or not they had experienced ECT whilst in hospital, and so to get some indication of how widespread this practice is (Rogers *et al.*, 1993, cited in Samson 1993). The survey findings are disturbing and should prove extremely useful to those involved in campaigns to protect the rights of psychiatric patients.

We should be wary of the naïve positivist assumption that quantitative research is somehow more 'scientific' than other types of investigation and that only 'hard' data stands free of subjectivity and prejudice. Surveys are not *the* one or best method for acquiring objective knowledge. But we should also recognise that survey methods are a valuable adjunct to other techniques. Surveys can play a vital role in confirming more qualitative research, in highlighting gaps in knowledge or issues that require further investigation, and in revealing broader patterns that might be missed if researchers relied solely upon qualitative methods.

Chapter 5

Interviewing

Although some social research relies purely upon observational techniques and some can be done without ever stepping outside a library, many types of research rely, to a greater or lesser degree, upon asking people for factual information, or questions about what they do and do not do, or about their beliefs, attitudes, aspirations, experiences and feelings. Interviewing people, whether for survey, case study or ethnographic research, presents the researcher with a number of practical problems. In particular, interviewers often face difficulties in:

- Obtaining *accurate and truthful* responses to relatively closed questions, such as 'How often?', or 'How many?'
- Obtaining *full and sincere* responses to open ended questions such as 'How did you feel about x?', 'Can you tell me what happened when y?'
- *Focusing* the interview, that is, getting people to talk about the issues which concern the researcher

Different methodological traditions emphasise different problems and different ways of dealing with them, and this chapter begins by looking at advice to interviewers from orthodox, qualitative and feminist methodologists. It then considers the techniques employed by Kinsey, Freud and Scully to highlight some of the issues raised by interviewing in the real world. This allows us to consider a methodological problem which is rarely dealt with in textbooks on interviewing. For while all manner of methodologists have a lot to say about how best to get people to give truthful, or full and sincere replies, less is said about how a researcher can tell whether an interviewee *is* telling the truth or being completely frank and open. Yet this issue is vital to the process of interviewing and to the reliability of the data that is collected.

THE ORTHODOX APPROACH TO ASKING QUESTIONS

Central to positivist philosophy is the assumption that there is a world of hard facts which have an existence independent of their social context and separate from the meanings that people attach to them. Take an example from the natural world. Mount Snowdon may strike someone from the Netherlands as being very tall, whilst to someone from the Himalayas, it may appear to be quite small. But though different people's subjective perceptions of the size of this mountain may differ, in reality, Mount Snowdon is a definite and particular height. The natural scientist's aim is to develop neutral instruments to measure this objective reality, rather than relying upon the subjective perceptions of individuals. Positivists hold that the same approach is necessary in the social sciences. We do not want to rely on the individual interviewer's subjective perceptions of how sexist or racist an interviewee is, for example, since the interviewer's subjective judgements are unreliable. The social sciences need a method which can strip away the subjective meanings that people attach to behaviours, ideas and events, and discover objective truths about the social world. It is therefore necessary to apply, as closely as possible, the methods of the natural sciences to the study of the social world. This is no easy task, especially when the research relies upon asking people questions.

When natural scientists investigate the molecular structure of a piece of metal, there is no danger that the subjective perceptions and beliefs of the piece of metal will interfere with and pollute the research process. Natural scientists need not concern themselves with the metal's reaction to the lab technician. The metal is hardly likely to refuse to be examined by someone because it does not like the look of them. Neither do natural scientists have to worry that the metal will attempt to deceive the lab technician in order to appear better endowed with molecules than it really is. The social scientist investigating the attitudes and behaviour of people, however, is dealing with conscious, purposive actors. In setting up interviews, the researcher is setting up a series of *social* interactions between interviewers and the human subjects of the research. Both interviewer and respondent bring to the interview a set of subjective beliefs, expectations, values and so on, which could potentially obscure or distort the truth. To give a rather obvious example, one of the things Kinsey asked male respondents was to estimate the length of their erect penis. Over 17 per cent of white college males estimated the length to be more than 7 inches, with four men even claiming that their members extended more than 10 inches (figures taken from Gebhard and Johnson

1979: 116). Had this question been put to them by a woman they found attractive, rather than Kinsey or one of his male associates, it is possible that their replies would have stretched the bounds of credulity still further. In other words, the interview is a social encounter, and how the respondent answers questions will depend to some degree upon what the respondent and interviewer think and feel about each other. For positivists, this raises *the* central methodological problem so far as interviewing is concerned. How can the researcher be certain that the respondent will give accurate and truthful information, rather than trying to please or impress the interviewer? How can researchers ensure that the data culled through interviewing is not coloured by the interviewer's subjective perceptions of the respondent and the respondent's subjective perceptions of the interviewer? Advice on interviewing techniques in orthodox textbooks reflects this central concern.

Whether interviews are being used in survey or case study research, orthodox textbooks hold that the researcher must take certain steps to avoid the bias that could arise from interviewer–respondent interaction. To begin with, the researcher must ensure that despite the fact that interviewers and respondents each have their own individual personality, history and mannerisms, each interview is standard and identical. An interviewer asking questions about sexual behaviour should ask every respondent the same questions about sexual contacts with animals, not omit these questions out of a sense of delicacy when interviewing nuns, for example. If nuns are not given an opportunity to answer these same questions, then the information from them will not be comparable with the information from the other respondents. The data must be gathered in a standard way. Similarly, in large-scale research where a number of different interviewers are used, the researcher must be wary of what is known as 'between interviewer variance'. Imagine two different interviewers collecting data for a survey on sexual behaviour. If the first asks someone how many times a month they have sex, and ticks the 'don't know' box as soon as the respondent replies 'I don't know', while the second gives all sorts of prompts to the respondent ('Is it about once a month, or maybe twice? With most people it's about two or three times, would you say you did it more or less than average?') and in this way finally extracts a figure, then the data culled by the two interviewers is not comparable. It was not gathered in a standard way.

Orthodox methodologists emphasise this need for standardisation. Regardless of whether a tightly structured, formal interview schedule or a very loosely structured, topic-based interview is employed, the important thing is to provide each interviewer with very clear and explicit instructions as to the questions to be asked or issues to be covered, the prompts that can be used, and the way in which responses are to be coded. In this way, the researcher ensures that even if every respondent were to be interviewed by a different person, they would each have a standard interview, coded in a standard way. To achieve this end, it is essential to provide interviewers with detailed training in how to approach respondents, how to tell respondents about the research, how to ask questions in the same way, how to code and record responses. Through standardisation, the researcher ensures that each respondent experiences an identical interview and that the data gathered through interviews is standard and comparable.

For large-scale survey research, interviewer selection is seen as vital. Orthodox textbooks often stress the need to recruit interviewers whose personal characteristics will not interfere with the subject's responses and to train them to undertake interviews in a neutral, professional fashion. The issue of interviewer selection ties in with what is, for many orthodox methodologists, the most insoluble paradox associated with interviewing. On the one hand, there must be a rapport between interviewer and interviewee. If respondents find the interviewer hostile, or unpleasant in some way, they are unlikely to co-operate with the interview, far less reveal any intimate truths. But on the other hand, researchers have to guard against bias that may arise as a consequence of subjects getting on with the interviewer *too* well. If there is too much rapport, the respondent may try to please the interviewer by saying what he or she thinks the interviewer wants to hear, rather than telling the whole truth. Moser and Kalton (1971) state that:

> There is something to be said for the interviewer who, while friendly and interested does not get too emotionally involved with the respondent and his problems. Interviewing on most surveys is a fairly straightforward job, not one calling for exceptional industry, charm or tact. Pleasantness and a business-like nature is the ideal combination.
>
> (1971: 286)

Questions must be asked as well as phrased in a neutral way, because if interviewers make it plain through facial expressions, intonation or verbal comment that certain views are either desired by, or unacceptable to them, the respondent is likely to modify his or her responses. No one would wish to confide details of a homosexual experience to an interviewer who was plainly homophobic, for example. The behaviour of the interviewer can thus lead to bias. Moser and Kalton hold that the way to reduce such bias is to carefully train the interviewer 'generally to deport herself in a way that is least likely to influence the respondent's answers' (1971: 272).

The concern with standardisation also leads orthodox methodologists to stress the need to control the subjectivity of the *respondent*. Because the respondent is a conscious, purposive actor, he or she can distort the interview by asking questions or making comments. If the interviewer responds to the respondent, striking up a conversation about the research and related issues, then there is no hope of ensuring standardisation, since that particular respondent will be provided with information that is not available to others, and furthermore, the interviewer's replies to questions might bias the respondent's future responses. For these reasons, orthodox textbooks hold that it is essential for the interviewer to retain complete control during the interview:

> [T]ight control is a central goal of the interviewer. The interviewer must take complete charge of the interaction, including such things as where people sit, when the interview begins and ends, what topics are covered, when they are covered, and so on. Losing control of the interview is almost always a methodological disaster that terminates useful data gathering.
>
> (Hessler 1992: 137)

The focus and scope of the interview must be controlled by the interviewer, and this both requires and implies a firmly hierarchical relationship between interviewer and respondent. The interviewer must be pleasant in order to secure co-operation, but must leave the respondent in no doubt as to who is in charge of the situation. The goal of standardisation further requires the interviewer to remain as neutral and as detached from the respondent as possible, whilst simultaneously maintaining a good rapport. Interviewers should politely but firmly refuse to engage in conversation with the interviewee, by saying something like 'I am much more interested in hearing what you have to say about these questions. I will be glad to answer any questions you might have after I have had the chance to hear you out' (Hessler 1992: 139). In short, orthodox methodologists hold that the key to extracting truthful replies lies in the reduction of bias from the interviewers, whose subjective beliefs and personalities might influence the way subjects respond, and the reduction of bias from respondents, whose subjective perceptions of the research aims, and of the interviewer, and of what is socially desirable and so on, might encourage them to lie, exaggerate, or otherwise conceal the truth.

For the orthodox social scientist, then, subjectivity is bias and ideally, the researcher should eliminate all traces of it in order to lay bare the objective truths behind it. Though it acknowledges the need for rapport, this approach demands that the interviewer performs the role, as far as possible, of a neutral instrument for extracting and recording a very specific and limited set of data. Any superfluous information provided by the respondent is ignored, his or her comments and questions, any detail of how the interviewer felt about the interview and so on, in fact, all traces of the interview as an interaction between two people are expunged from the final record. All this is in stark contrast to the approach recommended by qualitative and feminist methodologists.

QUALITATIVE APPROACHES TO ASKING QUESTIONS

Methods textbooks which take a more qualitative or an ethnographic approach to interviewing do not use the natural science language of 'variables', 'control', 'standardisation', and so on, but see the interview as an opportunity to delve and explore precisely those subjective meanings that positivists seek to strip away. Qualitative research is generally not so much concerned with obtaining accurate replies to closed ended questions, as with obtaining full and sincere responses to relatively open-ended enquiries. This is because most qualitative research is informed, to some degree, by the interpretative tradition described in Chapter 2. Where researchers wish to achieve some form of *verstehen* (interpretative understanding), both interviewer and interviewee will need to play very different roles to those set out above. The interviewee is not a research 'subject' to be controlled and systematically investigated by a 'scientist', but a reasoning, conscious human being to be engaged with. Hammersley and Atkinson (1989) observe that:

> The main difference between the way in which ethnographers and survey interviewers ask questions is not, as is sometimes suggested, that one form of interviewing is 'structured' and the other is 'unstructured'. . . . The important distinction to be made is between standardized and reflexive interviewing.
>
> (Hammersley and Atkinson 1989: 112–13)

Methodologists who take a more qualitative approach to interviewing argue that the interviewer must enter into an interaction with the interviewee and therefore needs to be prepared to respond flexibly to the interviewee as an individual, subjective being. Each interviewee and therefore each interview is accepted as different and individual, regardless of whether a structured interview schedule is being followed or not. Some qualitative methodologists see interviews as spontaneous and unpredictable encounters, rejecting the idea of formulating questions and probes in advance. Glesne and Peshkin (1992), for example, state that listening is one of the most important acts performed by the interviewer:

> At no time do you stop listening, because without the data your listening furnishes, you cannot make any of the decisions inherent in interviewing: . . . Has your question been answered, and is it time to move on? If so, move on to what question? Should you probe now or later? What form should your probe take? . . . The spontaneity and unpredictability of the interview exchange precludes planning your probes ahead of time; you must, accordingly, think and talk on your feet.
>
> (1992: 76)

This view of the qualitative interview is perhaps overdrawn. Certainly, in qualitative research, interviewers are far less controlling than survey interviewers, and the interview is a far more flexible and responsive tool. But this does not mean interviewing calls for no pre-planning, or that interviewers just sit back passively and allow topics or issues to emerge. Qualitative interviews are generally focused rather than completely free-flowing and spontaneous, though the degree of fluidity and improvisation will depend on the stage of the research and how much good and reliable data has already been gathered. Qualitative researchers may conduct completely unstructured interviews in the early stages of research, allowing the interviewee to talk about whatever seems most important to him or her, but in the later stages of research, they may wish to confirm particular points, or to focus on particular issues or topics and will then stick more closely to pre-set questions or topic headings.

The significant difference between qualitative and orthodox interviews is that, whether structured or unstructured, the qualitative interview has more the character of a dialogue than a quest for simple 'yes' and 'no' responses. For this reason, qualitative methodologists do not express the ambivalence about rapport which is to be found in orthodox accounts of interviewing. Establishing a good rapport is a vital element of the interviewing process; 'rapport is tantamount to trust, and trust is the foundation for acquiring the fullest, most accurate disclosure a respondent is able to make' (Glesne and Peshkin 1992: 79). Rather than trying to expunge the personality of the interviewer and to standardise interviews, this approach demands that interviewers should manage their appearance, behaviour and self presentation in such a way as to build rapport and trust with each individual respondent. If rapport is not developed, the quality of information gathered during the course of the interview will suffer. Good rapport also allows the interviewer to keep the interview focused on the topics he or she wishes to hear about. An interviewee is more likely to allow you to change the subject, interrupt or 'steer' the conversation if he or she warms to you as a person. This means that where orthodox researchers value interviewers with merely a 'pleasant and businesslike manner', qualitative methodologists tend to ask for much more. Interviewers must be empathetic and committed:

> When you are warm and caring, you promote rapport, you make yourself appealing to talk to, and, not least, you communicate to your respondents, 'I see you as a human being with interests, experience, and needs beyond those I tap for my own purposes.' . . . In an effective interview, both researcher and respondent feel good, rewarded and satisfied by the process and the outcomes. The warm and caring researcher is on the way to achieving such effectiveness.
>
> (Glesne and Peshkin 1992: 87)

Orthodox researchers see subjectivity as bias – something to be controlled or expunged. But in qualitative research, recognising the subjectivity of interviewer and interviewee is a key aspect of acquiring knowledge. Orthodox researchers assume that the people will tell the truth providing their responses are not contaminated by interaction between the interviewer and respondent as subjective beings. Qualitative methodologists, on the other hand, not only argue that interaction is necessary to develop a trusting relationship within which people will be prepared to disclose the truth, but also that a dialogue between the interviewer and interviewee as subjective beings is necessary to ensure that the interviewer has fully understood what is being disclosed. For the orthodox researcher, such a dialogue would prevent standardisation and require the interviewer to make subjective judgements and interpretations, and so would lead to bias. But for those who take a more interactive approach, double checking that the respondent understands the question and that the interviewer understands the reply is the only way to be sure of acquiring reliable, meaningful responses.

This concern with the interviewee as a subjective being does not require that the researcher abandons a commitment to objectivity, however. Qualitative methodologists, as much as those from the orthodox school, warn against the use of leading questions (see Glesne and Peshkin 1992), and stress that the interviewer should be conscious at all times of how his or her line of questioning may be affecting the inter-viewee's responses. Hammersley and Atkinson also note that 'a useful tactic is to make the question "lead" in a direction opposite to that in which one expects the answer to lie and thus avoid the danger of simply and misleadingly confirming one's expectations' (1989: 115–16). Essentially, then, qualitative methodologists recognise the interview as a far more complex phenomenon than do their orthodox counterparts. This is also evident in relation to the issue of researcher control, which is seen as a paradox, rather than simply asserted to be a requirement for 'objective' fact gathering. Glesne and Peshkin (1992) point out that whilst non-hierarchical relationships between researcher and researched are sometimes possible:

> In most instances . . . the researcher maintains a dominant role that reflects his or her definition of the inquiry purposes. As long as the purposes are his or her own, the researcher sustains a power imbalance that may or may not get redressed, depending on the researcher's opportunity for and commitment to reciprocity.
>
> (1992: 82)

But though researchers are dominant in this respect, they are simul-taneously submissive in as much as they 'cannot dictate the particulars of [the] interviewer–interviewee relationship' (Glesne and Peshkin 1992: 82). Getting access, eliciting continued co-operation throughout the course of the interview, how long the interview lasts, what is and is not discussed – all these crucial factors are within the gift of the interviewee, and thus outside the control of the interviewer. To this we could add that power relations external to the interview situation can further complicate the issue of control. A female researcher inter-viewing males may be in control in the sense that she is initiating the interview and using it to her own ends, but may simultaneously feel vulnerable because of her status as a woman. For example, O'Connell Davidson's research in the water industry involved her undertaking lengthy qualitative interviews, sometimes with solitary men in isolated geographical settings. For a woman to find herself in a secluded spot in the countryside, talking to a man she has never before met and unsure whether anyone else knows her whereabouts is extremely unnerving (see O'Connell Davidson 1991: 228). Likewise, for a female inter-viewer to be shut in an office with a lecherous senior manager is not conducive to a sense of full control.

The real point is that, for qualitative researchers, control is an ambiguous issue. Taking a non-directive approach to questioning and allowing the interviewee, at least in part, to set the agenda, is not necessarily 'a methodological disaster that terminates useful data gathering' as Hessler (1992: 137), quoted earlier, would have it. The interviewer is always an active agent in the process of data collection. By listening to what the respondent chooses to say, rather than forcing him or her to answer simply a pre-set list of questions, the interviewer is obtaining more and better quality information, information which can help to shape the future course of the research (Hammersley and Atkinson 1989: 114). Interviewers are not losing their 'objectivity', becoming partial or imposing a particular world view on the respondent, rather they are using the interview as an opportunity to explore the subjective values, beliefs and thoughts of the individual respondent. Many of these same themes and issues have recently been taken up by feminist methodologists.

THE FEMINIST APPROACH TO ASKING QUESTIONS

In recent years, a number of feminist writers have begun to argue for a distinctive feminist methodology (see, for example, Fonow and Cook 1991, Stanley and Wise 1993). They challenge the claim that traditional social scientists produce value-free, objective knowledge, arguing that sexist value judgements explicitly and implicitly inform what people choose to study, how they go about investigating social phenomena and how they interpret their findings. The idea that social research is coloured by the values and preconceptions of the researcher is by no means peculiar to feminist writers, but the emphasis upon a specifically masculine bias in social research has been an important part of the feminist critique of methods. So far as interviewing is concerned, some feminists assert that the orthodox methodologist's emphasis on control, hierarchy and the impersonal nature of scientific research reflects a masculine view of the world and of human relationships more generally. Oakley (1981) argues that the orthodox paradigm of the social research interview is characterised by the following features:

(a) its status as a mechanical instrument of data-collection; (b) its function as a specialised form of conversation in which one person asks the questions and another gives the answers; (c) its charac- terisation of interviewees as essentially passive individuals and (d) its reduction of interviewers to a question asking and rapport-promoting role.

(1981: 36–7)

This paradigm is rejected as morally indefensible, since it is controlling and exploitative, but Oakley also points to more practical reasons for ditching the advice of orthodox methods texts, noting that 'the goal of finding out about people through interviewing is best achieved when the relationship of interviewer and interviewee is non-hierarchical and when the interviewer is prepared to invest his or her own personal identity in the relationship' (1982: 41). Feminist methodologists therefore tend to recommend many of the techniques advocated by qualitative methodologists. Since they too are primarily concerned with obtaining full and sincere responses, the need for rapport and genuine interaction between interviewer and interviewee as subjective beings is stressed. The interviewer can answer the questions of the interviewee and enter into a genuine emotional relationship, possibly even a friendship with her research subjects. It is here that the similarities between feminist and qualitative approaches end. Qualitative methodologists make a strong distinction between conversations that are part of friendship and the research interview, noting that it is quite possible to achieve a rapport and learn a great deal from people that you do not like. They also recognise the complexity surrounding power and control in the interview relationship, whereas feminist methodologists often assume that where both interviewer and interviewee share the same gender socialisation and critical life-experiences, the interview can be a genuinely non-exploitative, non-hierarchical meeting of equals. Unlike qualitative methodologists, who recognise the need to retain some control over the focus and scope of the interview, many feminist methodologists seem to imply that researchers can and should just listen to women, allowing respondents to set their own agendas and focus on what is important to them. They insist that researchers should not try to control the research subject, but should instead attempt to work themselves into the mind of the social actor:

> and see the world as he or she sees it; this is not controlling the actor and manipulating his or her behaviour but rather respecting people's integrity . . . [This produces] an honest accounting empathetic of people and events and a most illuminating perspective.
>
> (Farganis 1989: 213)

This technique of simply letting women 'tell their stories' is supposed to enable the interviewer to enter the common-sense world of the women she studies and to document it. This non-exploitative, descriptive research is said to have an emancipatory potential. Since feminist methodologists explicitly seek to redress the gender imbalance in social

research, they direct their advice towards women researchers interviewing other women, 'sisters' researching 'sisters', and argue that the
knowledge such research produces can and should be returned to the
community to empower the female subjects of feminist research.

Thus far, the differences between these three approaches to interviewing
have been emphasised. Before turning to look at some examples of interviewing in the real world, it is worth noting that there are also some
similarities. Orthodox, qualitative and feminist methodologists could all
agree, for example, that an interview is not *merely* a conversation between
two (or more) people. They would not agree on what precisely the rules and
skills appropriate to interviewing are, but most would agree that interviewing is bound by rules of interaction and requires skills that are different
to those employed in everyday conversation. Interviewers will not glean
much information, for example, if they use the interview as an opportunity
to hold forth on their own life experiences or political beliefs, whereas this
might be acceptable as part of an ordinary conversation. Interviewers are
unlikely to get the interviewee to co-operate with any type of interview if
they are visibly bored, hostile or judgemental. The need for some degree of
rapport is recognised by all methodologists, and furthermore, all advocate
impartiality in as much as it is accepted that interviewers should not lead or
manipulate respondents into saying what the interviewer wishes or expects
to hear. The interviewing techniques used in a social services investigation
into child sex abuse in Britain recently caused much controversy precisely
because many people felt that interviewers put ideas into the children's
heads and used leading questions to extract the answers they expected. The
report of the inquiry commissioned to review the case describes one interview as follows:

> [T]he interviewers immediately raised with WB the question of
> whether she knew why she was there. They indicated that people had
> been saying that she had been hurt on parts of her body, and asked
> WB if at any time she gathered with a group of people where she or
> others were touched or hurt in any way . . . they had indicated to WB
> that they believed the information which had been given to them. . . .
> When WB insisted that nothing had happened to her, the interviewers
> tried to reassure her that they would listen to her, but they continued
> to indicate their belief that she had been hurt.
>
> (Report of the Inquiry into the Removal of Children from Orkney
> 1992: 185)

Orthodox, qualitative and feminist methodologists would all object to
such an approach, recognising that if interviewers doggedly push people

into giving the answers or story they wish to hear, the data they produce is biased and worthless. In short, whether researchers use highly structured interview schedules or take a completely unstructured approach, and whether they are pursuing standardisation or reflexivity, the interview is not a chance encounter or an aimless chat. It is initiated by the researcher and takes place with a particular goal in mind, namely data collection. Reliable data will not be collected if the interviewer leads the interviewee, suggesting appropriate responses and refusing to acknowledge others. The following outline of interviewing methods in the real world vividly illustrate the issues which have been raised thus far.

INTERVIEWING KINSEY STYLE

It was noted in the previous chapter that most of the methodological criticism of Kinsey's work has centred upon his sampling techniques. Even recent commentators comment favourably upon his interviewing methods. Shipman (1988), for example, describes Kinsey's interviews as follows:

> Complete confidentiality, absolute privacy during interviewing and no suggestions of right or wrong behaviour were the guides to rapport. Kinsey himself carried out 7,000 of the interviews lasting an hour to an hour and a half. This labour of love was conducted deadpan; friendly, but never with any expression of surprise or disapproval. The questions were asked as directly as possible to avoid interaction. The interviewer looked squarely at the subject and moved inexorably from factual background to intimate detail. . . . Questions were used to check others, husbands were checked against wives, reinterviewing after eighteen months was employed. This study is acknowledged as a classic.
>
> (1988: 84)

Kinsey's own descriptions of his interviewing methods certainly match this portrait of the impartial scientist, rigorously pursuing the truth, but accounts of the interviews offered by his associates Johnson, Pomeroy and Gebhard paint a rather different picture. Let us return to the central problem facing the orthodox interview researcher: how do you get people to give you truthful and accurate responses? Pomeroy states that there were only three possible ways that Kinsey's subjects could not tell the truth: they could exaggerate their sexual experience, they could remember events incorrectly, or they could deny and otherwise conceal their sexual experience. Only the last way of not telling the truth was believed by Kinsey and his associates to represent a real problem for his research:

> Exaggeration was almost impossible with the system we used for asking questions rapidly and in detail. People who tried reported little success. Not remembering accurately could be dealt with statistically; the errors one person might make were offset by errors another made in the opposite direction. Covering up was the most serious problem.
>
> (Pomeroy 1972: 120)

In other words, Kinsey and his associates assumed that the real problem was going to be getting people to admit the range and extent of their sexual experience, not that they might exaggerate it. Having decided in advance that 'covering up' would be the main barrier to truth, Kinsey held that respondents must be asked questions in such a way as to ensure that they felt free to admit anything. He therefore insisted that respondents should never be asked *whether* they had experienced sexual intercourse, cunnilingus, or whatever, but always asked *when* they had first done it. This was intended not only to show the interviewee how relaxed and non-judgemental the interviewer was, but also to make it more difficult for them to 'cover up' certain activities. As Pomeroy (1972) explains, it meant that 'The subject who might want to deny an experience had a heavier burden placed on him, *and since he knew from the way the question was asked that it would not surprise us if he had done it*, there seemed little reason to deny it' (1972: 112, emphasis added). This may have been all very well when they wanted to find out whether someone had ever masturbated an animal, but placing the burden of denial upon the interviewee could well have had the effect of exaggerating the incidence of more mundane forms of sexual activity. To ask a 17-year-old boy, for example, *when* he first had full penetrative sex, rather than *if* he has ever had full penetrative sex, or to ask a married man when he first, rather than if, he had extra-marital affairs, could be described as leading. The difference between asking a question in such a way as to suggest that a given response would not surprise the interviewer, and asking a question in such a way as to suggest that the interviewer *expects* that given response is rather fine.

To assess how likely Kinsey's respondents were to have been frank and open in the course of the interviews, it is also important to ask questions about the interviewers themselves.

The attributes of the interviewer would be identified by all three of the different approaches to interviewing outlined above as an important factor affecting how willing interviewees would be to disclose the truth.

Qualitative and feminist methodologists, for example, would probably recommend that interviewers be matched to respondents in terms of gender, and possibly also in terms of age and ethnicity, in order to set respondents at ease and encourage a good rapport to develop. Kinsey took a rather different view. Pomeroy explains that:

> It was suggested to us that we ought to have women interviewers to interview women, and Negro interviewers for blacks. By that logic, Kinsey pointed out, we would have to have prostitutes for prostitutes, drug addicts for drug addicts and so on. The qualities of the interviewer, not his sex, race or personal history, were the important variables.
>
> (1972: 102)

If sex and 'race' were really unimportant to Kinsey, it seems curious that all of his interviewers just happened to be white Anglo-Saxon Protestant (WASP) males, and that he even expressed concern about hiring anyone 'with a Jewish name because he thought some WASP interviewees might object' (Pomeroy 1972: 103). We are then hurriedly reassured that 'there was nothing bigoted' about Kinsey's refusal to employ women, Black people or people with Jewish names, it was simply that he believed 'only WASPs . . . could interview everybody' (1972: 102). This highlights a very real problem with various methodologists' assertion that the characteristics of the interviewer can either encourage or discourage people from partici- pating in the research. It is actually very hard to disentangle the researcher's own prejudices from his or her fears about potential interviewees' pre- judices. Were people really more likely to respond to a WASP interviewer than to a Jewish interviewer, or was it simply that Kinsey preferred to hire WASPs than to hire Jewish people?

Kinsey's assumption that women would tell the truth about their sexual lives to male interviewers certainly now appears as dated. How much effect this exclusive use of male interviewers had upon Kinsey's findings is, of course, impossible to determine, but it is interesting to note that Russell's research into incestuous abuse, which did match interviewers and respondents in terms of gender and ethnicity, found that 12 per cent of a random sample of women reported having been abused, whereas only around 2 to 3 per cent of Kinsey's female sample disclosed such experiences (see Russell 1986: 64–5). (This discrepancy may also reflect the different sampling methods employed. It may be that women who had suffered sexual abuse in childhood were less likely to volunteer to take part in sex research.) Similarly, the extent to which the exclusive use of WASP interviewers affected respondent's willing- ness to disclose the truth cannot be accurately determined, but the description of interviewing practice provided by Pomeroy is extremely offensive and suggests that Kinsey's faith in the WASP's ability to 'interview everybody' was misplaced. Moving immediately on from a discussion about how rapport was achieved with child respondents, Pomeroy explains:

> It was particularly important that we know the sexual viewpoint of the cultures from which our subjects came. Kinsey illustrated this point with the case of an older Negro male who at first had been wary and evasive in his answers. From the fact that he listed a number of minor jobs when asked about his occupation and seemed reluctant to go into any of them, [Kinsey] deduced that he might have been active in the underworld, so he began to follow up by asking the man whether he had ever been married. He denied it, at which Kinsey resorted to the vernacular and inquired if he had ever 'lived common law'. The man admitted he had, and that it had first happened when he was fourteen.
>
> 'How old was the woman?' [Kinsey] asked.
>
> 'Thirty-five,' he admitted, smiling.
>
> Kinsey showed no surprise. 'She was a hustler, wasn't she?' he said flatly. At this, the subject's eyes opened wide, he smiled in a friendly way for the first time, and said, 'Well, sir, since you appear to know something about these things, I'll tell you straight.'
>
> (Pomeroy 1972: 115–16)

Why was Kinsey so quick to assume that this man was 'active in the underworld' or that the woman he mentioned was a 'hustler'? Why did he not consider the possibility that the man was exaggerating the age difference, or that the smile and wide-eyed 'Well, sir' could have been a straightforward mockery of Kinsey's rather transparent line of thought? This really leads into another major problem with Kinsey's interviewing methods, namely the question of how Kinsey and his associates decided whether or not to accept an interviewee's replies as true. The extract quoted above gives an example of Kinsey suggesting to a respondent that he had lived with a 'hustler' at the age of 14 and accepting his failure to deny this as positive confirmation. On other occasions, however, the researchers did not accept the respondent's initial responses as gospel. Gebhard and Johnson (1979: 20) comment that when a respondent reported unusually high frequencies of sexual intercourse, for example, it was viewed with suspicion and the interviewer would ask a series of additional questions to double check. This generally led to the respondent modifying the original claim. However, 'we only utilized this technique in cases where our suspicions were aroused and, consequently, exaggerations which fell within the range of probability passed uncorrected' (1979: 21). Similarly, respondents were subjected to the third degree when the researchers thought that their answers were wrong or incomplete. The same question would be rephrased and asked again. Pomeroy notes that if he or Kinsey thought that an interviewee was lying, they would pretend to have mis-understood his reply and say things like: 'Yes, I know you have never done that, but how old were you the first time that you did it?' This approach was particularly fruitful with people termed by Pomeroy as 'of low mentality' (1972: 113). The questions placed the burden of denial upon the subject, but if the interviewer did not believe their denials, pressure was applied. Pomeroy explains how, if they were convinced a subject was lying, he and Kinsey would challenge them:

> It became necessary to say, with firmness, even vehemence, and yet always with kindness, 'Look, I don't give a damn what you've done, but if you don't tell me the straight of it, it's better that we stop this history right here. Now, how old were you the first time that this or that happened?' Surprisingly, in not a single case did a person refuse to continue.
>
> (Pomeroy 1972: 127)

Considered in the light of research into social conformity and the way in which people tend to comply with researchers who are perceived as authority figures, this makes Kinsey's figures on levels of sexual activity look even more suspect. If subjects did admit to being homo-sexual, or to having had animal contacts or whatever after being pressured in this way, their 'confession' would be recorded with no mention of what had gone on between interviewer and respondent in order to elicit the information. Pomeroy notes that 'To make it easy for subjects to correct answers, we ignored contradictions, accepting the correction as though it were a first reply' (1972: 113). The same approach was taken with the follow up interviews. If, after the interview was over, they began to suspect that it contained falsities they would return to the subject and '*demand* that he correct the record' (Pomeroy 1972: 113). This technique of demanding 'corrections', then accepting and recording them as if they were a first reply means that Kinsey's interviewing methods rather falls between two stools. He was using orthodox coding procedures (that is, recording only the limited and specific response and no detail of the interaction between interviewer

and interviewee that led to this response) combined with highly un-
orthodox procedures for extracting those responses.

More importantly though, we need to ask what it was that suddenly
made Kinsey and his associates recognise the 'falsity' of an interview?
What was it that made them able to tell whether a subject was lying or
covering up, and so decide to rephrase questions, interrogate further or
threaten to terminate the interview? Why was it that the African-
American respondent's claim to have lived with a 35-year-old woman at
the age of 14 was accepted and recorded without doubt or further
question, whilst other claims made by other respondents were dis-
believed and challenged? Could it have been that Kinsey chose only to
accept as true those replies which fitted his pre-existing theories and his
pre-existing stereotypes about what kind of sexual behaviour a given
'type' of person might indulge in? All this underlines the point that the
social research interview does not simply raise the question of how to
get people to disclose the truth, but also the more intractable methodological question of how researchers can and do decide which answers to
accept and record as true. This problem emerges equally forcefully in
relation to the interviewing techniques adopted by Sigmund Freud.

INTERVIEWS WITH SIGMUND FREUD

Any methodological critique of Freud's interviewing techniques is complicated by the fact that his interviews were not undertaken simply for
research purposes, but were also intended to be of therapeutic value to
the interviewee. He himself might therefore explain certain of his interviewing practices in relation to his role as a doctor, rather than as a
researcher. Freud may, for example, have insisted upon complete control of the interviews because he held this to be appropriate to the
doctor–patient relationship, rather than because he imagined this to be
the best way of extracting the truth in a researcher–researched relationship. Likewise, Freud held that the interviewee/patient's condition
precluded any genuinely intimate or equal relationship with him as
interviewer/doctor. Though Freud's interviewing methods undoubtedly
match the masculine paradigm described and criticised by feminist
methodologists, it is more difficult to condemn them as straightforwardly exploitative and morally indefensible, since psychotherapy
was ultimately intended to benefit the patient. However, as well as being
designed to serve therapeutic purposes, Freud's interviews served to
produce the data upon which he developed his psychoanalytic theories,

and here we are solely concerned with his interviewing techniques as a method of data collection. Freud claimed to have undertaken a scientific study of the unconscious, and it is therefore worth examining his interview practice in the light of the issues raised in the above sections.

Freud first graduated as doctor of medicine, and undertook research into the clinical use of cocaine. He then spent a year in Paris with Charcot, studying nervous diseases, particularly 'hysteria'. On his return to Vienna, Freud became interested in a method first pioneered by Josef Breuer, a consultant who argued that hysteria was the product of a trauma which had been forgotten by the patient (Bocock 1986: 1). The treatment consisted of using hypnosis to get the patient to recall the forgotten event and live through the appropriate emotional response to it. For Freud, the significance of hypnosis was that it revealed the existence of active parts of the mind that are not generally discernible either to the individual or the on-looker. He pointed out that in a hypnotic trance, people remember details about their lives that they cannot normally recall. Moreover, though people do not remember consciously what has been said to them during hypnosis, they will later act on suggestions made to them by the hypnotist. From this he concluded that there exists a part of the mind which is inaccessible to individuals at conscious level, yet still influences what they do, how they feel and so on. Freud called this hidden part of the mind the unconscious, and his aim was to scientifically explore its structure and content. However, whilst hypnosis had given Freud proof of the existence of this unconscious mind, he saw it as an imperfect research instrument. It was erratic and irregular. Sometimes it worked, at other times it did not. Some subjects were open to hypnosis, others were not. Freud explains:

> I soon came to dislike hypnosis, for it was a temperamental and, one might almost say, a mystical ally. . . . I set about working with patients in their normal state. At first, I must confess, this seemed a senseless and hopeless undertaking. I was set the task of learning from the patient something that I did not know and that he did not know himself. How could one hope to elicit it?
>
> (Freud 1974: 47)

How indeed? Freud wanted a method which would get people to tell the truth about their unconscious mind, something which, by definition, they did not consciously know anything about. The solution came to Freud when he realised that people were actually capable of dragging memories from the unconscious into the conscious mind without help of hypnosis. This he deduced from the fact that although people who had been hypnotised would initially say that they remembered nothing of what had been said during hypnosis, it would eventually be recalled if they were put under sufficient pressure. He therefore decided to use the same technique without hypnosis:

> When I reached a point with [my patients] at which they maintained they knew nothing more, I assured them that they *did* know it all the same, and that they had only to say it; and I ventured to declare that the right memory would occur to them at the moment at which I laid my hand on their forehead.
>
> (1974: 47)

Freud found this technique worked. Patients who at first told him they could not remember certain events or scenes from their childhood would produce memories when he laid his hand upon their forehead. As a form of scientific investigation this is problematic. If an interviewer asks 'Did you ever witness your parents *in flagrante*?' and refuses to accept the respondent's claim not to remember any such thing, saying 'Yes, you can remember, tell me about it,' it would certainly convey the impression that the interviewer both wanted and expected the respondent to produce a suitable memory. If the interviewer then said, 'When I lay my hand on your forehead, *the right memory* will occur to you,' an enormous pressure to comply would be exerted. To fail to come up with a memory in the face of such explicit expectations would appear uncooperative. Moreover, Freud's interviewees were typically unhappy or disturbed, probably feeling vulnerable having labelled themselves, or been labelled by their family as 'hysterical', and it is therefore likely that they were in a highly suggestible state. On top of this, as a doctor, Freud was an authority figure and the power relationship between him and his patients would presumably have added to this pressure to produce appropriate memories. A recent biography of Graham Greene notes that both Greene and his cousin Ave were sent to a Jungian therapist for treatment. This involved arriving at the therapist's office at 11 a.m. each morning and recounting their dreams of the previous night. Both Greene and his cousin often found it impossible to recall their dreams, and therefore, as Ave remarked, the two of them 'used to concoct dreams' for the therapist to analyse. Greene began all his fictitious dreams with a pig (Sherry 1989: 96).

Although Freud was keen to stress the 'scientific' nature of his research, there can be little doubt that his interaction with his patients affected what they told him. His line of questioning was leading in the extreme. He assumed that all neuroses originated in sublimated or repressed infantile wishes, interpreted everything the patient said and every dream they recounted through reference to childhood experiences, and then fed these interpretations back to the patient. Certainly orthodox methodologists would argue that such interviewing techniques would contaminate the responses provided by patients, for if respondents have a clear idea of the theory or hypothesis under investigation and the interviewer's concerns, they are likely to select out responses to please the interviewer – in this case to produce memories, dreams and ideas which fitted with Freud's obsession with repressed wishes and desires. Neither would Freud's approach be acceptable to qualitative methodologists. Freud was not engaging with his patients as subjective beings, but was quite relentlessly imposing his own agenda and beliefs upon them. It seems unlikely that such techniques are conducive to getting people to tell you the whole truth and nothing but the truth about their thoughts, dreams or experiences. Freud's theoretical pre-conceptions informed the questions he asked, and the way in which he asked his questions must surely have coloured the responses he elicited. His theoretical preconceptions also affected whether or not he accepted a patient's answers as true. Freud's abandonment of the seduction theory provides a clear example of how critical this issue is to research findings.

When Freud first started practising, he was visited by many 'hysterics', who displayed symptoms such as a nervous tic or cough, depression, or suicidal feelings and many of these people claimed that they had been sexually abused in their childhood. Following Breuer, Freud initially saw these traumatic childhood experiences as the source of the adult hysteria. In other words, he began by believing what his patients told him. He accepted their accounts of rape and molestation as true descriptions of events that had really taken place. The hysterical symptoms they developed in later life were a response to real events that had taken place. But as we saw in Chapter 1, these ideas were not well received by the medical establishment and Freud quickly abandoned his seduction theory. He came to see his former willingness to accept the word of his patients at face value as 'naïve'. He now thought that his female patients were describing to him their unconscious wishes and desires, rather than giving him accurate and reliable accounts of events. When women told him that their fathers had raped or molested them, Freud now believed that they were mistaking their *wish* for sexual contact with their father for reality. Nothing actually happened, but the girls longed for it to happen. They then came to see their longing as unacceptable and had to repress it, and it was this, not a real experience of abuse, which lay at the heart of their neurosis. What they told him in interviews was not truth but fantasy.

The question of whether a patient's account of childhood sexual traumas were accepted as true or rejected as fantasy was vital to the whole future development of Freud's research, theories and therapeutic practice. It meant the difference between searching for the origins of neuroses in the real world, or locating them in the internal world of the subject's unconscious mind (Masson 1984). The shift away from accepting patient's statements as true also means that the methodological foundations of Freud's theories are extremely shaky. He asked people questions, and concluded that the truth was the precise opposite of what they told him. He gathered together empirical evidence to the effect that many of his patients had suffered childhood sexual abuse, and used it to develop a theory which said they had not. Few methodologists could be happy with such an approach to data collection or analysis. The problem is well illustrated by one of Freud's case studies, that of a young woman, referred to as Dora. The following is a summary of Porter's (1989) excellent outline of her case.

Freud found Dora to have various 'hysterical' symptoms, including a nervous cough, general debility, migraine, and a disposition to flirt with suicide. She told Freud that an old family friend, Herr K., had kissed her when she was about 14-years-old, and sexually propositioned her three years later. When Dora said she found the man's advances disgusting, Freud took this to be a hysterical symptom, stating that a 'healthy' girl would find it pleasant and exciting to be kissed by a close friend of her father's. Freud claimed that in reality, Dora desired Herr K., but this desire conflicted with her Oedipal longing for her father, and she therefore had to deny and repress her true feelings for Herr K. When Freud put this to Dora, she denied it. So Freud explained that when she resisted and rejected his line of analysis, she was really confirming that it was true:

> To an objective observer like himself, such a denial really meant confirmation. Patients said 'No' in their consciousness. But, Freud explained, 'there is no such thing as an unconscious No'. . . . Likewise, Freud assured her, when a patient, denying an interpretation, says 'I didn't think like that,' the real meaning of the phrase is 'Yes, I was unconscious of that'. All this is, Freud assures his readers, an 'entirely trustworthy form of confirmation'.

> (Porter 1989: 115)

Again, we have to ask questions about when and why researchers accept that people are telling the truth, when and why they reject their informant's accounts. When Freud first lectured on his seduction theory, the orthodox medical profession rejected it because it was based on the word of 'hysterical' women. It seems that ultimately Freud came to share the view that such women are unreliable informants, especially when they make claims against those more powerful and better respected than themselves (i.e., against men). A researcher who accepts the word of a relatively weak and powerless group at face value risks vilification and professional isolation. The social pressure to make research findings acceptable, to record only that which fits with received ideas and commonly accepted views of the world can be immense.

If we concentrate solely upon Freud's interviewing techniques, asking whether they were likely to get people to talk openly and sincerely, and whether Freud was likely to judge accurately when the truth had been told, it is difficult to avoid concluding that Freud's own theoretical framework both affected what people told him, and coloured his judgements as to what was true and untrue. Equally, it is important to recognise that research does not take place in a social and political vacuum, but in the context of a particular set of normative and moral values. Freud undertook his work at a time when women were considered to be so intellectually and emotionally inferior that they did not even enjoy full rights of citizenship. The fact that, in this context, he jettisoned a theory which rested on the uncorroborated evidence of 'hysterical' women is perhaps unsurprising, but his willingness to shift blame away from the patriarchs and on to their victims is also a very clear example of the kind of sexism which feminist methodologists argue has distorted social and psychological research. The following section looks at the interview research Diana Scully recently conducted with convicted rapists. Again, it highlights the problem which interviewers face in trying to get respondents to give accurate, full and frank responses, but it also allows us to explore some of the limitations of the approach to interviewing recommended by feminist methodologists.

INTERVIEWING WITHOUT SYMPATHY

Diana Scully's *Understanding Sexual Violence* (1990) is based upon interviews, conducted in prisons by herself and a colleague, with 114 convicted rapists. Scully is a feminist and fiercely critical of the sexist bias in traditional social research, but she points out that, important as it is to do research into women's lives, feminist researchers must do more than simply describe the experiences of women:

> I continue to be concerned that feminist scholars are neglecting another . . . area of critical work on men's world. . . . While not

diminishing the continuing responsibility to illuminate women's subordinate condition, the debunking of patriarchy is not accomplished by focusing exclusively on the lives and experiences of women.

(Scully 1990: 3)

This raises important issues for advocates of a feminist methodology. If such writers wish to distinguish feminist methodology from orthodox methods by an insistence that feminist researchers be genuinely non-exploitative and truly care about their research subjects, they will pretty much preclude any feminist studies of men who oppress and/or brutalise women. Since orthodox methodology is held to be inadequate because it cannot accommodate the experience of one half of the population, it would be odd for feminists to champion a method which could *only* be applied to the other half. It also highlights the danger of a method which seeks only to 'give voice' to research subjects, rather than critically explore and analyse their worldviews. Feminists may be happy to empathetically describe the experiences of their female subjects, but presumably would not wish to use the same method with male subjects.

Scully argues that it is essential to understand the men and the ideologies that oppress women, and illustrates the point through reference to rape. Feminist researchers have undertaken important research into the experiences of women who have survived rape; they have looked at the psychological and legal problems such women experience, and have challenged the many horrific but widely accepted myths about women and rape. While such work is vital to the struggle to change things like the way that rape victims are treated by the police and legal system, it cannot hope to address the question of why some men are sexually violent. This area has been largely left to male researchers to investigate, and Scully argues that male researchers have tended to explain rape in terms of individual pathology, using a disease model, rather than linking sexual violence to social beliefs and attitudes. Furthermore, much of this research has done little more than reproduce and reinforce existing social attitudes towards rape, effectively blaming women for men's sexual violence (see Scully 1990: 33–60).

Scully therefore argues the case for feminist research with rapists and adopts a socio-cultural framework which considers rape not in terms of individual pathology, but as an extension of normal masculinity. She observes that far from being abberant, expressions of power and domination are socially prescribed and rewarded to men in North American society. The aim of her study was to discover what men who rape gain from their sexually violent behaviour and to explore their more general attitudes towards masculinity, femininity and sexual violence in an attempt to uncover links between their sexual violence and broader social ideas about women, masculinity and violence. This involved undertaking highly structured, but essentially qualitative interviews with convicted rapists, as well as with a control group of felons convicted of non-sexual offences. The first and most striking feature of her interviews is simply their length:

> The interviews were long – for rapists, 89 pages divided into three parts: Part 1 consisting of a complete background history including childhood, family, religious, marital, education, employment, sexual and criminal; Part 2 consisting of a series of scales measuring attitudes toward women, masculinity, interpersonal violence, and rape; and Part 3 consisting of 40 pages of open-ended questions about the rape and the victim. Those in the contrast group of other felons were given only Part 1 and 2 of the interview.
>
> (Scully 1990: 14)

Clearly getting people to even co-operate with an interview such as this is no easy task, as Scully notes 'the success of this research hinged on the ability to develop a good working relationship within a very brief span of time' (1990: 14). Without trust and rapport, no one is likely to disclose much about their marital and sexual history, far less details about their own criminal behaviour. Given the subject matter of the interviews, it would have been extremely difficult for Scully to follow the advice of orthodox methodologists to the letter. She explains that:

> I . . . found that it was impossible to adhere to a rigid sequence for questions. Quite simply, no matter how much probing was done, the men would not talk about certain things until they were ready and felt comfortable. So although all of the questions were asked of every man, the interviews, rather than being uniform, were all slightly different, *depending on the needs and readiness of the interviewee*.
>
> (1990: 14–15, emphasis added)

Yet it would also have been hard for Scully to feel genuinely 'warm and caring' about the interviewees, as some qualitative methodologists recommend, or to follow certain feminist methodologists' advice about respecting the subject's integrity and taking a non-hierarchical approach to the interview. Scully does actually manage to show the reader the world through the eyes of the rapists she interviewed. She shows how these men rationalised and justified their actions, how they made themselves believe that their horrific acts were acceptable, necessary or inevitable, and she is able to do this because during the course of the interviews she managed to get them to open up and talk in detail about their attitudes and their crimes, about how and why they chose to rape. But she did not enter into their worlds through a process of empathetic identification, she did not build trust and rapport upon a foundation of genuine warmth or sympathy. Instead she manipulated these men, encouraging them to see her in a particular way so that they would be willing to disclose information that they may perhaps not have disclosed had they known how she truly felt about them:

> The type of information sought in this research required a supportive, non judgmental neutral facade – one that I did not always genuinely feel. Frankly, some of the men were personally repulsive. . . . Additionally the stories they told were horrible and a few of the men were not overly co-operative. Indeed, some of the interviews required immense effort to remain neutral. But the fact is that no one tells his or her secrets to a visibly hostile and disapproving person.
>
> (Scully 1990: 18)

Few people would be filled by a sense of moral outrage at the idea of manipulating convicted rapists in this way, but it is worth noting that such an approach can generate other ethical dilemmas. Scully goes on to observe that her non-judgemental facade may have had unintended consequences; 'This was especially problematic with the men . . . who did not define their sexually violent behaviour as rape. I worried that some of these men might interpret neutrality as a signal of agreement or approval' (1990: 18–19). Her dilemma was intensified by the fact that if she interacted with these men as a person, rather than as a 'neutral' researcher, and disagreed with or challenged their views, they could have told other potential interviewees and 'who would volunteer to get shot down by the researcher?' (Scully 1990: 19). Scully's interviews also raise other ethical problems. She argues that in order to get convicted rapists to talk truthfully about their attitudes and behaviour, it was necessary to assure them that whatever they said to her would have no bearing on their future parole or release, and to guarantee them complete confidentiality (except if interviewees confided plans for future illegal acts outside the prison). She justifies this guarantee as follows:

> In the case of past criminal behaviour, confidentiality is justified because past acts do not pose a current threat, and since the individual is already in prison, no one is placed in danger from the continued activity. Likewise, the confidentiality of details about ongoing illegal

activities that occur within prisons, involving things like drugs or sexual behaviour, can be defended. Since staff are generally aware that these activities exist to some degree in all prisons, informing about a specific act would contribute little to what is already known or to a solution.

(1990: 23)

This formulation seems inadequate. What would have happened if a rapist, nearing the end of a relatively short sentence for one rape, had confessed to her a series of undetected rapes and murders? Surely under such circumstances the researcher would have a moral obligation to pass this information on to the authorities and so break the promise of confidentiality. The case for confidentiality as regards illegal sexual behaviour within the prison seems equally weak. If a man confessed to her that he was raping other men in prison, why should she protect him? It could equally well be argued that a researcher is under no obligation to inform the police if he or she extracts information about undetected rapes outside prison – after all, the police are generally aware that rapes occur, and informing about a specific act would likewise 'contribute little to what is already known or to a solution'. However, though all ethical issues are not resolved by the formulation quoted above, Scully was undoubtedly correct to assume that without a guarantee of confidentiality, her interviewees would have been less likely to disclose information, and that if they had believed that their chances of parole could be affected by what they told her, it would have been a positive incentive to lie or conceal the truth. In short, to encourage these men to tell the whole truth in the interviews, Scully had to build and maintain trust and rapport which involved concealing her true feelings about them, refraining from challenging or making negative comments about their assertions, and assuring them complete confidentiality. All of these things could, for one reason or another, be judged by a purist to be unethical, and yet without them it is unlikely that Scully would have gathered much useful data.

Scully also had to face the problem of how to decide whether or not her interviewees were telling the truth. Unlike many researchers, she confronts this issue directly in a section of her chapter on methodology. (Indeed, Scully should be more generally congratulated for her unusually detailed and thoughtful discussion of methodology.) So far as questions about the actual rapes for which the men were convicted, Scully had access to an independent source of verification in the form of pre-sentence reports, written by court workers at the time of conviction which provide information on both the offender's, victim's and police's versions of the details of the crime (Scully 1990: 31). Each interviewee was asked a list of 30 factual questions about his background and about the crime, and then, with the interviewee's permission, his responses were checked against these pre-sentence reports 'to establish the validity of the interview' (Scully 1990: 26). The availability of these records was of enormous value to the study. They allowed Scully to distinguish between three distinct types of rapists. First, there were those men who admitted the rape (admitters) and whose version of events in the interview broadly corresponded with that provided in the pre-sentence report. Scully notes, however, that whilst they did not actually tell lies:

> they did systematically understate the amount of force and violence they used. . . . Admitters also did not volunteer information about especially brutal or offensive aspects of their crimes. For example, a particularly anguished young man tearfully recounted the details of his rape, including the age of his 70 year old victim. His self-disgust was further clarified when the validity check revealed what he neglected to mention – that the victim had been his grandmother and that she suffered a heart attack as a result of the rape.
>
> (1990: 27)

Second, there were those who admitted having had sexual contact with their victims, but denied that they had raped them (deniers). The information they gave Scully in the interviews differed markedly from the victim's and police's versions of what had taken place. These men 'seemed genuinely to believe that their actions were not rape despite the admission, in some cases, that a weapon had been used' (1990: 27). Finally, there were 34 men who denied any contact at all with their victims, 'instead, they said that they themselves were the victims of mistaken identity, or that they had not raped the victims but had committed other crimes against them, such as robbery' (1990: 28).

Unlike Kinsey and Freud, Scully did not contradict her interviewees or challenge them to correct their answers if she suspected they were lying, but recorded their statements as they stood. The men who claimed to have no knowledge of the rapes they were convicted of were not questioned further about the rapes – Scully collected only background information and attitudinal data from them. So far as the men who admitted having had sexual contact but denied rape were concerned, Scully did not believe that what they told her was a true account of events, but she did believe they were sincerely describing what *they* saw as the truth. She suggests that deniers were not setting out to deceive her as a researcher, but rather were honestly describing to her how they deceived themselves. Accepting what they told her as a truthful portrayal of their self-deception actually formed an important part of her analysis. She argues that 'denials can also be taken at face value, and the content analysed as a statement on the cultural learning and socially derived perspective of sexually violent men' (1990: 28). It might be argued that Freud approached his patient's denials in a similar way, but a critical difference is that Freud had no way of knowing whether the denials were self-deception other than through reference to his own theories, whereas Scully was able to corroborate her suspicions through reference to documentary evidence compiled by others. Clearly, she could only independently verify issues covered by the pre-sentence report. Responses to other questions and attitudinal data could not be checked, and it is possible that these men expressed attitudes that they did not sincerely hold. But, as will be argued below, there is a sense in which interview research always relies on the good faith of the interviewee. Methodologists can argue the toss about which interviewing techniques are most likely to encourage people to be truthful, but the assumption that having volunteered or agreed to take part in research, the interviewee will not systematically and *deliberately* lie in response to every question remains an act of faith.

CONCLUSIONS

Earlier, we noted that all methodologists can agree upon the fact that interviews differ from ordinary conversations, and that it is wrong to lead or manipulate respondents into providing the answers that the researcher (for theoretical, political or moral reasons) wishes to hear. What orthodox, qualitative and feminist methodologists differ on is the role of the interviewer, the nature of the interviewer–interviewee relationship, and how exactly to go about extracting reliable data. Advice on these matters varies not simply because methodologists draw on very different philosophical traditions, but also because interviewing can be used in such a vast range of different types of research. The role of the interview in survey research is very different, and usually far more limited, than the interview is in ethnographic research. No one who wished to grasp the meanings that give form and content to social processes in an alien culture, for example, would set out to administer a pre-designed, standardised set of questions and no one who simply wanted to know whether people preferred butter or margarine would put enormous effort into establishing an excellent rapport and enter into a lengthy, in-depth, unstructured interview. The role of the interview in research which sets out to test a particular hypothesis is likewise different from that of the interview in theory-constructing research, and it is different in research which aims to produce an almost literary, descriptive account of, say, six prostitute's lives (see Jaget 1980) than in research which aims to systematically document the response of 30 women clerical workers to the introduction of new office technology (see O'Connell Davidson 1994). In other words, the scope of the interview (and therefore many of its characteristics) is powerfully affected by the researchers objectives and by other aspects of the research design. But whatever the aim and scope of the interview, it is always a social encounter, and this fact gives rise to the paradoxes which cannot be fully resolved by philosophical or methodological dogma. Let us spell these out before concluding.

Theorising about the virtues of various different interviewing techniques and actually conducting interviews are two rather different matters and, in part, this has to do with the fact that researchers cannot control for individual differences between respondents. When you talk to people who have conducted social research interviews or read accounts of the interviewing techniques adopted in particular research projects, you find that, no matter how committed the researcher was originally to a particular theoretical model of interviewing, the practice of interviewing diverged from the theoretical ideal to some degree. Interviewers who believe in the central importance of standardisation will come across people who are just plain awkward. Almost inevitably, there will be some people whose personalities are such that they cannot be put through a standard interview and who will manage to get even the best trained interviewer to answer some query or explain some item in more detail. Qualitative interviewers will also come up against people who they cannot interview in the recommended manner. Some people are just not expansive, and no matter how much effort is put into building trust and rapport they will still answer every question with a monosyllable and shrug their shoulders or look away in embarrassment when they are probed further. Even feminist interviewers interviewing women and committed to a non-directive, non-hierarchical approach can be confronted by 'sisters' who are so loquacious or so determined to discuss trivia that they are forced to adopt a more directive and controlling style.

Most methodologists observe that the success of the interview, in terms of extracting reliable data, relies to some degree on the personal characteristics and social identity of the interviewer. Some will insist that the blander the interviewer the better, others will argue that interviewers and respondents should be 'matched' in terms of gender and/or 'racialised' identity, some will call for interviewers to be caring, sharing, 'feely' people. Against this, we would argue that it is impossible to prescribe *the* 'best' or 'necessary' characteristics of an interviewer, other than to say that the interviewer should be able to exploit their personal characteristics to full advantage. Interviewers can and do employ what might appear to be a handicap, such as a stutter, to their advantage. Embarrassment sometimes encourages interviewees to keep talking and to say more than they otherwise would. In some situations, interviewers can and do exploit the negative stereotypes that certain people hold of them to their advantage. A young women interviewing relatively powerful male respondents, senior managers for example, can live up to their expectations by 'acting dumb' which can encourage them to disclose more information to her than they would to an older male interviewer, whom they might assume would know how to use the information against them. Kinsey's insistence on WASP male interviewers underlines the moral and political dangers of making the case for a certain 'type' of interviewer, while Scully's work demonstrates the fact that differences in gender are not necessarily a barrier to obtaining full and detailed information, even about topics of an extremely sensitive nature.

It is also important to recognise that there is no method or technique which actually *forces* people to provide truthful and accurate responses, far less full and sincere ones, and other than strapping your subjects to a lie-detector (which is, in any case, an unreliable instrument) there is no way of knowing with certainty whether or not they have told you the truth. Ultimately, deciding that an answer is true and complete is a subjective judgement on the part of the interviewer. This judgement can be informed by experience (both as a member of society and as a professional) and/or by more ephemeral qualities such as intuition. Certain skills, such as reading body language and facial movements, or being able to quickly cross-reference one statement with other previous statements, are obviously also useful. However, whatever this process of deciding whether a response is true or false may be, it is not 'scientific' in the natural science sense of the word. As a consumer of research, you therefore need to assess how likely the researcher was to have made good judgements about whether their informants were telling the truth. You need to ask yourself how likely the researcher was to be swayed by their own theoretical, moral and normative preconceptions. No matter which general approach to interviewing is taken (orthodox, qualitative or feminist), these preconceptions can lead interviewers to refuse to accept disconfirming statements from interviewees and to be too willing to accept confirming statements at face value, without further probing.

All this points to the following conclusion. There are certain interview practices which we can condemn universally. These include any techniques which lead or manipulate the respondent into saying that which the researcher wishes to hear, or which prevent the respondent from stating that which he or she wishes to state. But beyond this, it is not possible to lay down blanket rules and procedures to cover every conceivable social research interview that every single interviewer could successfully follow, any more than it would be possible to write a blueprint for how to behave in any other social encounter that every single person could use effectively. Any handbook which pretends otherwise is necessarily downplaying the complexity of the social interaction that interviewing involves, and the range of uses to which interviews can be put in social research.

Chapter 6

Observation in laboratories and other structured settings

Observation occupies a central role in the methodology of the natural sciences. Indeed, for positivist philosophers, scientific knowledge is distinguished from other more common-sense, traditional forms of knowledge because it is based upon empirical observations rather than blind acceptance of unsupported authority. The idea that the truth of statements of fact should be checked against observations is, according to Bertrand Russell 'an entirely modern conception, which hardly existed before the seventeenth century' (1976: 17). He continues:

> Aristotle maintained that women have fewer teeth than men; although he was twice married, it never occured to him to verify this statement by examining his wives' mouths. . . . When Galileo's telescope revealed Jupiter's moons, the orthodox refused to look through it, because they knew there could not be such bodies, and therefore the telescope must be deceptive. Respect for observation as opposed to tradition is difficult. . . . Science insists upon it, and this insistence was the source of the most desperate battles between science and authority.
>
> (Russell 1976: 17–19)

By the twentieth century, one might almost say that this situation had been reversed. Knowledge acquired through the methods of the natural sciences was now widely respected as the highest form of knowledge, and theories which could not be easily tested by experimental or structured observational methods, as well as research that relied on more qualitative techniques, were often dismissed as 'unscientific' and therefore worthless. Social scientists who share this regard for the natural science method therefore tend to see structured, observational research in laboratories as the purest form of scientific investigation. As ever, there are a number of methodological problems associated with such research techniques. This chapter begins by looking at some of the practical problems which face laboratory researchers, then moves on to consider some of the broader ethical and philosophical problems that experimental methods give rise to through a consideration of Milgram's classic social psychology experiment on obedience to authority.

OBSERVATION AND SEX RESEARCH

Social scientists who wish to apply the methods and procedures of the natural sciences to the study of human action face some rather obvious difficulties. They are often concerned with mental processes (such as thoughts, beliefs, motivations, values) rather than with actual behaviours and these processes are not open to direct observation. Even when researchers try to get around this problem by focusing on behaviours or actions alone, the fact that their subjects are human beings makes it difficult to achieve the kind of control that is exercised by natural scientists over their inanimate subject matter. Kinsey, for example, wanted only to know the 'plain facts' about human sexual behaviour and had no interest in the meanings people attached to their sexual acts, yet he still had to rely on their *accounts* of their sexual lives rather than being able to observe their sexual behaviour directly. As we saw in Chapter 5, this meant he was confronted by the question of how to ensure his subjects told the truth, a problem which natural scientists do not have to contend with.

In fact, Kinsey and his associates did also try to make use of more direct, observational techniques. Pomeroy explains that Kinsey felt 'a certain impatience' with the fact that the data he was collecting was 'necessarily secondhand' and 'it occurred to him that we ought to observe at first hand some of the behaviour we were recording' (1972: 172). Kinsey began his observational work by attending sex sessions held by a homosexual group in New York. For those who might be tempted to describe this as merely a foray into voyeurism, Pomeroy spends almost two entire pages to reassuring us that the experience of observation was entirely nonerotic:

> Kinsey possessed the ability to observe actual sexual behaviour with the same objectivity he maintained during interviews; he was always the scientist. . . . He was the absolute observer; there was no personal involvement whatever . . . There was, for us, no more erotic content in viewing the sexual activities of the human animal than in observing any other mammal. . . . I cannot recall a single instance of sexual arousal on my part when I was observing sex behaviour.
>
> (Pomeroy 1972: 175–6)

Subjects whose intercourse proved particularly 'intriguing' – for instance, 'a homosexual couple in which one of the partners had an orgasm of such intensity that he was in a frenzy of release, quite unconsciously beating the other man around the shoulders with his clenched fists' (Pomeroy 1972: 176) – were asked to perform on camera. In this sense, Kinsey anticipated the work of medical researchers like Masters and Johnson who conducted extensive observational research into human sexual responses, filming hundreds of couples in coitus. Masters and Johnson were pioneers in their field, and their research challenged much of the received wisdom about human sexuality at that time. As Parr (1975) puts it:

> Masters and Johnson are said to have shattered three sexual myths. The first is that male efficiency is related to the size of the penis. . . . The second . . . is that there is a difference between 'clitoral' and 'vaginal' orgasms. . . . The third 'myth' . . . is that female orgasm is always single rather than potentially multiple.
>
> (1975: 4)

Their work has been highly influential and numerous sex therapy techniques which are still in use today are based upon their laboratory investigations. Masters was an American medical doctor, trained in obstetrics and gynaecology. He spent several years researching hormone replacement before moving on to research into sexual responses in 1954. After three years, he hired Virginia Johnson (a 'professional student' who studied music, business studies, sociology and psychology but never received a degree) as his research assistant, because he believed that as a man, he would never be able to fully understand the sexual experiences described to him by female subjects (Belliveau and Richter 1970: 14–16). They began laboratory based research designed to explore the physiological and psychological response to sexual stimulation. Having investigated 'normal' sexual responses, they moved on to look at various forms of sexual 'dysfunction' and to develop therapeutic treatment programmes for a number of common 'disorders'. The research basically consisted of observing and monitoring the blood pressure, heart rate, respiratory rate, brain-wave patterns and other body activity of couples in coitus, single men masturbating and single women being penetrated by 'an artificial phallus which could be controlled voluntarily for size and for depth and for rapidity of thrust' (Belliveau and Richter 1970: 27, Masters and Johnson 1966: 21). The research subjects were taken to a moderate sized, windowless laboratory room in which there was a bed and various scientific instruments:

Couples were asked to relax for a while in this laboratory bedroom,
and then they were encouraged to engage in intercourse there, without being observed, before the recording of an actual experiment
began. . . . Couples were told ahead of time that they would be
observed during sexual activity not only by therapists but possibly by
assistants, artists, and cameramen. Many experiments were filmed.

(Belliveau and Richter 1970: 27)

A total of 382 women and 312 men took part in the research, and around
10,000 sexual responses were studied. Clearly, the 694 people who
volunteered to be observed in the laboratory were not a representative
cross-section of the population as a whole. Likewise, the sample of
individuals who co-operated with Kinsey's observational research were
not, almost by definition, typical of the broader population. It is not
usual to invite even the most 'scientific' observer to watch one masturbate, for example (though Pomeroy tells us that most of their observational subjects were ordinary, 'decent' folk, adding that 'the public
would have been astounded and disbelieving to know the names of the
eminent scientists who . . . volunteered . . . to be photographed in some
kind of sexual activity' 1972: 179). But even where laboratory research
is investigating rather more pedestrian phenomena, sampling still
proves something of a problem. A researcher using survey methods can
randomly select a sample of the population as a whole, pay interviewers
to travel to the respondents homes and badger them to participate in the
survey, and can hope for a reasonably high degree rate of co-operation.
But a researcher can hardly expect a large percentage of a randomly
selected sample to give up their time and travel all the way to his or her
laboratory in order to take part in an experiment. Such researchers
therefore tend to rely on less systematic methods of culling a sample,
generally upon volunteer sampling. Because laboratories are typically
located on university campuses, and because students can be expected
to be reasonably well disposed towards academic research (especially
when paid a small fee), the bulk of social scientific experimental
research has relied upon volunteer samples drawn from a student population. Samples therefore reflect the social class, gender and 'racialised'
composition of university undergraduates, that is, they typically over-
represent white, middle-class males. When reading research based on
experimental or observational methods in laboratories, then, it is important to ask how the researcher obtained the sample, to look carefully at
the composition of that sample, and to think about how it may have
biased the research findings.

Masters and Johnson were well aware of the fact that their sample was not representative of the population as a whole, and they made no generalised claims about sexual *behaviour* on the basis of their work with this sample: 'All they claim is that they were sexually *responsive* people. Studying sexually functioning people made it possible to establish some of the physiologic facts of sexual response never observed and recorded before' (Belliveau and Richter 1970: 28 emphasis added). In other words, they held that because they were observing physiological responses, it did not matter whether their subjects were a representative cross-section of the population in terms of their sexual activities. However, they did actually attempt to screen out what they termed 'obvious exhibitionists' and also decided after 18 months of study that female prostitutes were not suitable subjects for normal sexual response studies, noting that because 'they frequently experience sexual arousal without having orgasm, prostitutes often develop a chronic pelvic congestion which makes their physical reactions different from those of the average woman' (Belliveau and Richter 1970: 25). Being sexually responsive was not the only selection criterion Masters and Johnson used to pick a sample, then. They also filtered out certain subjects on the basis of their own preconceptions about 'normal' sexuality. They assumed (some would say over-optimistically) that unlike prostitutes, 'the average woman' does not frequently experience sexual arousal without having orgasm, and that people who openly display their exhibitionist tendencies are sexually different from people who conceal, deny or do not have them.

Laboratory based sex research raises a number of other practical problems, and again whilst sex research illustrates these clearly, they are problems which confront all laboratory researchers no matter what topic they are investigating. To begin with there is the question of funding. Almost all research requires funding, either in the form of grants from government, industry or charitible trusts or in the form of support from the university in which the research is based. Experimental and structured observational research can be expensive, especially if the researcher needs specialist equipment, and obviously the subject matter of the proposed research affects the willingness of funding bodies to provide cash support for the project. Masters and Johnson, for example, found it extremely difficult to obtain funding. In 1963, Masters is said to have spent more time writing grant applications than writing up or conducting research. Money problems can critically affect the course of research, and the need to attract continued funding, combined with the need to secure or maintain professional reputation, places enormous pressure on researchers to come up with conclusive, quotable results. Masters once remarked that:

> If you do cancer research for ten years and don't come up with anything noteworthy, nobody is going to question you professionally. I went into sex research with the full knowledge that I had to win. I had to come up with something or I would have been destroyed professionally. Even with results, sex research invites criticism.
>
> (cited in Belliveau and Richter 1970: 20)

This underlines the fact that academic researchers, much as they might like to see themselves as erudite and unworldly scholars, are actually participating in a labour process. Like other wage workers, they have to concern themselves to some extent with mundane vulgarities, such as money, job security and professional advancement, and this impacts on the kind of questions they choose to address in their research, the methods they adopt and the way in which they disseminate their research findings. In the current climate of recession and cuts to public spending in both Britain and the USA, such matters are increasingly affecting the nature and scope of academic research.

The fact that the research process is also a labour process is significant for another reason. Laboratory research, like survey research, is rarely conducted by a single individual. Instead, there is generally a division of labour, with one person or group designing the research, and others, employed as research assistants, technicians and so on, helping to execute it. The work of this latter group is often far from scintillating. There are many boring, routine tasks associated with laboratory research which have to be performed over and over again, and so many possibilities for human error, especially if research assistants and technicians are disaffected with their employer or the research itself. Even laboratory research on human sexuality is said to become extremely dull after a time: 'Sex research is boring. It is interesting to note the variations and differences, to see changes on the records, but apart from that, watching someone masturbating or a couple in coitus hour after hour is boring' (Hartman cited in Radford 1992).

Like other workers, laboratory sex researchers also face health and safety hazards. For example, a researcher at the Center for Marital and Sexual Studies in California recently contracted gonorrhoea of the eye after failing to 'follow the proper procedures for fitting sensors to intimate parts of a volunteer' (Radford 1992). The real point is that laboratory research is itself a social process, and the power relations between those involved in funding, designing and executing research has an effect on the nature and reliability of the research findings. But these practical and political problems are not the only issues raised by laboratory research. As the following sections show, it also raises a number of ethical and philosophical problems.

EXPERIMENTAL RESEARCH IN THE SOCIAL SCIENCES

Orthodox positivist textbooks often present experiments as *the* most scientific and therefore the most desirable research technique. They are preferable to other methods 'whenever . . . feasible' (Simon 1969: 230). Indeed, for methodologists like Stouffer (1950), all other research methods are merely inadequate compromises with or approximations to the experimental method, having some but not all of its components (see Hessler 1992: 167). Why are laboratory experiments so highly prized by positivist methodologists? One reason is simply that the experimental method places the researcher firmly in control of the research environment and the research subject. The researcher designs the experiment and sets up the laboratory situation exactly as he or she wants it. No unexpected or unwanted interruptions need occur, the experiment begins and ends at the behest of the researcher. Standardisation is easy to achieve. Because the researcher is in control it is simple to arrange a series of identical experiments with different subjects and, providing the researcher writes down the details of the research procedure, the experiment can be replicated, and so validated, by other researchers.

This desire for control is underpinned by more basic philosophical assumptions about the nature of scientific research. Positivists who champion the experimental method believe that the social world can and should be scientifically investigated in the same way as the natural world. The natural sciences are essentially concerned with the abstract properties of objects, such as their mass, length, force, velocity and mollecular structure, rather than with objects as whole or complete entities in themselves (see Hughes 1990: 41–3). These abstract properties are referred to as 'variables' – they are properties which vary along a scale, for example, the mass of any given object varies and can be measured on a numerical scale. The goal of experiments is generally to discover law-like relationships between two or more variables. Physicists, for instance, conduct experiments to discover the relationship between an object's mass and the velocity with which it falls through the air and use their observations to make generalised statements about the law of gravity. The experimental method allows the physicist to isolate one variable (such as mass) and study its effects.

Positivists hold that the social scientific laboratory experiment, like the natural science experiment, is a method 'of getting knowledge about the relationships between (or among) variables, most especially about the *causal* relationships between variables' (Simon 1969: 228). The assumption is that the social scientist, like the natural scientist, can identify certain abstract properties possessed by the object of their study (i.e. human beings), isolate them, measure them along some kind of scale and look for relationships between them.

The first step in designing a social scientific experiment is, then, to decide which observable variables will be the focus of study (Simon 1969: 231). A researcher might want to investigate the effects of viewing violent pornographic videos on men's attitudes towards rape, for example. The men's attitudes towards rape would be one variable (the 'dependent' variable) and you could measure this by using a scaled questionnaire or attitude inventory. The video material would be the independent variable which could be varied – some men could be shown videos depicting non-sexual violence, others videos depicting no violence at all, and some shown videos depicting sexual violence. Indeed, this is the crux of the experiment. The experimenter 'intentionally manipulates one or more of the independent variables . . . thus exposing various groups of subjects to the different variables . . . and then observes changes in the dependent variables' (Simon 1969: 228). After exposure to the material, subjects' attitudes towards rape would again be measured to see whether any change had occurred. If changes to the attitudes of subjects that had been exposed to the sexually violent material were more pronounced than changes to the attitudes of those who had viewed non-sexually violent material, the investigator would probably conclude that some kind of relationship existed between the two variables.

Positivist methodologists hold that, as with natural science experiments, the key to good design is to ensure that the effects of the independent variable are isolated from other conditions. It would be no good, for instance, to re-measure subject's attitudes towards rape several days after they had been exposed to the video material, since the experimenter would not be able to tell whether it was exposure to the video that had affected their attitudes, or exposure to some other variable(s) in the interim period. A number of studies in this vein have been conducted (particularly by Malamuth, see for example Malamuth 1986) and the findings widely used in the feminist anti-pornography campaign. For an excellent feminist critique of both these experiments and the feminist anti-pornography literature which relies so heavily upon them, see King (1993).

Social scientific laboratory research does not always entail using the experimental method or hypothesis testing. It can simply involve observation. Psychologists have, for example, investigated various forms of human interaction, such as non-verbal communication, simply by observing subjects interacting in the laboratory through one-way mirrors. What both these forms of laboratory research have in common is a very particular kind of observation, namely observation that is structured and controlled along the same lines as observation in the natural sciences. One of the recurrent themes of this book is the idea that attempts to replicate the methods of the natural sciences in the study of the social world are highly problematic, and the following sections reiterate this point through a focus on some of the ethical and philosophical issues raised by a classic social psychology experiment.

MILGRAM'S EXPERIMENTAL RESEARCH ON OBEDIENCE: ETHICS AND INTERPRETATION

Milgram's (1963) experimental study of obedience is well known. He wanted to investigate the extent to which ordinary people would be prepared to obey an authority figure. Would they be willing to inflict pain on others if commanded to do so, or would their own moral and normative values lead them to resist such instructions? His subjects were deceived into believing they were taking part in a learning study. They were asked to sit in a cubicle, next door to a 'student', and told that the control panel in front of them would allow them to administer increasingly severe electric shocks to that student if he or she gave the wrong answers to questions. When the ficticious shocks were administered, the subject heard cries and screams from the 'student' through the partition walls:

> Painful groans were heard on administration of the 135-volt shock and at 150 volts the victim called out 'Experimenter, get me out of here! I won't be in this experiment any more! I refuse to go on!' Cries of this type continued with generally rising intensity, so that at 180 volts the victim cried out 'I can't stand the pain' and by 270 volts his response to the shock was definitely an agonized scream.
>
> (Milgram 1974: 23)

Many subjects exhibited extreme doubt and anxiety about administering these shocks, but were urged by the experimenter to continue regardless. A large number of subjects continued to obey the experimenter and administer shocks up to the maximum level, despite hearing the 'student's' distress, and Milgram's conclusions about the degree to which people are prepared to obey authority were therefore extremely depressing. Quite 'normal' individuals, it seemed, like the good citizens of Nazi Germany, were more likely to obey orders from an authority figure than to follow their own moral code.

Ethical issues

It is difficult to read about this experiment without questioning the ethics that underpin it. Milgram's experiment not only caused subjects a great deal of emotional stress, but was all the more unpleasant because of the way he deliberately deceived them. As a consequence, it has been heavily criticised for being unethical in its use of subjects. The atrocities committed by Nazi medical researchers led to the formulation of what is known as the Nuremburg Code, which provides ethical guidelines for experimental research in psychological as well as medical science research, and Milgram's study certainly violates some of the principles embodied in this code. Homan (1991) observes that 'the Nuremburg Code lays emphasis upon the need . . . to use only voluntary subjects and to relieve them of the pressure or pain of the experiment if this becomes excessive' (1991: 10). Milgram's subjects were pressed to continue with the experiment even when they begged to stop. Had he felt bound by the Nuremburg Code, which insists that 'subjects should be free and know that they are free to withdraw from an experiment, even once it is in progress' (Homan 1991: 10), he would have responded to his subject's requests to end their ordeal. The Nuremburg Code further holds that it is the responsibility of the researcher to end an experiment if it is causing 'undue discomfort or harm to a subject' (Homan 1991: 11), and Milgram can be accused of negligence in this regard.

This kind of ethical code can be applied to all types of research, not simply laboratory work, but because experimental and laboratory research concentrates power and control so utterly in the hands of the researcher, abuse of power in this setting is especially worrying. Milgram himself defended his research by saying that the experiment provided subjects with an opportunity to learn something about them-selves, and about the conditions of human action. But as Milgram deceived his subjects about the nature of the research so elaborately, they were unable to exercise any choice over whether or not to take advantage of this 'opportunity'. Through his deception of research subjects, Milgram violated another ethical principle central to the Nuremburg Code, namely the principle of informed consent which holds that 'the human subjects of research should be allowed to agree or refuse to participate in the light of comprehensive information concerning the nature and purpose of the research' (Homan 1991: 69). The idea is that it is not good enough for researchers to assume that as scientists they are able to decide what is and is not harmful or beneficial to the research subject. The individual must be allowed to exercise choice and can only do so if he or she fully understands what is involved in the research. Even when experimental research does not involve overt deception, it can still raise ethical problems about consent. If subjects are paid to participate, for instance, they may feel obliged to continue with the experiment even when they actually want to stop.

When the question of consent is considered further, it becomes apparent that ethical and practical concerns can often produce conflicting demands of the researcher. If, for ethical reasons, a researcher gave subjects *fully* comprehensive information about the nature and purpose of experimental or observational research, it could make it impossible to conduct the experiment. On the one hand, fully informed subjects might well refuse to take part in experiments such as that conducted by Milgram. Even when less controversial methods such as survey interviewing are being used, the moral imperative to secure informed consent often conflicts with the practical imperative to gain access or co-operation. On the other hand, subjects who know exactly what the researcher is investigating may alter their behaviour in view of this knowledge. Milgram's subjects, for example, would hardly have behaved in the way they did if they had known exactly what he was doing and why. Some researchers justify being less than frank with their research subjects on precisely these grounds, arguing that to provide comprehensive information about the nature and purpose of the research would influence and bias the subject's behaviour in the experimental or observational situation.

This dilemma springs from the positivist philosophy that underpins such research. If researchers recognised and accepted the fact that the human subject of social research, unlike the subject matter of natural science research, is a conscious, purposive being, they would be forced to also recognise that there is no hope of a social scientific experimenter achieving the level of control exercised by the natural science experimenter. For once the human subject is acknowledged to be a conscious, intelligent actor, it becomes obvious that refusing to tell them what the experiment is all about does not secure total control for the researcher. If research subjects are *not* told what the experiment is investigating, they will simply look at what is being done and draw their own inferences about the experiment's nature and purpose. These inferences, whether right or wrong, will then affect subjects' behaviour in the laboratory. In other words, whether duped and deceived or fully informed, research subjects are thinking human beings who interpret the situations in which they find themselves and impose meaning upon it, and their perception of the situation will inevitably affect their actions. As the following section shows, this issue can be central to the interpretation of experimental and observational laboratory research.

Issues of interpretation

Methodologists who favour the use of experimental methods in the social sciences seem to assume that the difference between the subject matter of the natural and social sciences is insignificant and that the methods of the natural sciences are therefore suitable for the investigation of human action. The trouble with this view is that it ignores the critical role played by subjective interpretations and beliefs in determining action. The research subjects that the positivist experimenter tries to manipulate and control in the laboratory are not blank, empty ciphers waiting passively to respond to any stimulus that the experimenter presents. They are human beings, and as such actively engage in interpreting and making sense of the 'variables' that the scientist seeks to isolate, observe, vary and control. For the experimenter to interpret their actions, then, it is necessary for her or him to understand these subjective interpretations and beliefs. As well as being censured on ethical grounds, Milgram has been criticised for failing to do just this. Harre (1979) argues that because Milgram did not consider the way in which his subjects perceived the situation in which he placed them, he fundamentally misinterpreted his findings. Milgram's study 'was not an experiment about obedience. It was an experiment about trust' (1979: 105). Harre holds that the actions of Milgram's subjects are only explicable through reference to their trust in Milgram and his assistants' scientific knowledge:

> Nearly every one of the subjects, at the point where the supposed learner was showing signs of distress, protested against the procedure they had been told to carry out. At this point they were reassured by the assistant in words which ran something as follows: 'I assure you that the learner is suffering no tissue damage. You may proceed with the treatment'. Under the conditions of trust that obtained between the subjects and Milgram's assistant, that lie . . . was taken by the subjects to be true.

> (Harre 1979: 105)

If Milgram's subjects did genuinely believe that administering the supposed electric shocks caused no damage to the learner, and even, perhaps, that the shocks were a form of 'treatment', then their behaviour in the laboratory may not have been a measure simply of their willingness to obey an authority figure, as Milgram took it to be. Instead, the experiment may have revealed 'how much trust [subjects] were prepared to put in the word of someone who seemed to have something of the aura of a scientist about him' (Harre 1979: 106). The real point is that observing *what* people do in given situations cannot answer questions about *why* they do it. This is because it is impossible for the social scientist to faithfully imitate the natural scientist by holding a situation constant and manipulating one 'independent variable' to observe its effects, for human experience simply cannot be decomposed into a number of separate, independently variable parts. A person's willingness to obey an authority figure, for example, cannot be isolated from a host of other factors, including, in Milgram's case, the subject's pre-existing knowledge of electricity. We cannot assume that because subjects obeyed the orders of white-coated scientists in the setting of a university laboratory in a liberal democratic state, having been deceived into thinking they were taking part in valuable educational research, that they would unquestioningly obey the orders of other authority figures in other settings. The individual's subjective beliefs about the legitimacy of the authority figure, about the purpose of the orders being given and about the consequences of obedience are inseparable from the act of obeying.

These problems of interpretation are not confined to Milgram's work. Harre argues that all experimental research in laboratories produce the same problems, and that these are irresolvable. His argument is that when people are placed in the bizarre and unfamiliar environment of the scientific laboratory, they are unsure how to behave:

> Actors simply do not know which rule-meaning system to draw upon in acting. Every one of their actions is fraught with a kind of uncertainty. In the end, of course, one presumes, the most generalised and unspecific kind of responses are given, as they would be in the most ambiguous conditions of real life, such as, for example, a meeting between strangers in an undifferentiated public space.
>
> (1979: 107)

Harre is referring to the kind of uncertainty that people feel when placed in a situation without any clear guidelines or socially established rules about how to respond. All of us know how to react when we bump into an acquaintance or colleague leaving the cinema with their spouse or partner, for example. There are social rules that tell us to smile, greet both of them, wait for an introduction to the spouse or partner, and so on. If we bump into the same acquaintance or colleague leaving the cinema locked in the embrace of someone who is definitely not a spouse or partner, we experience a sense of uncertainty. There are no recognised, established social rules for dealing with the situation, and we tend to make ambiguous responses, perhaps only half acknowledging the person, so that these responses can be reinterpreted at a later date. In the unknown setting of the laboratory, people are generally at something of a loss. They are therefore likely to make what Harre refers to as 'generalised and unspecific' responses, or to grab for clues as to how to behave from the scientist who has set up the situation (as Milgram's subjects probably did), or to look to stereotypical beliefs about what is and is not appropriate to the role they have been asked to take on. Without knowing what rules and meanings subjects drew on to guide their action, the experimenter has no hope of understanding why people acted as they did in a given experimental setting, and so no hope of interpreting his or her findings.

The idea of the research subject as an actor who consciously tries to make sense of events in the laboratory, rather than as a passive *rea*ctor to the manipulation of the experimenter also highlights another problem with laboratory based and highly structured observational research techniques; namely the problem of researcher effects.

THE EFFECT OF THE OBSERVER ON THE OBSERVED

As well as being afflicted by the problems discussed above, laboratory research raises a methodological problem known as 'observer effects' or 'reactivity'. This basically refers to the way in which observers can exert an influence over what they are observing. The simple presence of the observer can have an effect on events in the laboratory. Laboratory based sex research provides a good illustration of this point. It seems highly likely, for instance, that there are people who are not 'obvious exhibitionists' yet still have some tendencies towards exhibitionism and would find a sexual act more physically stimulating and enjoyable when they know they are being observed even by a 'disinterested' scientist. Meanwhile, people who definitely do not have such tendencies would find any given sexual act *less* pleasurable under these conditions. The physiological responses of both exhibitionists and non-exhibitionists, such as the length of time taken to climax, would thus be affected by the presence of the researcher.

Such problems are compounded by the fact that, as with interview and survey research, the researcher's expectations and the subject's perceptions of them can critically affect the subject's behaviour. Laboratory experiments and observational research involve a social encounter between two human beings – the researcher and the researched – and responses in the laboratory, as much as spoken responses in interviews or written responses on questionnaires, can be affected by the subject's ideas about what the researcher wants. A story told by Pomeroy about an episode of filmed observation clearly illustrates how the research subject's perceptions of what will interest and please the researcher can shape their behaviour:

> During a session recording male masturbation, the subject went on and on with the act until the camera began to overheat and [the camera man] knew he was about to run out of film. He made a despairing gesture to Kinsey, indicating what was happening. [Kinsey] leaned forward to the subject and said gently, politely, 'If you would just come now . . .'
> 'Oh, sure,' the subject said and immediately came to orgasm just as the film ran out. The man had misunderstood and thought Kinsey wanted a lengthy sequence of masturbation which he was prepared to keep up indefinitely.
>
> (Pomeroy 1972: 175)

In other words, Kinsey was unable to watch human sexual behaviour as a 'fly on the wall'. His presence coloured what he saw, just as his questions and interviewing techniques coloured what people told him about their sexual behaviour. Because his subjects were human beings, not just 'any other mammal', they interpreted the bizarre situation in which they found themselves, tried to work out what Kinsey wanted to see, and provided just that.

The real point is that while positivists would celebrate experimental and structured observational methods for the control they afford the researcher, this control is largely illusory. Because research subjects are conscious actors whose behaviour is crucially shaped not only by their subjective beliefs and values but also by the meanings they attach to a given social situation (even if that situation is an experiment in a laboratory), it is not possible for the social scientific researcher to isolate and manipulate variables in the same way that the natural scientist does, nor is it possible to avoid influencing the very events that he or she has set out to passively observe. Moreover, the behaviour of the social scientist's human research subject is also affected by the extremely artificial context in which he or she is being observed. Harre observes that:

> Experiments take place in special places, often called social-psychological laboratories, where a simplified environment consisting of undecorated walls, plain furnishings, rarely more than two chairs, the mysterious blank face of the one-way mirror, and perhaps the intrusion of the unblinking eye of the television camera. . . . But in real life social events occur in highly differentiated environments, rich in sights and sounds, well furnished with symbolic objects, which direct or determine the interpretative procedures and the choice of rule-systems of the actors.
>
> (Harre 1979: 106)

In such artificial settings, people are hardly likely to behave *exactly* as they would in their own bedroom, or as they would in any real social encounter. There is a sense in which the artificiality of the laboratory influences, or sometimes even creates, the very behaviours that the experimenter wishes to observe, and this renders the whole project dangerously close to pointless. Who, after all, would want to conduct an experiment to find out only what people do in experimental situations? Dissatisfaction with the artificiality of laboratory and other structured observational research leads some methodologists and researchers to favour the ethnographic techniques first developed by anthropologists, techniques which allow human research subjects to be observed in more natural settings. This type of observational research is the focus of the following chapter.

Chapter 7

Ethnography and qualitative analysis

Ethnography is concerned with the 'discovery' and description of the culture and social structure of particular social groups. Originally, ethnographic techniques were used by anthropologists such as Malinowski (1929) who studied, among other things, the sexual practices of the Trobriand Islanders of New Guinea. The anthropologist's technique was to immerse him or herself in the particular culture of the society under study in order to be able to describe life in such a community in vivid detail. This entailed becoming an accepted member of the group in question and participating in its cultural life and practices. Since the early anthropological studies, sociologists have adopted a version of this method to gain information on small groups and communities existing within particular enclaves of modern society. In the 1940s and 50s, Chicago University was particularly influential in encouraging and producing ethnographic studies of urban communities. However, since then the method has become very widely used as a standard technique in social research.

The distinctiveness of the approach is most easily seen by comparing it with the forms of observation used in laboratory and other structured settings discussed in the previous chapter. In these settings, there is an attempt to impose rigorous control over the environment in which people are acting, so as to identify the causal variables that are thought to be influencing that behaviour. This approach makes the positivist assumption that people can be viewed as objects of scientific investigation and that the observer can eliminate subjective bias (the influence of emotional responses, of preconceptions and prejudices, and so on) by taking an impersonal, detached 'scientific' stance. Ethnographic research is based on a rather different set of assumptions, the most important of which is that we should study people in their natural environments, rather than in artificially controlled ones (as in experimental research). Contemporary ethnography thus belongs to a tradition of 'naturalism' which centralises the importance of understanding the meanings and cultural practices of people from *within* the everyday settings in which they take place and shares much in common with the *verstehen* tradition of interpretative analysis.

Some ethnographers have stressed the need for the researcher to avoid becoming over involved with the people being studied, disturbing the natural setting and thereby compromising the scientific credibility of the research. Against this view, it has recently been argued that in order to truly grasp the lived experience of people from their point of view, one *has* to enter into relationships with them, and hence disturb the natural setting. There is no point in trying to control what is an unavoidable consequence of becoming involved in people's lives in this way. In fact this involvement is a requirement for unearthing good and reliable information about what is going on and why, the rules and values that guide behaviour, the forms of language that are commonly used, and so on, within the group or community under study. The ethnographer must therefore take this fact on board, and consider its impact on the actual research process. This is registered in the notion of 'reflexivity' in which the researcher constantly asks questions about the way her or his presence is influencing what is being observed and the findings that result from the study (Hammersley and Atkinson 1989).

It is tempting to view ethnography simply as an antidote to naïve positivist views of the social world. Certainly, much of the distinctiveness of ethnography can be understood as an attempt to reveal the complexity of people's lives, their experience and their subjective attitudes in a way that is impossible simply through the use of surveys, interviews, documents or experimental or structured observations, which take an exclusively impersonal and detached viewpoint. Because of this, the method of 'participant observation' which the ethnographer uses has often been identified with interpretative (particularly interactionist or phenomenological) schools of thought, but this link should not be exaggerated. Many ethnographic techniques have been, and continue to be, used in association with a diverse array of theoretical frameworks and approaches, including Marxism, critical theory, feminism and postmodernism. Furthermore, contemporary ethnography is likely to be seen as an adjunct to more conventional approaches which depend rather more on the use of quantitative data. In this sense, traditional boundaries between approaches and the use of different sources and types of data are tending to break down, or at least, be the subject of question and debate (Bryman 1988, Silverman 1985, Layder 1993). All in all, ethnographic data and techniques have proven to be flexible allies to a range of approaches and theories which otherwise may be viewed as somewhat antagonistic to each other. Moreover, the range of topics and areas that have been covered by this method is likewise formidable. Virtually every nook and cranny of society, conventional and deviant, has been, or could potentially be, investigated using this technique.

Some advocates have underlined the use of ethnography for the production of mainly descriptive data/information about a particular group. Such writers have stressed its 'anti-formal' nature or its attempt to undermine the pretensions of a more scientific attitude to the study of social life (Becker cited in Rock 1979). On this view, the whole point of 'involved observation' is to come close to the human texture of the lived experience of those in whom we are interested and this means dispensing with any prior assumptions or pet theories held about the group. We should rid ourselves of formalised concepts and frameworks that we assume to be important in understanding the milieu and the behaviour of others, and try to see it afresh. This attitude is often tied to a distrust of theorising of any sort. However, other commentators and practitioners have pointed out that ethnography can be just as useful to research which has the development of theory as a general concern (Glaser and Strauss 1967, Hammersley 1985, Layder 1993 and 1994). In this sense it can be linked to theory-testing and theory-generating in a number of different ways. There is certainly no reason to preclude an interest in social theory since one of the main purposes of social research is to provide evidence in support of explanations of a theoretical kind.

This is not to undervalue the sort of descriptive data relatively free from imposed formal concepts and ideas that is frequently claimed to be the purpose and great virtue of this qualitative approach. Very often our knowledge of particular practices within various sectors or subcultures is scant, and one way to increase our fund of information about the area is to observe and collect data without much in the way of reaching for theoretical explanations. The goal of this kind of research is simply to provide textured evidence or 'thick description' (Geerz 1973), which allows us to understand the subculture from the inside in terms that the participants themselves use to describe their behaviour and practices. Stoller's (1991) study of the sadomasochist (S & M) scene in West Hollywood is a case in point. His attempt to convey the nature of consensual sadomasochistic practices through the use of transcriptions of audio-taped conversations with some of the people involved is based on the assumption that little is known about these practices and that an open-minded presentation of the attitudes and behaviour of practitioners will lead to the breaking down of preconceptions and stereotypical assumptions about it. In fact, Stoller deliberately refrains from explaining such behaviour since he felt it would be premature in a situation in which so little information has been gathered. None the less, his data does allow us to increase our store of knowledge about this area of human sexuality, suggesting, for instance, that sadomasochism includes a very wide range of behaviours and cannot be viewed as a unitary phenomenon. Similarly, he illustrates the idea that sadomasochistic games (master–slave, parent–child fantasies) do not typically involve real acts of punishment but rather offer an arena in which past suffering, pain and humiliation can be enacted (this time with happier endings), and thus underlines the theatrical and mastery elements in erotic life.

Such information is extremely important both in plugging gaps in our existing knowledge of human sexuality and also as preparatory material for generating later, more theoretical explanations. In other areas, where there has been a great deal of research and amassed information, such as that on school pupils, further ethnographic work could be used in the service of testing out hypotheses, say about conditions under which disruptive behaviour occurs (Hammersley 1985, reviewing the work of Lacey 1966, Hargreaves 1967 and Ball 1981). Whether there is a lack of information or a glut, Glaser and Strauss (1967) have argued strongly that an eye should always be kept on the development of new theory from the primary data uncovered by such qualitative methods. They suggest that if a concern with theory is only linked to the testing of hypotheses and propositions, then the growth of theory and of knowledge in general will stagnate. Similarly, if ethnographic studies are limited to the amassing of detailed information and descriptions of cultural practices, they will not contribute to the cumulative development of knowledge through theory.

TYPES OF OBSERVATION, FIELD ROLES AND ACCESS

Participating or involving ourselves in the community of an unfamiliar group (or at least one to which we do not normally belong) can be achieved in a number of different ways and can entail differing levels of involvement with, or closeness to, members of the community and their culture. Gold's (1958) classic discussion of field roles remains a good starting point for exploring this issue. He identifies four types of field role adopted by the researcher using forms of participant observation. These roles do not necessarily have to be distinct or exclusive. The researcher may move between them at different phases of the research, and sometimes they merge imperceptibly into one another. None the less, they enable us to discern differences in emphasis in the form of observation and the kinds of relationship that are struck up with those who are the subjects of the research.

The first of these is the 'complete participant' role, in which the researcher attempts to pass as a member of the group. Sometimes this involves a deliberate concealment of one's identity as a researcher in order to make covert observations. At other times, researchers may actually utilise occupational or other social skills so as to join in the activities of the group members. Classic studies undertaken in this vein include Humphreys' (1975) study of homosexual behaviour in public restrooms in which he acted as a 'watchqueen' or lookout for those engaging in sexual activity in the toilets. Becker (1963) drew upon his musical abilities in his study of Jazz musicians and their occupational culture, while Polsky (1967) employed his pool-playing skills to gain access to the world of pool-room hustlers. While these latter studies did not require too much concealment of the real 'motives' of the researcher, Humphreys' study involved deliberate deception in order to gain access and information, as did Rosenhan's (1973) study of a psychiatric hospital. Such covert studies raise serious ethical questions and dilemmas to which there are no easy answers, and we shall return to this topic presently.

Acting as a complete participant means that the researcher has to adopt an almost passive demeanour, absorbing information through observation and conversation in a non-directive manner. To be a sympathetic listener is perhaps the best means of achieving rapport in this kind of situation. One problem with this role is that the required level of immersion and involvement in the activity itself may lead to neglect of the kind of analytic observation that is needed to develop an overview of the issues or to otherwise be analytic and questioning as a researcher. This role can also present the ethnographer with ethical dilemmas around the issue of how complete 'complete participation' should be. Should a researcher participate in any illegal activities of a 'deviant' group under study? When studying the National Front (an extreme right-wing, virulently racist British political organisation), should Fielding have offered to assist in its election campaign (see Fielding 1982)? The practical requirement to get as close as possible to subjects in order to see the world through their eyes can sometimes conflict with ethical considerations about what kind of activities are morally acceptable.

The next role is that of 'participant as observer' in which the researcher makes it known that she or he is undertaking social research and that this is the primary purpose of the observations and conversations. This role has the virtue of giving more freedom to the researcher to concentrate on what seem to be the most interesting facets of the activities in question, while at the same time allowing the development of in-depth relationships with informants. Thirdly, Gold identified the 'observer as participant' role, in which contact with informants is brief and formally defined in terms of the research interests of the observer. This role does not facilitate the closeness and depth of involvement that is generally required to appreciate and gain access to the meanings, values and traditions of the group. Finally, there is the 'complete observer' role, wherein the researcher remains, to all intents and purposes, external to the group and does not engage in sustained interaction with informants (Burgess 1984). Overheard conversations and observations from a distance are the means by which data is gathered and this, of course, means that there is the strong possibility the researcher will interpret what is going on from the point of view of his or her own cultural and social position. Bias may thus occur through the imposition of preconceptions and stereotypical assumptions.

As noted earlier, the researcher may move between different roles during different phases of the research. In this sense, field roles are continually negotiated and renegotiated during the investigation in terms of such things as the employment of different strategies by the researcher, the development of unpredictable problems and circumstances, and the general give and take of encounters and relationships with people. Among other role attributes that are important are the age, sex and 'racialised' identity of the researcher (it would have been impossible for a female to undertake Humphreys' research into male homosexual activities in public restrooms or for an African Caribbean researcher to undertake Fielding's study of the National Front), the degree to which the researcher is accepted by the members of the group, and so on. Sometimes the roles adopted by the researcher merge with general emotions associated with different levels of rapport, such as feelings of marginality or a sense of being able to 'get on' with certain people. Hammersley and Atkinson (1989) suggest that the most effective demeanour involves a non-aggressive, non-threatening personal style. The researcher comports him- or herself as a socially acceptable 'incompetent' who is there to learn from others.

The kinds of field roles that pose most problems from an ethical point of view concern those which involve some kind of deception in order to gain access. Both Humphreys' study of the 'tearoom trade' and Rosenhan's study of a psychiatric hospital have been criticised on these grounds. Humphreys' study involved a highly sensitive subject and though he recalls that it was suggested to him that he should avoid it altogether (1975: 168), he insists that we should not shy away from such topics. The main concern, according to Humphreys, should be with the protection of the researcher's subjects. In this case, he argues, the protection of the harassed gay community is not improved simply by ignoring them or refusing to study the area of 'sex without commitment'. According to Humphreys, as long as confidentiality is preserved and the consequences of the research do not produce a negative reaction from the forces of social control, then there have been no infringements of ethical principles. Humphreys couples this argument with the defence that, in practice, he was no different from all of the men he observed engaged in sexual acts (principally fellatio) in public toilets who misrepresented or failed to represent their true identities. Indeed, one of his findings was that the anonymity and impersonality of the settings and the sexual activity itself were centrally valued aspects of the tearoom trade (sex without commitment).

Humphreys may well be right to assert that men engaged in sexual activities in public toilets neither expect nor require formal introductions to other participants, and do not typically enjoin watchqueens for details of their employment status, family background and suchlike. But what this defence fails to justify is the fact that Humphreys also noted the licence plate numbers of the cars owned by the men using the restrooms, in order to track down their names and addresses and subsequently interview them. Critics point out that the very existence of such information would have severely compromised the confidentiality of the research subjects if it had fallen into the wrong hands. Humphreys also failed to properly take the ethical principle of informed consent into account. When he asked for interviews, he concealed the true purpose of the research and did not tell the men concerned that he had previously witnessed their sexual acts in restrooms.

Rosenhan's (1973) study, which involved the successful deception of medical personnel, also highlights this problem. The whole point of this study was to probe the issue of whether mental illness is detectable in any clear manner and, in order to do this, researchers pretended to be suffering from the symptoms normally associated with mental illness (mainly hearing voices, a particularly common feature of schizophrenia). Once they had been admitted to the psychiatric hospital on this basis, they also intended to observe how medical staff interacted with patients, and to determine how easy or difficult it was to become redefined as healthy and therefore to be allowed to leave the hospital.

Given this set of objectives, it is clear that they could not be carried through or investigated if the researchers had been open about them in the first place. As it was, Rosenhan's study revealed many things about attitudes towards, and the treatment of, mental illness within the context of the hospital, including the fact that although it was relatively easy to feign symptoms and to be diagnosed as mentally ill, it was much more difficult to persuade medical staff that the researchers (pseudo-patients) who had been so labelled were not, in fact, ill. Also, much about the way staff tend to avoid or minimise contact and conversations with patients was revealed by the study. None the less, much debate has centred around whether this kind of deception in order to gain access to sensitive information gives social research a bad name, thus making it more difficult for subsequent research with a critical intent. Obviously, the power and autonomy of the medical profession was challenged by the research and this brings into relief the power of vested interests to close down areas of investigation which could be used as a basis upon which to question or challenge this power.

This raises the question of access. The entry into particular kinds of settings is often controlled by 'gatekeepers' who are concerned with the way in which the setting or organisation and its practices are to be depicted in the published research. This kind of worry can lead gate-keepers to block off lines of enquiry, which in turn requires the researcher to establish or re-establish trust with a view to securing full access. Sometimes this is not a problem, so long as a *bona fide* research identity and commitment is demonstrated in advance. Erving Goffman's (1961) famous study published under the title of *Asylums* was accomplished with the full consent of the hospital administrators who even provided him with a plausible cover role, that of assistant to the athletic director (Manning 1992). This allowed him to roam freely while gathering his ethnographic materials on the patient's experience of hospital-isation. It is also worth noting that negotiating access is an on-going process, rather than a one-off event. When the research is being undertaken covertly, the researcher must daily reproduce the deception of subjects and win their acceptance. If the researcher falls out with a key informant, or if his or her true identity is discovered, for example, it may lead to access being closed off. In some cases, such revelations could physically endanger the researcher. Even if a researcher secures full co-operation from gatekeepers in the first instance, his or her continued access throughout the course of the research rests on maintaining good relations with those gatekeepers.

GATHERING DATA AND SELECTING INFORMANTS

Lofland (1971) suggests that once in the field, the researcher can employ three kinds of note taking in order to develop a store of data. While actively participating in events, the researcher should take 'mental notes' of things, events and the physical character of the places in which they occur. Secondly, 'jotted notes' comprising little phrases, key words and remembered quotes should be written inconspicuously in cars, hallways, coffee bars or restrooms. Such notes can be valuable memory aids for later use. One complication relating to this is illustrated by the experience of a researcher on Rosenhan's team. After having been admitted to hospital because of apparent mental illness, one of the pseudo-patients made a habit of taking notes on his experiences with staff and patients. His 'note-taking activity' was itself noticed by the medical staff and viewed as evidence of mental instability, thus making his task of convincing them of his good health all the more difficult. Finally Lofland states that at the end of the day, full field notes would be written up to provide a log of what has happened in the setting, including descriptions of events and people, and conversations with and among people.

Apart from making notes on the casual conversations that one has as part of routine daily life, it is also possible in some instances (and desirable from the point of view of the research) to conduct more in-depth interviews with informants who have revealing views and important information to impart. This is where ethnography joins forces with other qualitative approaches and the discussion in Chapter 5 is pertinent. The use of interviews as a supplement to observation and casual conversation enables the researcher to be more directive and systematic in probing certain topics and issues. Usually such interviews would be of the intensive, semi-structured variety in which the interviewer uses an interview guide (a list of topics or issues expressed in the form of loose questions) to focus the conversation, but which does not rigidly determine the interchanges. The interview will depart from any pre-set agenda as and when such flexibility is required (for instance when an informant proves to be particularly forthcoming on a difficult or sensitive topic or when some unanticipated topic of relevance emerges).

Depending on the focus of the interview and the selection of infor-mants, the interviews can be turned towards purposes and methodo-logical techniques other than the gathering of descriptions of everyday life and experiences in a particular social location. For example, the use of 'life history' studies which require in-depth interviews focusing on the narrative sequencing of events in a person's life course are closely related to general ethnographic techniques, but are none the less concerned with somewhat different issues. Connell's (1992) study of the construction of masculinity in the lives of gay men, the interplay between heterosexual and homosexual identities, and the experience of change in gender relations is a good example of the use of this method and its relatedness to ethnographic concerns.

As Connell's study highlights, and as is the case with all research dealing primarily with qualitative data, the whole philosophy behind the selection of informants – the 'sampling procedure' in formal terms – is very different from that which applies to analyses dealing with quantitative data, such as surveys. Generally, qualitative research is concerned with smaller numbers of cases but with more intensive analyses. In formal terms, qualitative enquiry deals with non-random samples in which there is no way of estimating the probability of the units in the universe (the total population of the group or community) being included in the sample that is actually studied. This is especially the case with deviant forms of activity for which it is often impossible to gauge the total number of people in a given location involved in the practices in question. Stoller (1991), for example, would have found it hard to assemble a sampling frame for his research into sadomasochism which listed every single dominatrix in West Hollywood, or every man who played 'slave' to such women. Sometimes the inaccessibility of unconventional or deviant groups adds to the problems of generating a representative sample. None the less, representativeness is aimed for, although in less precise terms. Moreover, as noted above, the whole point of selecting informants for qualitative investigation is to concentrate on an intensive analysis of a limited number of cases which represent, or are in some way tailored to, the central objectives of the research.

As Patton (1990) puts it, the logic and power of purposeful sampling lies in selecting information-rich cases from which we can learn a great deal about issues of importance to the central purposes of the research. The size of the sample is thus of secondary importance to the quality of information that is elicited from it. In some cases, the parameters of a sample are defined by the boundaries of the immediate setting, as in Goffman's analysis of the mental hospital as a 'total institution' (one which controls every aspect of a person's life, including self-identity). This makes it easier to judge the representativeness of informants by understanding their position within this milieu. In other cases, such as Jodelet's (1991) study of the Family Colony of Ainy-le Chateau, in which more than 1,000 psychiatric hospital patients are placed in nearly

500 local homes to be 'fostered' by the families in this community, the dispersal of the research subjects was such that more careful and systematic selection of informants was necessary to investigate the issue of how the patients are treated in the community and how the community responds to the presence of the mentally ill.

In any case, even if the immediate setting provides convenient boundaries from which to draw a sample of informants, some attention to the wider social structure and context is necessary, otherwise the study itself would be open to the criticism that its focus was too narrow to be realistic. Connell, for instance, argues that even the life history approach with its concentration on the biographical aspects of informant's lives requires 'prior analysis of the social structure involved' (1992: 739). In the case of his analysis of gay masculinity, this includes an analysis of gender as a structure of practices and a structure of power. Also, Harvey's version of critical social research 'attempts to link the detailed analysis of ethnography to wider social structures and systems of power relationships in order to get beneath the surface of oppressive social relationships' (1990: 11). Layder (1993) has further stressed the importance of the historical context and the way that this shapes the context of power relations which both feed into everyday life and which are reproduced by these same activities.

As these examples show, the issue of sampling is not simply about the selection of people as informants but about the selection of the unit of time in which one is interested, and various aspects of the setting and context which figure importantly in people's lives. For instance, life history methods focus on a person's whole biography, while much ethnographic research concentrates on a fairly narrow time frame, centring around a particular everyday activity occupying a small segment of people's lifetimes. This is why it is necessary to bear in mind the time spans involved in the larger sense of history and their impact on the contemporary area of interest. For example, Jodelet's investigation of the history of the Family Colony of Ainy-le-Chateau provided essential contextual information in this respect.

Similarly, the researcher has to select the sites and events that are to be studied. Many ethnographic studies appear to be located on a single site such as a factory (Roy 1973), a hospital (Glaser and Strauss 1965) or a school (Burgess 1983) although the possibility of cross-site analyses has been discussed in the literature (Miles and Huberman 1984). Indeed, the dispersed nature of some forms of social organisation requires that the researcher tries to identify and describe the networks of social relationships that produce the links between the different segments (see the discussion of the acting profession in Layder 1993). However, even studying within a single site means that decisions must be taken about which sub-sites need to be observed. For example, in studying a hospital, which wards should be observed? If one ward is chosen should the researcher remain at one nurses' station or move around? Should she or he attend meetings? Where should the researcher eat and take rest breaks? Hammersley and Atkinson (1989) have pointed out that such decisions are crucial because observations in all these places might yield important and different information.

Drawing on Goffman's (1959) work on the 'presentation of self', they suggest that people behave differently in different places and in front of different audiences. For example, Goffman himself would not have been able to identify and analyse the flourishing 'underlife' of the mental hospital (wherein patients 'work the system' to their own advantage and thus maintain some sense of self that is independent of the hospital's attempt to control their lives completely) unless he had talked to the patients in locations away from staff interference. Rosenhan's study may not have revealed the extent of avoidant behaviour exhibited by medical staff towards the mentally ill patients if the staff had known that their behaviour was being monitored by outsiders. Of course, the ability to pick and choose between observational vantage points is to some extent dependent upon the accessibility of locations, the un-obtrusiveness of the observer and, last but not least, obtaining 'permission' to move freely about.

Returning to the selection of people, it is important to recognise that sampling may take place around specific criteria such as age, gender and 'racialised' identity, or the amount of experience of a particular activity a person has had and so on. Also important are the sorts of categorisation that members of a group use in relation to other members. Stoller (1991) found that people involved in the S & M scene categorised themselves and others as 'tops' (dominant role), 'bottoms' (subordinate roles) and even 'pushy bottoms' (those who make demands and exercise control through their submission) and 'killer bottoms' (those who can never be satisfied 'no matter how long or how hard they are played'). This 'member identified' terminology is useful as a way of selecting informants on a representative basis. Also important are the categories identified by the researcher. Lofland's study of waiting behaviour in public, for example, yielded a number of waiting modes such as 'the nester' (a person who arranges and rearranges their props in the manner of a bird building a nest) or 'the maverick' (people who do not protect themselves in public settings, such as children, the stigmatised and eccentrics) (cited in Hammersley and Atkinson 1989: 51). The different types mentioned overlap with the settings of activity, particularly in terms of what Goffman calls 'front' and 'back' regions, since people tend to behave differently when in the presence of different audiences. Teachers behave differently in the setting of the classroom and the setting of the staff-room (see Burgess 1983). Likewise, Stoller (1991) found that S & M brothel owners presented themselves differently according to whether he arrived to interview them alone or accompanied by a police officer, and that dominatrixes presented themselves differently according to whether they were alone, in the presence of a 'master' or in the presence of a 'slave'. Some attempt to find out about non-public behaviour is essential to a rounded understanding of the subculture of the group being studied.

Sometimes it is very difficult to contact potential informants for reasons of confidentiality, or because of the illegal or deviant nature of the activity or the sheer difficulty of finding relevant people. This may lead to a dependence on a few key informants. Stoller's entrée into the S & M scene, for example, came about as a result of being introduced to a police officer who was at the time drawing up rules regulating com-mercial 'bondage & discipline' establishments. His initial contact with owners of these establishments allowed him to develop relationships with three or four key informants, upon whom the study relies extremely heavily (some would say too heavily). But even when faced with extreme difficulties in contacting potential informants, the researcher should try to ensure that he or she gets in touch with a sample of people who are representative of the population under investigation (in Stoller's case, all those involved in the S & M scene). Researchers should not merely pick a *convenient* sample or the validity of the findings and the conclusions of the research will be questionable. Fas-cinating as Stoller's study is, it is perhaps over dependent upon one very articulate, keenly intelligent and analytic key informant, 'Ron'. Such informants are, of course, godsends to ethnographers, but it is important to bear in mind that the very qualities which make them so useful are perhaps also the ones which make them less than representative of the rest of the community under study. Data in general (and this includes documentary evidence as well as pure observation) should be gathered either in pursuit of some theoretical purpose, or because of the nature of already gathered empirical information, or ideally, some combination of both. In cases where it is difficult to identify or contact informants, the method of 'snowball sampling' (asking informants to put you in touch with friends or acquaintances in the same line of business) can be a useful strategy. But to avoid bias in the sample, it is necessary to break the chain of contacts at various points and restart the 'snowball' of informants.

To stress the usefulness of the snowball technique here may seem to conflict with points made in Chapter 4 where the bias produced by Kinsey's use of this technique was described. In practice, however, it simply points up some crucial differences between survey and ethnographic methods. Surveys are particularly useful when dealing with a highly generalised research topic (such as 'typical' sexual behaviour) and a large universe (all males and females) whose characteristics are fairly well known through census statistics and so on. The unthinking use of a snowball technique in these circumstances may indeed lead to bias. In qualitative analysis researchers are often dealing with universes whose parameters and characteristics are unknown and cannot be precisely measured (people who enjoy 'deviant' sexual activities, sufferers from existential neurosis or free-floating anxiety). In cases where it is difficult to obtain any information at all, then the only possibility is to talk to, and observe, those people we manage to contact through personal networks. It is in these circumstances that the snowball sample is of most use (bearing in mind that minimising bias should always be a priority).

It also has to be remembered that the whole philosophy behind sampling in qualitative research is very different from that which applies in more quantitative techniques such as surveys. The qualitative researcher is looking for information-rich cases that are relevant to the specific purposes of the research. In this respect, Glaser and Strauss's (1967) notion of 'theoretical sampling' has several advantageous features. By this they refer to the selecting of events, people, settings and so forth in terms of the emergent nature of the research. The researcher collects data and analyses it simultaneously and this provides the basis upon which new data will be collected. The emerging theoretical ideas will suggest which people need to be interviewed next and what questions need to be asked of them, or which documentary sources need to be consulted. Glaser and Strauss's ideas apply particularly to researchers who wish to generate theory directly from research data and this is certainly a very important consideration. However, more generally this kind of flexible adaptation to the ideas and information generated by the research is one of the great advantages of ethnographic and other qualitative approaches over more rigidly structured methods, such as the survey, in which assumptions (theoretical and otherwise) are built into the instruments of data collection and cannot be revised during data collection.

CODING AND ANALYSIS

As soon as the researcher enters the field, she or he begins to collect data either in the form of notes on observations and conversations or in terms of transcribed tape recordings of interviews (as well as possible documentary evidence). Eventually, this may result in a massive amount of collected data, much of which, in the end, will not be required to substantiate the findings and conclusions of the research. The main practical problem for the researcher is to reduce this data to manageable proportions. Coding the data in terms of the main themes or concepts that are the focus of the research allows the researcher to condense the data. Coding also enables manipulation of the data so that two further processes may take place. First it facilitates the identification of particular segments of field notes or interview text so that they can be spotlighted and shuffled around at will for comparative purposes. Second, and this is the main purpose, by identifying the data in terms of main themes, concepts, categories and issues, coding allows the researcher to begin to analyse the findings. By ordering the data in this way it becomes possible to construct forms of description and explanation for the activities and behaviour that have been observed and recorded in terms of these themes and concepts.

For example, in *Asylums*, Goffman (1961) analyses key aspects of the behaviour of the inmates in terms of strategies of adaptation to the humiliating circumstances encountered in the hospital (especially the system of privileges whereby, for example, inmates are rewarded for obedience with candy bars). One of these strategies he terms 'situational withdrawal' which involves elements of daydreaming or fantasising (such as reliving newspaper accounts of sporting events). Another strategy involves establishing an 'intransigent line', that is, a limit below which the inmate will not tolerate further assaults on her or his self-identity. Beyond this limit, inmates may engage in retaliatory action such as barricades, hunger strikes or dirty protests (smearing walls of cells/rooms with excrement). In these examples, we can see that the themes and concepts of 'situational withdrawal' and an 'intransigent line' are core analytic units. By coding the data (field/interview notes) in terms of these, the researcher is able to identify all those segments of the data that are directly or indirectly relevant to them. Eventually the data may fill-out or modify categories, revealing exceptions to the rule or making refinements and elaborations. In this particular case, Goffman appears to have developed these categories directly out of the data he gathered, rather than deciding in advance that they would be relevant.

This highlights the way in which coding may begin with an 'open' stage early on in which the researcher is attempting to understand everything and is experimenting with many different coding categories. This eventually gives way to the establishment of a provisional set of categories. For instance, in Goffman's study, 'daydreaming' and 'fantasising' may have functioned as provisional codes until he was led to review examples of these in relation to the more general question of how inmates maintain a sense of identity. Thus the core category of 'situational withdrawal' may have emerged through a process in which essentially descriptive, provisional categories give way to more refined and general ones, which begin to *explain* the behaviour in question. This contrasts with research that has less of an exploratory character than Goffman's – for example, in an area on which much research has been done already. In those cases, many of the central categories, hypotheses and so on may have already been established and the current research may have the aim of testing them out in various ways. It also highlights the flexibility of ethnographic techniques in comparison with the survey method. As was seen in Chapter 4, both the interview schedule and the coding techniques employed by Kinsey prevented him from responding to unanticipated information and acted as a barrier to exploring certain facets of the data.

INTERPRETATION AND VALIDITY OF FINDINGS

Although ethnographic research attends primarily to the subjective worlds, lived experience and forms of communication within various groups, the validity of such studies is no less important an issue than it is with other methods and techniques. As we have seen, the demands of involved observation mean that the researcher cannot view behaviour in a neutral and detached manner. This raises the question of how we and other researchers can be sure of the validity of our findings. How can we be sure that they give us an accurate and truthful picture of the social milieu in which we are interested? Essentially these questions concern the researcher's ability to merge with, and join in, the routine activities of the group by becoming accepted and trusted, in order to gain access to the meanings that the group holds dear (Rock 1979). Bruyn (1966) identifies what he calls criteria of 'subjective adequacy' which are directed precisely at the above questions. These include the amount of time spent with the group and proximity to them attained, which affect the likelihood of the researcher's interpretations being valid. Similarly, the more the researcher can view the group from a number of different vantage points (both in terms of social position and physical settings), the more likely he or she will produce accurate findings. Stoller (1991) describes how his view of one dominatrix, 'Tammy', changed over time. In a series of interviews over a number of years, she presented herself to him in different ways, and he also obtained information about her from other informants which led him to question certain details of her own accounts. He comments:

> If I were an ethnographer born and raised in New Guinea trying to bring back to New Guinea the truth about this bizarre erotic Western institution S & M, what would I report to my readers if Tammy and I had talked only that first time five years ago? . . . When can the historian rely on his texts? Which biographers shall we trust? . . . There is no end, no final, correct version. . . . Tammy's case helps us confirm the well-confirmed and well-denied idea that everything is complex. One version is not enough.
>
> (Stoller 1991: 237)

By watching people over time and in different situations, and by talking to them and to others about what you have seen and how you interpret it, you obtain richer and more reliable data. This accords with Goffman's notion that people behave differently and display different selves, or aspects of themselves, to different audiences. It also has much in common with Denzin's (1970) ideas about 'triangulation' as a means of ensuring accuracy and validity. Here, triangulation involves cross-checking the accuracy of findings by using different sources and types of data to study the same phenomenon. For instance, Hickson *et al.* (1990) in their study of 'Southern rednecks' in the USA used a variety of techniques including participant observation, unstructured interviews, analyses of diaries, family histories, legal documents and Southern folklore (1990: 105).

The other criteria of subjective adequacy identified by Bruyn concerns familiarity with the language of the group (including non-verbal communication), the degree of intimacy achieved and the extent to which the researcher is able to communicate to other people his or her understanding of the culture of the group. To a certain extent, but without their concern with theory generation, Bruyn's criteria resemble Glaser and Strauss's (1967) idea that theory produced directly from research data is more adequate and less speculative than other more abstract theories because it is more securely grounded in empirical evidence. In this sense, Glaser and Strauss's insistence that grounded theory should 'fit' the data and be relevant to the people involved mirrors Bruyn's criteria of subjective adequacy. By 'fit' and relevance, they mean that the researcher's concepts and categories of analysis should grow from the research data itself and not be 'imposed' on it because of the researcher's prior commitment to a particular theory or theoretical approach. Moreover, the analysis and interpretation of the findings must be recognisable and 'make sense' to the people who are subjects of the study.

In Jodelet's study of mentally ill lodgers and their foster parents, she identifies a number of techniques used to control the lodgers. As she points out, 'the whole art of controlling the lodgers can be reduced to mastery, in accordance with the different partners and events, of the variations of fear and kindness' (1991: 124). She outlines a repertoire of control techniques and modes of employment based on the one hand on fear (of rejection, intimidation, punishment and so on) and on the other on kindness (by appeals to responsibility, giving rewards, flattery and so forth). These repressive and incentive techniques of control are directly related to the forms of discrimination that operate in the colony community and form barriers to the integration of the mentally ill, which contradict the supposedly integrative purpose of the community in the first place (Jodelet 1991: 73–114). In terms of Glaser and Strauss's notions of fit and relevance and Bruyn's criteria of subjective adequacy, these techniques of control and modes of discrimination must be recognisable to the people involved. The researcher must describe or explain observed behaviour in such a way that the people themselves understand as a depiction of their own activities.

Clearly, such criteria are important in ensuring that researchers' findings and interpretations adequately reflect the intersubjective world being studied. However, an exclusive concern with subjective adequacy deflects attention away from social structural issues such as power and domination which provide the wider social context. Ethnographic approaches are notoriously prone to a restricted focus on the 'micro' world of face-to-face conduct to the neglect of wider macro issues of class, 'racialisation', gender and power. Jodelet's foster families may not all, for example, be able or willing to recognise and understand their 'kindnesses' to lodgers as a 'control technique', and if an ethnographer were to describe some of the practices that are all too common in our schools (such as the deliberate segregation of boy and girl children in the playground, or the consistent channelling of African-Caribbean children towards sport and vocational subjects and away from academic subjects) as sexist or racist, not all teachers would be able to understand it as an accurate depiction of their own activities. It is therefore important to balance the emphasis on subjective adequacy with an appreciation of the fact that macro and micro features are interconnected. Tracing such interconnections in the data should be a central part of ethnographic studies and therefore must not be overlooked as a result of a preoccupation with criteria of subjective adequacy (Smith 1988, Troyna and Hatcher 1992, Layder 1993).

VARIETIES OF ETHNOGRAPHIC WORK

Let us conclude by examining some of the assumptions underlying different approaches to ethnographic work. Although ethnography has been closely associated with interactionist and phenomenological schools of thought, currently it is allied to a number of rather different theoretical frameworks or approaches. The above section stressed the importance of viewing ethnography in partnership with macro analyses and structural issues of power and domination. Here we examine some feminist and postmodernist ideas on the use of ethnography.

Some feminist scholars believe that ethnography and qualitative analyses in general are uniquely suited to the study of women and women's issues. However, there are differences of emphasis even among feminists. Some believe that quantitative studies represent a 'masculine' approach to social analysis whereby a supposedly all-knowing 'objective' observer records the facts in a detached, unemotional manner. The control of 'variables' and the quantification of findings through the application of reason (as opposed to intuition or feelings) represents the male need to eradicate subjectivity in social analysis. These feminists thus identify naïve positivism as a quintessentially 'male' philosophy, sometimes using the terms 'mainstream analysis' and 'malestream analysis' interchangeably. As a consequence, they believe that ethnography and qualitative analysis cuts through this blinkered view by upgrading the value of experience, subjectivity, feeling and emotion, both in the researcher and the subjects of her research (Reinharz 1985, Millman and Kanter 1987). Some feminists have taken this valuation of subjectivity and experience to an extreme which almost seems to deny the existence of a real world independent of our interpretations (Stanley and Wise 1983: 130–1). As with conventional ethnography influenced by interactionist schools of thought, this simply makes it much more difficult to recognise, and so to analyse, the real conditions of oppression of various subordinate groups (not just women). Also, the idea that individuals and groups define reality for themselves, unconstrained as it were by wider structures of power, implies a naïve and unrealistic faith in people's capacity to change society and social reality at will. Moreover, to deny the 'intellectual authority' of the researcher on the grounds that everyone's opinion is as important as everyone else's ignores the whole point of research, which is to generate opinions informed by evidence gathered in ways which are open to the scrutiny of (any) other researchers (Hammersley 1990).

Ethnography can certainly be brought into the service of oppressed or subordinate groups by virtue of its lack of attempt to control variables or to manipulate the environment of the research subjects in any way. But even if a study genuinely had no exploitative objective, and merely attempted to give voice to an oppressed group, it would not follow that the researcher's claims to knowledge were automatically more valid than anyone else's. It is possible to be both well intentioned and wrong. Other feminist scholars have recognised this and, while holding to the unique value of ethnography, suggest that a complete analysis of women's position must go beyond the level of observed appearances and lived experience to explore and understand the social relations which determine them. Dorothy Smith (1988) in particular has argued for such a position with her version of 'institutional ethnography'. Smith insists that the value of ethnography resides in its starting point of lived experience. In the case of women, this is necessary in order to understand their social invisibility in public life and in their exclusion from what she calls the 'relations of ruling'. But to understand the domain of women's lived experience (primarily the private sphere of housework and childrearing), one has to understand the social relations of domination which are external to it and which underpin it. Thus a sociology for women must go beyond and supplement ethnographic analysis by taking into account the wider context of capitalist social organisation as well as patriarchal power and domination.

So called 'postmodern' ethnography shares much with feminism, although its concerns are with a wider range of oppressed groups. Denzin's (1990) ethnographic study of alcoholics and alcoholism reflects these overlaps. Denzin claims that postmodernism rejects all the positivist criteria of objective knowledge and instead presents accounts of experience that are much closer to fiction, autobiography and folklore than they are to scientific 'truth'. As a result, 'fieldwork becomes a gendered experience overflowing with the emotions, subjectivities and experiences of the ethnographer and of those being studied' (1990: 86). His study of Alcoholics Anonymous (AA) treatment centres revealed that they regarded alcoholism as an 'emotional disease' and encouraged the expression of feelings and emotions. The AA's ethical, spiritual and philosophical stance, he claims, offers an emotional understanding of alcoholism and challenges the scientific approach which rejects emotion and offers rational causal explanations. Denzin, following Foucault, suggests that modern science has created oppressive structures of experience for certain groups (in this case alcoholics). Moreover, locally based forms of knowledge as exemplified in the AA self-help groups re-inject a more authentic language of feelings and emotionality into the treatment programmes. This challenges the idea that science can liberate humanity from its ills and that it represents a neutral, objective truth. The local narratives of the alcoholics themselves (including the auto-biographical experience of the researchers) must take precedence over the narrative of scientific knowledge, and in this way, oppressed groups like alcoholics can begin to take control of their own destinies. As this brief account makes clear, the postmodern ethnographer, like many feminist ethnographers, takes an unashamedly committed stance towards her or his subjects. There is, however, a greater willingness than in feminism to see a multiplicity of groups as 'oppressed' and to insist upon the validity of their viewpoints.

One of the obvious problems with such approaches is their extreme relativism. While it is easy to agree that local narratives should be given a voice, to say that their voice should be 'privileged' over other points of view simply replaces one form of dogmatism with another. It also suggests an unnecessarily pessimistic view of research by implying that it can do no more than give voice to the special interests of various (albeit oppressed) groups. Against this we would argue that first, research should not simply be restricted to oppressed groups. The systems of power and forms of domination on a society-wide scale must always be taken into account and in any political or ideological struggle for equality and freedom it is as important to know about the lived experience of oppressors as it is to learn about that of the oppressed. Scully's (1990) study of convicted rapists must rank as valuable as a study examining the experience of women survivors of rape, for example. If this need to explore the world of oppressors is accepted, it becomes obvious that we must do more than just give voice to research subjects – the last thing the world needs is yet another platform upon which racists and misogynists can advertise their views. Second, it is important to note that researchers produce claims to knowledge based on evidence and through procedures and criteria that are open to public scrutiny. At times this may be at variance with the local narratives of oppressed groups. In such situations, the judgement as to which form of knowledge has greater validity is essentially a political one and will depend in any case on the particular circumstances in question. It does not depend on a claim that one form of knowledge has unique access to the truth.

CONCLUSION

As we have seen, ethnography cannot be completely divorced from other qualitative approaches to research. None the less, perhaps more than any other method, participant observation requires that we reject the notion of researcher as a detached 'objective' scientist who manipulates the subjects of the research by controlling the variables that affect their behaviour. In this sense, the whole thrust of ethnography opposes the naïve positivist view of research as an attempt to construct hard and fast universal laws and principles of social behaviour. However, although ethnography tries to deliver more textured data on meanings and the lived experience of research subjects, it does not follow that it is completely incompatible with other methods and approaches such as the survey or structured interviews. Thus ethnography has come to be associated with feminists, critical theorists, postmodernists, even management consultants (Gummesson 1991) and psychoanalysts (Stoller 1991), as well as more traditional interpretativist schools of social theory. Ethnographic data has been, and will continue to be, used in conjunction with an array of other approaches, including those that favour quantitative analysis and the search for causes of behaviour in the wider 'macro' social environment. In particular, the unique entrée into the world of intersubjective experience that ethnography provides has been fashioned to meet the purposes of a diverse range of theorists and researchers with different political priorities.

Chapter 8

Documentary sources and textual analysis

As well as the techniques discussed in previous chapters, social researchers can make use of a range of documentary sources. A document is essentially any written text, but as Scott (1990) notes, documents may 'comprise a range of research sources, varied in origin and access, stretching from the archetypal government papers to the more marginal cases of photographs, invoices and stamps, and merging imperceptibly with printed ephemera and material remains' (1990: 19). The state produces official documents (not just statistics but also reports of various kinds) which can be used by sociologists, political scientists and historians. White papers and the Hansard Records (transcripts of speeches in the Houses of Parliament) are also useful sources. Prisons, schools, churches, organisations like the Confederation of British Industry (CBI), trade unions and particular firms, also keep records (annual reports and accounts, the minutes of meetings, lists of employee or membership numbers, contract documents and so on) which can provide vital information. Such documents are often the *only* source of certain information. Researchers are unlikely to find an informant who would be able to tell them, without checking the documentary records, what proportion of the company's workforce had been engaged in manual work every year for the past two decades, or how union membership figures for 1953 compare with those for 1993. Other documentary sources from the public sphere include those which are 'regarded as media for mass communication' such as newspapers, books, pamphlets, magazines (and more recently film, television programmes and videos) as well as others 'with more limited circulation, such as directories, almanacs and yearbooks' (Scott 1990: 137). Personal documents, such as letters, diaries, household accounts, personal memoirs, family photos and portraits and address books can also be used to give some insight into family life, business and politics in a specific period, to generate hypotheses, to provide illustrations of more general points and so on. There exists, then, a multitude of documentary sources which can be exploited in the course of research, and the classical sociologists made extensive use of them. Durkheim used official suicide statistics, Weber used religious tracts and pamphlets to support his arguments about the Protestant ethic and the spirit of capitalism, and in the first volume of *Capital* alone, Marx:

> cites thirty reports of HM Inspectors . . . five reports of the Medical Officer of the Privy Council on public health . . . reports of select committees, Royal Commissions, and others on the adulteration of food, on the baking trade, mines, railways and agricultural labourers, the employment of children in factories, the Banking Acts, and the Corn Laws; the report of the Commissioners on Transportation and Penal Servitude (1863); Inland Revenue Reports . . . the report of the Social Science Congress in Edinburgh (1863); the *Report of the Committee of the Master Spinners' and Manufacturers' Defence Fund* (1854); and the report of the Registrar General on births, death and marriages in England. . . . Finally he cites *Correspondence with Her Majesty's Missions Abroad regarding Industrial Questions and Trades Unions* (1867) and Hansard.
>
> (Harvey 1990: 42)

Documents can be the sole data source for a piece of research. Alternatively, they may be used to supplement other sources of data derived from other research techniques. In either case, and as with any research method, documentary research raises a number of methodological problems and these are the focus of this chapter. In a book which critically examines this method, Scott (1990: 19) argues that the key to documentary techniques is to apply 'the quality control criteria of authenticity, credibility, representativeness and meaning'. This chapter begins by examining these four criteria, and then moves on to look in more detail at a form of textual analysis known as content analysis.

DOCUMENTARY EVIDENCE AND WITCHCRAFT

This section will outline Scott's criteria for assessing documentary sources, and apply them to the example of research into seventeenth-century witch-hunts – a phenomenon which is commonly associated with both a form of collective madness and a preoccupation with sexuality. The first two criteria which Scott suggests researchers must use are authenticity and credibility.

Authenticity and credibility

Assessing a document's *authenticity* involves asking how genuine it is. Documents, especially historical ones, can be copies of the original. It is clearly important to know whether a document is an original or a copy, and to ask questions about the author of the document, its date and, for published works, the place of publication. Documents may be forgeries and, though forged documents may be of interest in their own right, it is impossible to use a source properly without knowing whether or not it is authentic. Assessing the *credibility* of a document 'involves an appraisal of how distorted its contents are likely to be' (Scott 1990: 22). In much the same way that interviewers have to form judgements about how knowledgeable and truthful their informants are, researchers working with documentary sources need to consider the sincerity or otherwise of the author, and the likely accuracy of their version of events.

There are a number of primary sources to which a researcher interested in witchcraft could turn. ('Primary' sources are those written by witnesses at the time of the events, 'secondary' sources are those written after the event by people who were not present at the time.) Best known of these would be the *Malleus Maleficarum* or 'Witches' Hammer', written by two witch-hunters, Jakob Sprenger and Heinrich Institoris at the request of Pope Innocent VIII, and first published in 1487 (Lewinsohn 1958: 133). But there are also other lesser known works which would be of interest, for example, John Stearne's *A Confirmation and Discovery of Witchcraft* (1973), first published in 1648. Stearne was a close associate of Witch-Finder General Matthew Hopkins and was involved in an intense campaign to root out witches in East Anglia between 1645 and 1647. The British Museum acquired a copy of *A Confirmation* in the nineteenth century (shelf mark C. 54.e.6.), and in 1973 The Rota Press at the University of Exeter reproduced the work with permission from the Trustees of the British Museum. Any researcher who wished to use Stearne's work would need to ask questions about the authenticity of the copy held in the British Museum. Where was the manuscript between 1648 and the nineteenth century? Is it an original or a copy? If a copy, when was it produced and by whom? Are there likely to have been errors in copying, and if so, how might these have affected the data? Is the Rota Press's edition a complete and accurate copy of the British Museum's version?

Once the researcher establishes that the work is authentic, and has considered the possibility of errors, he or she can turn to the question of Stearne's sincerity and how accurate and authoritative a witness he was likely to have been. *A Confirmation*, as the title suggests, is a work which asserts the existence, and describes the nature and practices of, witches. Stearne writes, for example:

> Witches worship Devills, they invocate them, crave helpe of them, worke by them, and doe them homage, sacrifice to them, and they do it not to stockes and stones, and so mediately to the Devill, as other Idolaters doe, but immediately to the Devill himselfe, and therefire the greatest Idolaters that can be; and are not they then more worthy of death?

(Stearne 1973: A2)

Few people today would believe that this passage provides us with an accurate description of events. If Stearne were describing what he had eaten for breakfast (as Samuel Pepys does in his dairies), a researcher might accept this as evidence that in the seventeenth century some people ate bread (or whatever was mentioned) first thing in the morning. However, in Western cultures, where scientific rationalism has largely replaced magical, superstitious and religious thinking, a primary source asserting the existence of supernatural forces is unlikely to be taken as *evidence* of the existence of such forces. The importance of the passage quoted above, then, would be seen as its contribution to our under-standing of seventeenth-century *ideas* about witchcraft. Even so, a researcher should not uncritically accept this as documentary evidence that men like Stearne believed in the existence of fully fledged, prac-tising, devil worshipping witches. Just as a researcher in 300 years time would need to ask whether tabloid journalists truly believe in some of the stories they write, it is important to ask whether Stearne really believed what he wrote in *A Confirmation*. Scott observes that:

> One of the most important considerations in assessing sincerity is the material interest that the author has in the contents of the document, the extent to which he or she seeks some practical advantage which might involve deceiving his or her readers.

(1990: 22–3)

Such matters can only be assessed by setting the document in its historical context, which involves drawing on knowledge about the period from other sources. It is known that witch-finders were paid substantial fees for hunting out witches and bringing them to trial, and that by the seventeenth century there were those who accused witch-finders of 'hypocrisy and chicanery' (The Rota 1973) and held that they were motivated more by the desire for wealth and notoriety than by religious sentiment. *A Confirmation* was, in fact, written in response to precisely these kinds of criticisms and Stearne provides a clear statement of his motives in writing the text:

> I desire to give some satisfaction to the world, that it may appeare, what hath beene done, hath beene for the good of the commonwealth, and we free from those aspersions cast upon us, and that I never favored any, or unjustly prosecuted others, but that all that be guilty of this, ought to die.
>
> (Stearne 1973: A3)

Stearne further attempts to reassure his audience of his own sincerity, stating that 'I neither formerly, in any of my proceedings concerning this matter, or in penning of this, ayme at mine owne private ends rather than the publique good' (1973: A3). A researcher would thus need to confront the fact that Stearne recognised his sincerity was questioned by his contemporaries and that he was at pains to exonerate himself from a variety of charges, against himself and witch-finders more generally, before arriving at any conclusion about how reliable a statement of seventeenth-century beliefs about witchcraft *A Confirmation* provides. It may be that after careful consideration, the researcher would conclude that though Stearne profited by his profession, he was sincere in his insistence that witches existed and were evil, that 'white witches' did not exist, that it was every person's spiritual duty to hunt out witches, and so on. But accepting the author's sincerity is only half the battle. Even the most sincere authors can write inaccurate descriptions of events. They may misinterpret what they have seen, they may forget, they may exaggerate. Consider the following passage in which Stearne describes a confession:

> John Bysack . . . confessed that the devil came in at his window in the shape of a rugged sandy-coloured dog, which asked him to deny God, Christ, and his Baptism, which he spake with a great hollow voice; and he consented. . . . Satan promised to free him of hell-torments, and that he would send him other things which he must let suck his blood, and they should avenge him of all his enemies . . . and soon after those came, which he called his Imps, and sucked on those marks or teats which I found on his body, neer twenty yeers together, sometimes once a week, sometimes once a fortnight, which he confessed came in the likenesse of Snails, onely they differed from another in colour and bigness.
>
> (Stearne 1973: 41)

How accurate a report of Bysack's confession is this? Given prevailing ideas about the nature of the devil and witchcraft, it is possible that Bysack did 'confess' exactly this (in rather the same way that many homosexuals who enter psychotherapy 'confess' to having had an over-dependent relationship with a 'domineering' mother). But it is also possible that Stearne was partial and selective in the way he memorised and recorded 'confessions'. The account might be inaccurate because of what it omits, or because Stearne remembered what he wanted to have heard, rather than what he actually did hear. It is also possible that Stearne exaggerated features of the confession. He may have felt that 20 years of having teats sucked by imps in the shape of snails carried more dramatic effect than, say a mere eight or ten years, or that saying Satan spoke with a 'big hollow voice' made the whole thing more convincing. In short, before attempting to use a documentary source as a piece of research data, it is necessary to ask questions about the sincerity of the author and how accurate their account is likely to be.

Representativeness

As well as considering the authenticity and credibility of a document, Scott argues that:

> The intelligent use of documents involves a judgement as to whether the documents consulted are representative of the totality of relevant documents. This is not to say that good research cannot be carried out with an unrepresentative selection; but the user must know to what extent and in what respects those documents are unrepresentative.
>
> (1990: 24)

In a sense, this is similar to the issue of sampling. Often documentary research involves examining only a small portion of all the relevant documents. This can be simply because there is just too much docu-mentary evidence to be analysed. Few researchers would have the resources to analyse *all* the newspaper articles ever written on sexual assaults, for example. But it can also be because the totality of docu-ments has not survived or is unavailable and this is especially relevant for historical research. For instance, in his study of witchcraft in seventeenth-century New England, John Demos (1982) used a range of primary documentary sources including court records, depositions and warrants, public and town records, journals and letters, but he clearly did not have, and could not have had, access to every single document ever written by, or in relation to, those tried for witchcraft in New England.

As he was working with only a partial sample of the relevant documents, he encountered numerous problems, even when simply trying to provide a portrait of the kind of people who were tried as witches:

> To investigate the witches as a biographical type is no easy task. With rare exceptions . . . the record of their experience is scattered and fragmentary. Much of the surviving evidence derives from their various trial proceedings; in short, we can visualize them quite fully as *suspects*, but only here and there in other aspects of their lives. We lack, most especially, a chance to approach them directly, to hear their side of their own story. Most of what we do hear comes to us second- or third-hand, and from obviously hostile sources. It is hard enough to simply count their number.
>
> (Demos 1982: 57)

Court records pertaining to witchcraft trials, like all official publications (see Chapter 3), do not tell the whole story even in the most basic numerical terms. Demos observes that figures drawn from official sources 'certainly under-represent the total of witchcraft suspects in seventeenth-century New England. The court records are riddled with gaps and defects; it is possible, even probable, that important cases have been lost from sight' (1982: 57). In other words, such records cannot even tell us how many people were tried for witchcraft, because not all court records have survived and those that have survived are imperfect or incomplete. More importantly, so far as the issue of representativeness goes, the incompleteness of the documentary evidence means that the researcher must be extremely cautious about making generalisations on the basis of any partial sample.

As part of his study, Demos wanted some very basic background information about the kind of people who were accused of witchcraft – their sex, their age, their marital status, their social and economic position, and so on. He found court records pertaining to 114 individual suspects. If he could have been certain that only these 114 people had ever been tried for witchcraft, and that the court records were reliable, accurate and complete, it would have been possible to simply count how many suspects were male and how many female, and so on, and to make general statements such as 'x per cent of suspects were female', 'x per cent were aged 50 or over', 'male suspects were typically younger than female suspects'. But Demos knew that he only had access to part of the totality of relevant documents and the question of representativeness was therefore important. Were these 114 cases likely to be representative of all other seventeenth-century New England witchcraft suspects? Did the documents pertaining to these particular cases survive for a particular reason, perhaps precisely because they were qualitatively different to other cases? In this case, they would be highly *un*representative and it would be quite wrong to make any general statements along the lines of those above. After considering the representativeness of the documents upon which he relied, Demos (1982: 59) argued that even if the 114 cases were merely the 'tip of the iceberg' in terms of the total number of people tried for witchcraft, the 'substantive and structural features [of these cases] still merit investigation. There is no reason to imagine any considerable difference between the known witches and their unknown counterparts.'

In order to assess the representativeness of documentary evidence, therefore, it is necessary to ask why particular documents survived, how many similar documents survived, whether the documents you have are typical of those that did not survive, and to ask why is this document available when others like it are not. Unless the researcher knows the answer to at least some of these questions, it is possible that the 'facts' he or she constructs from the documents will be '*purely* functions of the bias inherent in selective survival and availability' (Scott 1990: 28).

Meaning

The final and most difficult methodological problem to confront the documentary researcher is that of assessing the meaning and significance of a document. To begin with, there may be difficulties in grasping the literal meaning of documentary sources. Even if the writing is decipherable and the words familiar (which is not always the case when working with historical documents – seventeenth-century handwriting is particularly difficult for contemporary researchers), the literal meaning may not be immediately apparent. In *A Confirmation*, for example, Stearne speaks of a woman who confessed that 'the devill had the use of her body, but she said she could not tell whether he performed nature or not' (1973: 30). To a modern day reader, this sounds as though the woman meant she had some form of sexual contact with the devil, but what exactly does 'the use of her body' and 'performing nature' mean? To understand this sentence in its literal sense would require knowledge of seventeenth-century sexual terminology and euphemisms.

Simply grasping the literal meaning of a document can be problematic. But difficulties here are as nothing compared to the methodological and philosophical problems which arise when the researcher attempts to interpret the deeper meaning and broader significance of a document. Can the researcher speak with certainty about what a given document *really* means (i.e. say that this or that is the one, true interpretation), or is the meaning of a document inextricably bound up with the subjectivity of the author, the reader, the researcher? For researchers who take an essentially positivistic approach to research, this problem is often glossed over. Such researchers are generally looking for 'facts' and figures, and often assume that all texts have an objective meaning which can be uncovered through rigorous scientific analysis. But just as interpretative methodologists question the notion that there are objective truths which have an existence external to the subjective meanings and perceptions of social actors, so they would question this idea that texts can have a single, eternal meaning that exists across time and across cultures.

Stearne's work highlights this problem clearly. He states that his intention in writing his treatise was to prove that witches did exist and to explain how he discovered them. The work was meant, as the title implies, to confirm certain 'facts' about witchcraft. But though modern readers can use a process of *verstehen* to try to grasp what the author intended (they can attempt to empathetically reconstruct the world through Stearne's eyes in order to understand what he meant), they cannot accept that the document literally means that witches exist. In other words, what is written in *A Confirmation* cannot possibly mean the same to a reader in the twentieth century as it meant to Stearne. If you do not believe in witchcraft, then descriptions of people being visited by the devil in the form of rats, mice and moles that speak in great hollow voices and suck blood cannot be read as factual accounts of real events. Though the words in the text remain unchanged over three centuries, the meaning the text carries has changed. It cannot be interpreted through reference to ideas about supernatural forces, and modern day readers are likely to use some alternative framework for making sense of such texts. Demos (1982), for example, makes use of psychoanalytic theory to interpret the meaning of one of his sources – a treatise written by The Revd Samuel Willard in 1672. The treatise describes the possession of a 16-year-old girl called Elizabeth Knapp and Willard's attempts to help her. Willard provides a detailed account of the girl's violent physical fits, which were followed by periods of contrite, self-accusatory melancholy and, drawing on his belief in witchcraft and the supernatural, he interprets this as a manifestation of her struggle with Satan. Demos notes that twentieth-century commentators necessarily interpret Elizabeth Knapp's behaviour rather differently:

From fits and demonic possession we move to 'conversion symptoms' and 'intrapsychic conflict.' It is an abrupt transition, and yet a
necessary one. We should not shrink from concluding that Elizabeth
Knapp was truly ill – by our standards, if not by theirs.

(Demos 1982: 117)

Demos accepts The Revd Willard's account of Elizabeth's behaviour
and his own interventions as an accurate description of events, but uses
a psychoanalytic model to interpret the meaning of events and to evaluate what the text *really* tells us. Referring closely to the text, Demos
explains Elizabeth's 'illness' in terms of 'exhibitionism, dependency
[and] rage' (1982: 118) and presents Willard as playing a role analogous
to that of a 'therapist'. He then explores possible erotic motives and
conflicts behind Elizabeth's state, talking about repressed sexual wishes
and Oedipal conflicts, and concludes that her dependency on Willard
stemmed from her need to protect a fragmenting self by projecting an
idealised version of herself onto him. Demos asserts that:

It should now be evident that her relation to her own 'therapist' – the
Rev. Willard – approximates the narcissistic, rather than the libidinal,
transferences. . . . Recall that her fits began when Willard had left
home on a trip of several days – in short, when the 'narcissistic
object' had abandoned her. It is reasonable to speculate that her
symptoms expressed a disguised aim to bring the minister back. She
needed his regularly available presence to maintain the integrity of
her all-too-fragile self.

(1982: 120)

The way in which Demos reworks the text, weaving it with psychoanalytic theory and tying it in with fragments of evidence from other
sources is impressive. His analysis of this seventeenth-century New
England girl is as coherent as many of the case studies in the contemporary psychoanalytic literature and, if you accept the model upon
which it is based, it is a convincing interpretation of the meaning of the
text. But this is a big 'if'. It is, for example, only 'reasonable to
speculate' that Elizabeth's behaviour expressed unconscious wishes if
you believe in the existence of an unconscious mind. There are those
who would see an unhappy parallel between Demos' analysis and that
originally offered by Willard, noting that since neither the unconscious
mind nor Satan are open to empirical observation, a belief in the existence of the unconscious is as much an article of faith as a belief in the
existence of Satan. The real point, however, is that the meaning of a text

appears to be affected by the reader's pre-existing beliefs about the world. The meaning changes over time not because of what is *in* the text, but because of what the reader or researcher *brings to* the text. If the reader comes equipped with a belief in supernatural powers, Revd Willard's treatise is a factual account of his own attempts to help a girl possessed by the devil. If the reader arrives with a belief in psycho-analytic theory, Revd Willard's treatise is a description of the behaviour of a girl suffering from a gross 'narcissistic imbalance'. Which reader is deciphering the *true* meaning of the text? Or should we conclude that texts have no single, true meaning but rather a number of meanings that vary according to the subjective perceptions of the people that read and interpret them? It is important to note, of course, that some beliefs do not change. We still believe in the existence of food, and when we read a seventeenth-century description of what was eaten for breakfast we do not question its authority in this way. Scott's criteria of 'credibility' cannot therefore be neatly separated from that of 'meaning', since to assess how distorted the contents of a text are likely to be, we must first decipher their meaning.

To deal with these kinds of problems, many interpretativist theorists draw on a philosophical tradition known as 'hermeneutics'. Hermen-eutic philosophy has a long history and is not a unitary body of thought, but more recent authors have tended to share an emphasis on the rules, interpretations and meanings ('frames of meaning' or 'forms of life') through which people produce and reproduce social life. The idea is that people of any given culture or 'tradition' learn a set of implicit rules which govern social practices and learn to interpret cultural symbols and linguistic signs and it is this tacit knowledge which guides their actions and allows them to make sense of the actions of others. There are, for example, a whole set of complex rules which govern how people in Britain and North America greet each other, and although individuals would probably be unable to describe all these rules to someone from another culture, they know when the rules are broken. People know that it may be appropriate to greet a close friend with a slap on the back and 'How are you mate?', but that to greet a new boss or a head of state in the same manner would be insulting. It is also our knowledge of the rules and meanings which make up a 'form of life' that allows us to understand and interpret the written word, for instance, to distinguish between news reporting and satire, between a respectful and a sarcastic letter, between a despairing and a mildly irritable entry in a diary. The problem for the documentary researcher working with a text from another culture or era is that he or she does not possess this tacit knowledge which is so crucial to interpretation. Could a modern day reader hope to discern if or when Stearne or Willard were being ironic?

Hermeneutics represents an attempt to deal with this problem. It directs researchers to try to engage with other 'traditions' or 'forms of life', to see how the rules and meanings that guide social life in one era or culture differ from those in their own and by so doing, to understand meaning in a given context – in other words, to try to achieve a form of *verstehen*. The hermeneutic philosopher recognises researchers cannot simply detach themselves from their own frame of meaning and read a 300-year-old text as its author would have read it. However, this inability to disengage from one tradition does not make understanding impossible. For philosophers such as Gadamer, once words have been written down as text, that text takes on an existence of its own, independent of the author's intentions and 'since the understanding of a text is a creative mediation of traditions, such understanding is an unending process; it can never be "completed", because new meanings are continually brought into being through readings of the work within fresh traditions' (Giddens 1982: 63). The hermeneutic researcher is not so much looking for the one, true, objective meaning of a text, but is searching for understanding. As Scott puts it:

> Textual analysis involves mediation between the frames of reference of the researcher and those who produced the text. The aim of this dialogue is to move within the 'hermeneutic circle' in which we comprehend a text by understanding the frame of reference from which it was produced, and appreciate that frame of reference by understanding the text. The researcher's own frame of reference becomes the springboard from which the circle is entered, and so the circle reaches back to encompass the dialogue between the researcher and the text.
>
> (1990: 31)

Hermeneutic approaches are not without problems of their own. If scholars from two different 'traditions' come up with two different interpretations of the same text, must we accept both as correct? Equally problematic, what if two different researchers from the *same* 'tradition' or 'form of life' come up with very different interpretations of a historical text through hermeneutic enquiry? Contemporary feminist scholars, for example, do not always interpret documentary evidence on witchcraft in the same way as orthodox male academics. The trouble is that once a text is assumed to have an existence and meaning of its own, separate from the intentions of its author and comprehensible only through reference to the interplay between different 'traditions', it is difficult to avoid the sort of relativism which says that a text means anything that any individual wants it to mean. If neo-Nazis use their world view as a springboard to understanding *Mein Kampf* as a harmless piece of idealism, we cannot say their interpretation is wrong, merely that from the vantage point of a different world view, we would offer a different interpretation. It is in an attempt to avoid this relativist trap that authors like Giddens (1982) and Scott (1990) insist that texts must be 'approached in terms of the intentions of its author and the social context in which it was produced' (May 1993: 140). Without returning to the naïve positivist's uncritical assumption that texts have an objective meaning which can simply be uncovered through proper 'scientific' analysis, Scott suggests that documents cannot be usefully employed in social research if they are thought of as wholly disconnected from the author's intentions. He argues that:

> We must recognise three aspects of the meaning of a text – three 'moments' in the movement of a text from author to audience. The *intended content* of a text is the meaning which the author of the text intended to produce, while the *received content* is the meaning constructed by its audience. Both author and audience may be socially differentiated entities, and so there may be numerous intended and received meanings for the same text. Intervening between the intended and the received meanings is the . . . *internal meaning*.
>
> (Scott, original emphasis 1990: 34)

We will return to this point in the concluding section of the chapter. Before doing so, it is worth looking at a widely used research technique known as *content analysis*. This technique is essentially concerned with the last aspect of meaning mentioned by Scott, looking at the messages contained in a text as though they could be separated from the author's intentions and their reception by a given audience and it therefore highlights a number of philosophical and methodological problems.

CONTENT ANALYSIS

At its most basic, content analysis is a research technique which allows the researcher to quantify the content of communications. The more elaborate forms of content analysis were developed by those working in the field of communications and the technique is most commonly used in studies of the media, but it is also applied in other disciplines (including political science, literary criticism, history, psychoanalysis and linguistics), and to a diverse range of data such as newspapers, books, transcripts of speeches, interviews, and psychotherapy sessions, television, film, art, children's drawings, postage stamps (see Krippendorff 1980). In essence, content analysis simply consists of deciding on a *unit of analysis* (a word, a paragraph, an article, a photograph), devising *categories* and then counting how often the unit of analysis falls into each category. A very basic example would be where news photos in tabloid papers were the unit of analysis, and 'male' and 'female' were the categories. The content analyst would then calculate the frequency with which news photos fell into each category to produce results in the form of percentages: 95 per cent of news photos depicted males, 5 per cent depicted females. The categories could be made more complex, for instance, 'men at work', 'women at work', 'semi-naked men', 'semi-naked women' and so on.

Since the late 1950s numerous research handbooks on content analysis have been produced, the vast majority of which take an essentially positivist approach to research. Berelson's (1952) definition of content analysis is typical. He claims that content analysis is 'the objective, systematic, and quantitative description of the manifest content of communication'. Content analysis is thus presented as a technique for uncovering and describing what Scott terms the *internal meaning* of a text. The idea is that this 'manifest content' can be analysed independently of the author's intentions and the audience that receives it and 'the objectivity of content analysis is said to be guaranteed by the use of rigorous and replicable procedures' (Scott 1990: 130). According to the orthodox textbooks, this objective and systematic analysis should be conducted as follows.

The first step is to select a sample of documents (or film footage or whatever) systematically. Next, the researcher needs to decide on the coding unit and the categories that will be used. The coding unit can be virtually anything at all – a word, a paragraph, a column inch in newspapers, a photograph, a theme – depending on what is being analysed. The researcher may wish to count how many times certain words are used to describe rapists in magazines or newspapers or television news, or how often certain themes emerged in newspaper coverage of rapes, or how many column inches tabloid papers devote to sexual assaults by known assailants. In each case, a different coding unit would be appropriate – a word, a theme, a column inch respectively. Having decided on a coding unit, it is necessary to define it very precisely. If column inches had been selected as the unit of analysis, for example, it would be important to specify in advance whether the space taken by the headline would be included as well as that taken by the text, how articles of the same length but different column width would be compared and so on. The point of this exercise is to ensure that standard techniques are employed throughout the study.

The researcher must also decide whether to collect *nominal* or *ordinal* data. Nominal data come from simple frequency counts – categories such as 'semi-naked men' and 'semi-naked women' are decided upon, and the researcher counts how many published photographs fall into each category. Ordinal data come from ranking items on a scale – for example, newspaper articles about a particular government policy could be ranked as favourable to the policy, neutral or unfavourable. If ordinal data is required, it is necessary to decide what kind of scale the material will be ranked along.

The researcher then selects the analytic categories into which the content of the coding units will be fitted. Imagine a researcher is concerned with newspaper coverage of sexual attacks upon women, and has decided to use the column inch as the coding unit. He or she could use one catch-all category 'sexual attack' and count how many column inches are devoted to attacks of any type. It is more likely that the researcher would want to differentiate between, say, rape and workplace sexual harassment, and so would decide on a number of categories: 'sexual harassment', 'indecent assault', 'rape', 'rape murders' and so on. Textbooks on content analysis stress that the definition of categories should be a rigorous and precise process. If the categories are not rigorously defined, the possibility of researcher bias increases. Say that our imaginary researcher did use one all embracing category of 'sexual attack'. How would she or he decide whether to include in this category articles reporting an unfair dismissal hearing at an industrial tribunal in which a woman described having been repeatedly subjected to un-wanted physical attention from her boss? If there were no pre-established, precise guidelines telling the coder what should and should not be included under the category 'sexual assault', she or he would have to rely on personal judgements and opinions about whether these attentions constituted a sexual assault.

Holsti (1969) argues that categories should be 'exhaustive' and 'mutually exclusive'. By 'exhaustive' he means that the categories should cover every possibility otherwise it may prove impossible to classify, and therefore to measure certain items. In their study of media coverage of sex crimes, Soothill and Walby (1991) observe that a previous study by Soothill and Jack (1975) 'masked the amount of sex crime being reported in newspapers' because they only counted articles which covered 'cases which would appear as rape in the *Criminal Statistics* for the relevant year . . . this provided a narrow definition of sex crime' (1991: 19). The absence of categories to cover sexual assaults that never got to court, non-rape trials that nevertheless involved extensive coverage of sexual activities and of categories to cover reports of rapes in other countries made the research findings less reliable. 'Mutual exclusiveness' refers to the fact that categories should not overlap. The categories should be defined in such a way as to make it impossible for any one item to be classified in more than one category. It would be no good having two categories called 'rape' and 'sexual attack', since rape is a sexual attack. The categories would need to be more explicitly defined: 'rape' and 'all sexual attacks other than rape'. The selection and definition of analytic categories is seen as central to good research. As Budd *et al.* (1967) put it, 'No content analysis is better than its categories, for a system or set of categories is, in essence, a conceptual scheme . . . categories are not mere labels, but compartments with explicitly defined boundaries into which material is grouped for analysis' (1967: 39).

The idea is that if categories are defined rigorously and precisely enough, coding will be a straightforward and systematic process that requires no subjective, interpretative effort on the part of the coder. Indeed, the process of coding should be so straightforward that even a computer could do it, and attempts have been made to design software packages for computerised content analysis. It is the rigour of these techniques which leads methodologists like Holsti (1969) to claim that content analysis is an 'objective' method. They serve to standardise the process of analysis and so make it possible for other researchers to replicate (and therefore verify) the study. The categories and coding system are held to be akin to the neutral measuring instruments of the natural sciences that can be used by anyone to produce reliable value-free knowledge since, if specified closely enough, anyone could apply the same coding unit and categories to the same material and come up with exactly the same results. In other words, positivist textbooks on content analysis suggest that it is a method of textual analysis which overcomes one of the problems discussed in the previous section, namely the fact that different audiences find different meanings in the same text. If seventeenth-century treatises on witchcraft were being analysed, for example, a researcher could categorise a number of different themes ('devil taking the form of animals', 'devil engaging in sexual relations with women', 'devil speaking through women'). Once these categories had been rigorously defined, anyone, whether they be a fundamentalist Christian, a psychoanalyst, a feminist historian or a practising Satanist, could count how often these themes occurred in a sample of texts and come up with the same results. Content analysis is therefore held to produce objective knowledge about the 'internal meaning' or 'manifest content' of texts.

There are a number of problems with this positivist approach to textual analysis. To begin with, the simple quantification of words or themes or images in communications is a flawed project, no matter how rigorously it is done, for the very simple reason that the same words or images can mean and convey very different things in different contexts. The words 'Jesus Christ', for example, mean and convey something different according to whether they are spoken at the start of a prayer, or in response to spilling a cup of tea, or in reply to the question 'Who are you?'. The problem of context is equally, if not more pressing, when material is being ranked in some way (e.g., as favourable, neutral or unfavourable), not simply counted. Here it is often necessary to set words or images in the context of the author's political and moral views as well as in that of the text as a whole. Take the word 'militant'. Is it favourable, unfavourable or neutral to describe a feminist as militant? Consider the following examples:

i   'She was a militant advocate of women's rights, unceasing in her fight against oppression' (obituary in a feminist journal);
ii 'Local politics are being taken over by militant feminists, lesbians, queers and communists' (letter to right-wing local newspaper);
iii 'Ms X., one of the union's leading feminists, made some fairly militant demands' (Minutes of consultative meeting between managers and workers).

In an attempt to surmount such problems, Holsti (1969) suggests that researchers should not only decide on a coding unit before beginning analysis, but also identify 'context units'. He thus allows that to determine how to code a given word or statement, it is sometimes necessary to refer to the whole sentence or paragraph, perhaps even the whole article. But this concession actually changes the whole ball game. Coding is no longer simply the straightforward application of rules, it now involves the *interpretation* of meaning from context. Scott (1990) observes:

> This contextual determination of meaning is one of the crucial obstacles to the computerisation of content analysis, and also a major limitation on the reliability and replicability of the technique, as

comprehension of the meaning of an item in context is a matter of interpretation and, therefore, of individual discretion.

(1990: 131)

If coding relies on researchers interpreting meaning from context, then the cultural knowledge and subjective values of the researcher cannot help but impinge on the process. Once we accept this, content analysis is no longer so easy to distinguish from other, more interpretative, forms of textual analysis. The coder has to understand the literal meaning of the words and the literary conventions governing the way the text was written (genre and style), and will also need to form judgements about the intentions of the author in writing the text. Deciding whether a statement is favourable, unfavourable or neutral in a given context, meanwhile, involves drawing on moral and political values. Budd *et al.* (1967) note that such evaluations are one of the 'most frustrating problems facing the researcher, because it is one area in which the element of subjectivity is difficult to control and impossible to eliminate entirely' (1967: 50). They go on to advise the would-be content analyst to define as neutral 'those items which reflect neither favourable or unfavourable conditions either through a balance of content or a lack of controversial material' (1967: 53). But how can a coder decide what is to count as 'balance' and what is to count as 'controversial' except through reference to their own values and beliefs? Return to statement iii above for a moment. To decide whether the word 'militant' is being used in a favourable, unfavourable or neutral way, the coder would read on and find out what these 'demands' were. If Ms X. was demanding the reinstatement of a woman sacked for complaining about sexual harassment and the coder agreed with the author that this was a 'fairly militant' demand, then he or she would code the statement as 'neutral' – a straight description of 'facts'. But if the coder disagreed, seeing Ms X.'s demand as eminently reasonable, the term 'militant' would seem pejorative. All this seriously undermines Holsti's (1969) claim that the systematic methods of content analysis make it more objective, and hence scientific, than literary approaches.

The context-dependency of meaning is highly problematic, then. The issues raised by the drawing up of categories are equally troubling. There are both practical and philosophical problems. Orthodox handbooks instruct researchers to do this at the start of the study, but in practice this may be difficult. For instance, the Glasgow Media Group, which has conducted a number of excellent studies of the British media, found it virtually impossible to follow such guidelines in their research on BBC news reporting. The group made some preliminary studies and drew up a draft of twenty-four categories, which they then tested and modified. A data sheet was produced onto which information was to be logged, and this allowed for recording the length, placement and running order of news items, its category (crime, industrial, disasters and so on), who presented it, what interviews were involved, what use was made of news film (Glasgow University Media Group 1976). But even with such elaborate planning, difficulties arose with the categorisation of data. The group found that the same story often appeared in different categories according to the news angle adopted by the news room and stories were often bundled together by broadcasters into a package. Three separate industrial disputes could appear linked together as one news item. In short, it proved extremely hard to draw up mutually exclusive categories prior to actually analysing the data, since the researchers could not anticipate all the different ways in which information would be presented.

At a philosophical level, there are problems surrounding how researchers arrive at categories in the first place. It is all very well to insist that content analysis is 'scientific' because other researchers could reproduce and verify results using the same categories and coding system, but this ignores the fact that researchers of very different political persuasions or from different cultures are unlikely to come up with the same categories in the first place. A feminist scholar and a fundamentalist Christian undertaking a study of seventeenth-century religious tracts, for example, would have very different theoretical concerns and interests. The fundamentalist Christian would not, presumably, be primarily concerned to count the number of hostile references to women's sexuality or the number of phallocentric images in the text. Selecting categories is a theory-laden process and content analysis, as much as any other form of textual analysis, therefore begins with a theory-impregnated rather than a neutral classification system.

Again, champions of the method are not blind to such problems. Krippendorff (1980), for example, accepts that messages can be examined from a number of different perspectives and interpreted in a number of different ways – psychologically, sociologically, politically – and holds that all of these interpretations may be simultaneously valid. He argues that researchers must decide on the boundaries of their research using the conventions of their academic discipline to decide what to concentrate on. Thus a feminist sociologist looking at pornographic materials can decide not to include psychoanalytic categories referring to various 'perversions' or 'personality disorders', while a psychoanalyst analysing the same material need not explore the content in relation to, say, aspects of patriarchal ideology. Though this advice sounds sensible from a practical viewpoint and would help to guarantee internally coherent studies, it also takes us straight back to the problems discussed in the previous section in relation to hermeneutics. Krippendorf's position allows for numerous different 'readings' of the same text, and gives no clue as to how we could judge between them. Analyses of the same documents produced by a psychoanalyst and by a feminist, for instance, may directly contradict each other, but we would have to accept both as 'simultaneously valid'. Again, this problem arises because the text has been detached from author and audience, and is being approached as if it has an internal meaning that can be analysed in a vacuum. Yet the researcher, in his or her attempt to interpret this meaning, immediately becomes part of the text's audience and cannot neatly separate the internal from the received meaning. As Scott (1990) puts it:

> The most that can be achieved by a researcher is an analysis which shows how the inferred internal meaning of the text opens up some possibilities for interpretation by its audience and closes off others . . . the interpretation of a text cannot be separated from the questions of its production and its effects. The reading of a text is validated by relating it to the intentions of the author, and by taking account of the fact that its 'objective meaning' goes beyond these intentions, and also by relating the text to its audience.
>
> (Scott 1990: 34)

Kobena Mercer's (1993) discussion of the gay photographer Robert Mapplethorpe's work illustrates these points well.

CONTENT, AUTHOR AND AUDIENCE: MERCER ON MAPPLETHORPE

The homo-erotic photography of Robert Mapplethorpe is controversial. There are, of course, those who object to it simply because it celebrates male homosexuality, but his portraits of naked children, his images of gay male sadomasochism and his studies of nude Black males also disturb many lesbian and gay people as well as liberals and feminists. In an article entitled 'Just looking for trouble', Kobena Mercer considers Mapplethorpe's work from a Black gay male perspective. He describes his own initial response to the photographs and then outlines how and why he came to 'read' Mapplethorpe's work in a rather different way. In so doing, Mercer shows very neatly how any interpretation of a text (or work of art) that fails to consider its effects on audiences and the intentions of the author (or artist) is necessarily incomplete.

Mercer's first reaction to Mapplethorpe's studies of Black men in *Black Males* (1982) and *The Black Book* (1986) was outrage at the way in which the photographs 'seemed to perpetuate the racist stereotype that, essentially, the black man is nothing more than his penis' (1993: 96). Mercer shows how, if the images are considered on their own, separate from the intentions of the photographer and their reception by different audiences, it appears that 'racial fetishism is an important element in the pleasures (and displeasures) which the photographs bring into play' (1993: 99). He observes that:

> Whereas the white gay male sadomasochist pictures portray a sub-cultural sexuality that consists of 'doing' something, the black men are defined and confined to 'being' purely sexual and nothing but sexual – hence hypersexual. We look through a sequence of individually named African-American men, but we see only sexuality as the sum-total meaning of their black male identity. . . . Such racial fetishism not only eroticizes the most visible aspect of racial difference – skin colour – but also lubricates the ideological reproduction of 'colonial fantasy', in which the white male subject is positioned at the centre of representation by a desire for mastery, power and control over the racialized and inferiorized black Other.
>
> (1993: 98–9)

But, as current debate amongst feminists about pornography also reveals (see Segal and McIntosh 1993, Assiter and Carol 1993), photographs, like other cultural texts, are ambiguous. They can be interpreted in a number of ways, they are received differently by different audiences. As Mercer notes, 'the variety of conflicting interpretations of the value of Mapplethorpe's work would imply that the text does not bear one, singular and unequivocal meaning, but is open to a number of competing readings' (1993: 102). Mapplethorpe's images can be read as straightforwardly racist, but they can also be read as an ironic comment on racist stereotypes. Moreover, there are audiences (for example, certain homophobic and/or racist audiences) who read these pictures as neither racist nor about racism, but simply find it deeply disturbing and threatening to be presented with images of Black men's bodies. Indeed, it was partly the reception of Mapplethorpe's work by the New Right, the 'vitriol and anxiety expressed in hostile attacks on Mapplethorpe's *oeuvre*' (Mercer 1993: 102), which prompted Mercer to rethink his own position on the photographs. He points out that conflicting 'readings' of the pictures are not randomly produced by different individuals but are informed by 'the social identity of the audience' (1993: 106). It is therefore necessary to consider the relationship between the text and its various audiences in order to evaluate different readings. But considering the internal meaning of a text and its effects on different audiences is not enough on its own. It is also necessary to look at the identity and intentions of the author. Mercer argues that Mapplethorpe's identity as a gay artist must be taken into account. He continues:

> As Mapplethorpe put it in an interview shortly before his death, 'At some point I started photographing black men. It was an area that hadn't been explored intensively. If you went through the history of nude male photography, there were very few black subjects. I found that I could take pictures of black men that were so subtle, and the form was so photographical.' An awareness of the exclusion of the black subject from one of the most valued canonical genres of Western art – the nude – suggests that it is both possible and necessary to reread Mapplethorpe's work as part of an artistic inquiry into the hegemonic force of a Eurocentric aesthetics which historically rendered invisible not only black people, but women, lesbians and gays and others.
>
> (Mercer 1993: 106)

So far, then, Mercer's article has served to emphasise Scott's argument that to focus solely on the 'objective' content or internal meaning of a text is inadequate – we must also consider the meanings attached to it by its audiences and by its author. But Mercer also reveals something else about textual analysis. He makes it clear that the interpretation of texts is necessarily political. Mapplethorpe died from Aids in 1989 and his work became the centre of a political controversy in the USA during 1989 and 1990, when Senator Jesse Helms led a campaign 'to prevent the National Endowment for the Arts from funding exhibitions of so called "indecent and obscene materials"' (Mercer 1993: 95). The political right has, of course, long claimed to be the champion of decency, moral order and 'family values' and firmly opposes progressive social movements. Recently, however, it has started to take on and exploit some of the arguments made by the feminist anti-pornography movement, and in both Britain and the USA, somewhat bizarre political alliances between certain feminists and the New Right have been developing around the issue of pornography. Such alliances are perceived by many as extremely dangerous. Wilson (1993), for example, observes that 'feminist fundamentalists' who present pornography as the main cause and expression of women's oppression are effectively wiping out 'almost the whole of the feminist agenda and [creating] a new moral purity movement for our new (authoritarian) times' (1993: 28). Mercer, meanwhile, argues that the New Right are making use of liberal and feminist rhetoric to prepare the ground for coercive legislation:

> Under these conditions – when, despite its initial emancipatory intentions, elements of the radical feminist anti-porn movement of the 1980s have entered into alliance with neo-conservative forces – it is not inconceivable that a reading of Robert Mapplethorpe's work as racist, however well intended, could serve the ends of the authoritarian trend supported by this new alliance of social actors.
>
> (1993: 109)

When evaluating various interpretations of the same text, researchers are confronted with the fact that different readings have different political implications. It is not just the text, but also *the interpretation of a text* which cannot be separated from the conditions of its production and its effects. In the current climate, when the Aids crisis is being manipulated to whip up homophobia, when moral conservatives are making political gains by focusing on pornography and hijacking the rhetoric and tactics of the feminist anti-pornography movement (see Segal 1993), Mercer clearly feels that to interpret Mapplethorpe's work as racist is to give succour to the homophobic 'moral majority'. This not only underlines the fact that researchers necessarily make political decisions (something many academics refuse to acknowledge) but also the fact that researchers are part of the audience of a text. They come to a text with their own social identities, their own political and moral values, and they also live and work in a particular political, social and economic context. Decisions about which cultural texts to analyse and how to interpret them therefore involve political as well as methodological choices.

Chapter 9

The practice of research

This book has been concerned not simply with the technical problems and issues associated with a range of research methods, but also with the relationship between social research and social power, with the ethical dilemmas raised by social investigation, the need for reflexivity and the relevance of social research to our daily lives. This chapter aims to reiterate these themes and spell out their implications for the practice of research. It does so primarily through reference to a piece of research which is currently being undertaken by one of the authors, Julia O'Connell Davidson, into prostitution.

RESEARCHING PROSTITUTION

At the time of writing, I am involved in a small-scale ethnographic study of a prostitute, her receptionists, her clients and a number of her 'hangers on'. The prostitute (to whom I shall refer as 'Desiree') is, her receptionists tell prospective clients, 'a beautiful brown-eyed brunnette, with a stunning figure measuring 44–26–40'. She is neither a street prostitute nor a Madam. She works from home and runs what is effectively a fairly lucrative small business, although like other small businesses, Desiree's is adversely affected by the somewhat unsteady progress of the British economy under the stewardship, at the time of writing, of the less than convincing Major Government. She provides clients with a range of services 'from a basic massage through to a full personal service, which includes everything' and 'offers a selection of toys and uniforms'. Because she alone provides sexual services to clients, and because she does not solicit men to visit her, this business is quite legal. My research with Desiree has evolved in a fairly *ad hoc* way. One of her part-time receptionists, 'Angie', was a student of mine, and knowing my interest in sex research, she arranged an interview with

Desiree for me. I did not have a clear research agenda but spent about three hours talking to her. What she told me was not only fascinating in its own right but also tied in with a number of my theoretical pre-occupations. Desiree gave me an open invitation to return, and after several weeks I did, this time with a rather sharper focus for the research.

First and foremost, I was interested in the issue of power and control. For some radical feminists, prostitution is one of the purest expressions of patriarchal domination, reducing women to nothing more than bought objects. Prostitution not only allows men to secure temporary (but direct) control over the prostitute, but also increases their existing social control over all women by developing and enhancing their powers of 'sexual aggression'. The prostitute's consent is explained primarily through reference to male hegemony. Other feminists contest this vision. They emphasise the skills and control of the prostitute in the commercial exchange itself and further hold that prostitutes effectively resist and defy male power by refusing to allow any one man ownership of their sexuality. According to Roberts, the 'whore is dangerously free' (1992: 354), enjoying both the financial and the sexual autonomy that is denied to the majority of women in patriarchal societies. My initial interview with Desiree had led me to believe that issues of power, control and consent may be rather more complex than either of these positions suggest, and I therefore wanted to use ethnographic techniques to explore some of the contradictions of control within the prostitute–client relationship. I did not intend to limit the research to simply testing out this hypothesis, however. Since very little empirical research has been conducted in this field, I believe it will produce useful descriptive data. Such research also has potential for theory-constructing. All in all, I am adopting a flexible approach rather than restricting the research to theory-testing, empirical descripton or theory-constructing *per se*.

These ambitions have implications for the actual techniques employed in the research. There would be little point in administering a formal questionnaire to Desiree and her receptionists not just because they would be a minuscule and unrepresentative sample, but also because I could hardly hope to tease out the subtle and complex contradictions which interest me with such a blunt and unresponsive instrument. Besides, as Chapter 4 showed, unless a researcher already has a fairly clear idea of the questions that need answering, the survey method is inappropriate. I have therefore employed a range of techniques, including formal, topic based interviews, informal conversations, observation, participation (as a receptionist – answering phone calls, making appointments, taking coffee to waiting clients). I am also now collecting data on clients of a more systematic kind. Because there are large numbers of clients – Desiree sees between 30 and 40 men per week – it would be too time consuming to conduct taped interviews about each one. Yet I want to know something about the range, nature and pattern of demand. Though Desiree could give me an impressionistic account, she finds it difficult to recall the exact details of every punter she saw in a week. I therefore used interviews and conversations with Desiree to develop a questionnaire that monitors the sexual services each client receives (reproduced below), and she now fills one of these in after clients leave.

There is an obvious problem with this technique, namely it relies upon Desiree, who is often very busy, remembering to fill forms out and remembering details accurately. Any data on client's marital status and employment will also have to be treated with extreme caution. Although some clients display a rather extraordinary wish to 'share' their lives with Desiree (showing her photographs of their wives or children after having received a sexual service, describing the details of their work life as she chains them up, even supplying her with a written curriculum vitae in one case 'because we don't get a chance to talk much'), common-sense suggests that many will lie or conceal the truth about such matters. Furthermore, the questionnaire – like all questionnaires – has proved to have certain limitations. It is incapable of encompassing unanticipated sexual requirements, such as rectal examinations using Deep Heat cream or watching Desiree crush a live beetle underfoot. It has also overlooked some 'extras'. Anal stimulation, for example, is included only in the 'method of achieving orgasm' category, but in practice there are clients who ask for ice cubes to be inserted in the anus as an accompaniment to penetration, or for anal stimulation as a pre-cursor to a 'hand job'. Desiree kindly makes a note of such things, but these limitations will none the less have to be borne in mind when the data is analysed and presented.

At present, I spend a day or an afternoon each week at the house, observing, participating and interviewing. I write up fieldnotes and transcribe taped interviews, code up the questionnaires and will soon begin to analyse them using SPSS (Statistical Package for the Social Sciences). But even though the research is in its infancy, it has already raised many of the key methodological, ethical and political issues which are the focus of this book.

APPROXIMATE AGE

> 20	21–30	31–40	41–50	51–60	61–70	71+

MARITAL STATUS

Has Partner	No Partner	Unknown

FREQUENCY OF VISITS

Weekly	Monthly	Less Often	Never seen before

OCCUPATION ....
METHOD OF ATTAINING ORGASM

Boob job		Penetration	
Blow job		Beating/whip	
Foot job		Anal stimulation	
Hand job (you)		Other (please specify)	
Wank (him)			

SETTING/EXTRAS

Beating/whip		Videos	
Bondage		Talk dirty (fantasy)	
Watch you with vibrator		Talk dirty (you love it)	
Cross dresser		He insults you	
Uniform		You insult him	
Shoes/strutting		Water sports	

FANTASY

You as dominatrix		You as hypersexual	
Love affair		He as lesbian	
You as object		He makes pro happy	
You as schoolgirl		He as great lover	
You as maid		He as virile (dysfunctional men)	
You as nurse		Other, please specify	

Figure 9.1 Client questionnaire

DEGREE OF SPECIFICATION

Client has fixed idea – closely scripted	Client has general idea – loose role play, improvised	Client has no clear idea – you devise role & script

HOW DEMANDING/DRAINING?

Not very – 1	2	3	4	5 – Extremely

Any other comments?

Figure 9.1 (continued) Client questionnaire

Sampling

Desiree, her receptionists and her 'hangers on' are an opportunistic sample, and it would be impossible for me to make generalised claims about all such prostitutes and their receptionists on the basis of interviews with these people. It would be better to broaden out the research by interviewing other women operating the same kind of set up. But this is extremely difficult to arrange. There are magazines and newspapers which advertise their phone numbers, but so far I have found it impossible to get past their receptionists, who are highly skilled at putting an end to 'nuisance' and 'time-wasting' calls. Receptionists treat a phone call from a woman with particular suspicion, since, Angie tells me, such calls are generally from other prostitutes doing a little market research on prices. In any event, a receptionist is hardly likely to agree to an interview on her employer's account. I could ask a male colleague or friend to phone and make a bogus appointment, thereby obtaining the addresses of other prostitutes, but wonder whether this would be ethical or even an effective way of securing access. I will probably have to rely on snowballing or volunteer methods to expand my sample, and there is thus little prospect of my ever being able to advance *generalised* claims about home-working prostitutes on the basis of the research.

The lack of a large or randomly selected or completely representative sample does not make the research worthless, however. To discover the ways in which Desiree exercises control within the prostitute–client relationship is informative and useful whether or not she is typical of *all* self-employed prostitutes, for example. Likewise, though the sample of clients is not a random selection of all men who visit prostitutes (Desiree's advertisement will attract a sample with particular sexual interests and from particular geographical locations), information about the nature and pattern of these particular men's demand for sexual services can make a valuable contribution to an area about which very little empirical data have been collected.

Ethical issues

Although I have full and informed consent from Desiree, her receptionists and her 'hangers on', my research involves covert observation of her clients and this raises some of the ethical issues which were discussed in Chapters 6 and 7. When I answer the phone and offer to provide details of services offered and prices charged, the men making enquiries (often masturbating as they do so) take me to be either a prostitute or a receptionist. Clients do not know that a sociologist is listening to their conversations and rows with Desiree in the hallway, or observing their fleeting forms as they run from the house having, as Desiree puts it, 'shot their load'. They have not consented to Desiree imparting information about their sexual preferences, commenting extensively and wittily on their physical and psychological defects. When I take coffee to a waiting punter, he is not aware that I am making mental notes on his presentation of self, or that I will later be told whether he is a cross-dresser or a masochist or suffers from erection problems – or indeed all three.

It could be argued that I am invading these men's privacy and that, since I am firmly convinced few would give their informed consent, this is unethical. Yet I find myself untroubled by my uninvited intrusion into these men's world. This is mainly because the clients remain completely anonymous to me, and I am not therefore in a position to secure, store or disclose any information which could harm them. Moreover, Desiree has willingly offered to provide me with the details of their interaction, and since this knowledge belongs to her (in the sense that it is part of her lived experience, not a private experience of the client's and that she has not entered into any formal agreement with the client not to talk about their interaction), it seems to me that she is entitled to do what she likes with it. I recognise that purists could still make a case against my research practice. Some of the criticisms levelled against Humphreys' observational research in public toilets could also be levelled against me (although I hasten to add that I have no intention of noting the licence plates of punters' cars in order to track them down for interviews). But such purism is a luxury that most researchers cannot afford. Virtually all social research is intrusive and exploitative to some degree, because though researchers may truly believe that their work is in the *interests* of their human subjects, it is seldom undertaken at the *behest* of these subjects and rarely, if ever, is it undertaken without a view to the professional advancement of the researcher. It therefore inevitably poses moral dilemmas, which, at the end of the day, can only be resolved through reference to the researcher's own moral and political values.

I feel a certain commitment towards Desiree and her receptionists, for example. I do not imagine for a moment that my research will help them as individuals, but I absolutely do not want it to damage them in any way. I would not want to deceive them about the research aims and feel obliged to allow them to make an informed choice about whether, and how much, to participate in the research. This is partly because I actually like and respect these women, and partly because I have no moral or political objection to the way they live their lives – rather the reverse. Desiree is an able, intelligent, independent and ambitious woman who lives in a society that does not value such qualities in women very highly. I am sympathetic towards her desire for financial and emotional autonomy, even though I personally would not wish to achieve it in the way she has chosen and have my doubts about whether she will ultimately attain it by engaging in commercial sex. But this sense of commitment does not extend towards her clients. I have no wish to advance their interests through the research, no personal liking and no real sympathy for them. I have a professional obligation to preserve and protect their anonymity and to ensure that they are not harmed by my research, but I feel no qualms about being less than frank with them, and no obligation to allow them to choose whether or not their actions are recorded.

In fact, my lack of sympathy for punters as a collective group actually raises another, rather different, set of ethical problems. Desiree introduced me to, then arranged an interview with, a man who I shall call 'Dick'. Dick's status at Desiree's house is ambiguous. He is useful to her in the sense of doing bits of DIY, walking the dogs, shopping and so on, but he is also a rather sad and lonely man, who might variously be described as an odd-ball, a misfit, perhaps a bit 'simple'. He does not buy sexual services from Desiree, but hangs around her, apparently dependent upon her in a number of ways. Though he does not buy sex in Britain, he takes an annual holiday in Thailand, where he spends three or four weeks 'going through' as many prostitutes as he can. Desiree suggested that I might find it interesting to talk to him. I chatted to him once informally, and then conducted a two-hour, topic-based interview with him. It was certainly interesting, but I also found talking to him the most difficult and unpleasant experience I have ever had as a researcher. What he told me sickened and disturbed me. He spoke of the Thai prostitutes (many probably only 16 years of age or less) as nothing more than objects. He described, in profoundly racist terms, how the Otherness of 'Orientals' made these 'girls' especially appealing to him. He told me that the fact these women are from a 'Third World' country makes him feel rich and powerful and how 'fantastic' it is for the single man to get the choice of thousands of young and beautiful girls. He told me that he effectively haggles with human life, using safer sex as bargaining counter by offering them less money for sex with a condom. He described his experiences with what he terms 'brand new' girls (those who have only just started to work as prostitutes) how they emerge from the shower clutching a towel to shield their naked bodies and try to get under the bedclothes without him seeing them – 'I soon put a stop to that. I rip the towel off them and chuck it across the room'. He described visits to brothels where women who are effectively owned by the pimp sit behind a glass screen with numbers round their necks waiting to be bought by men like Dick, and taken to be used and abused in anonymous hotel rooms.

Obviously, Dick would hardly have continued to disclose such information if I had openly expressed my horror and disgust. To maintain the rapport which makes an interview possible, I felt constrained to appear neutral and non-judgemental. This meant I was confronted by the dilemma which Scully faced in her research with rapists – neutrality could be interpreted as a signal of approval, but disagreement or negative comments could destroy rapport (Scully 1990: 19). To Dick, I am an educated woman of relatively high social standing – a university lecturer. If I appear to accept his appallingly callous attitudes towards and exploitation of these women, will he see it as somehow more legitimate? Am I endorsing his activities by failing to outrightly and vigorously condemn them? For me, this is a far more serious ethical dilemma than any issue about invading Desiree's clients' privacy. I cannot claim to have resolved this problem, even to my own satisfaction. In defence of having thus far failed to roundly condemn him, I would argue as follows. My initial work with Desiree makes me think that the whole question of what exactly it is that men buy from prostitutes, and what exactly it is that prostitutes sell, is highly problematic. Though ostensibly a commercial exchange, because sex is so powerfully attached to ideologies about gender, biology and the proper relations between the sexes, the transaction between prostitute and client is not a simple market exchange. The interview with Dick made me begin to think about broadening my research to explore such ideas in more depth. The fact that he (and thousands of other men) apparently find it necessary or desirable to travel to Thailand to buy something from women, many of whom are kept as virtual slaves (thereby helping to sustain and reproduce the conditions of their oppression) seems to me to be worth investigating further. For the time being, therefore, I need Dick. He has information and contacts that may be invaluable to such research and I do not wish to alienate him by fully expressing my views.

I am not entirely happy with this formulation, but I do not believe that my failure to condemn him is actively encouraging him to persist with his activities. Moreover, if we insist that researchers are morally obliged to directly challenge the sexism and racism of their subjects during the research *process* (rather than in the work they publish), we will make it virtually impossible to undertake empirical research with such people. As a researcher, then, I can justify presenting a neutral facade to Dick and men like him. As a private individual, listening to such offensive views without attacking them leaves me with a sense of discomfort.

Feminist methodology

The above discussion can also be used to underline the points made about feminist methodology in previous chapters. Our position has been that whilst the feminist critique of orthodox social science research provides important and valuable insights, claims for a distinctive feminist methodology are problematic. Feminist methodologists are not the only, and are by no means the first, people to call for research which is empathetic, non-hierarchical and non-exploitative. But this emphasis is especially difficult when coupled with an insistence that research should be emancipatory. To fully understand women's subordination it is necessary to study not just women, but also the men who oppress them. Of course, no feminist would recommend a non-hierarchical and non-exploitative approach to such research, insisting that I should enter into a genuinely caring and empathetic relationship with Dick, for example. (It is worth noting that the fact he actually sat back, spread his legs and started masturbating through his trousers towards the end of the interview made it difficult for me to go through even the most orthodox, polite, end-of-interview formalities.) Most would presumably agree that my approach is justifiable under the circumstances, and merely insist that my emotional responses to Dick (and to everyone else) should be discussed and included in written accounts of the research. I should be aware that 'being alive involves us in having emotions and involvements; and in doing research we cannot leave behind what is to be a person alive in the world' (Stanley and Wise 1993: 161). In other words, I should be reflexive. But again, there is nothing unique or distinctive about feminist methodologist's stress on the need for reflexivity in social research.

What is more distinctive, perhaps, is the way in which feminists like Stanley and Wise use and celebrate the notion of 'experience'. We are told that women experience reality differently from men; that women have not been allowed to 'name' their own experience:

> These experiences have been named for us by men; but men have used what Shiela Rowbotham has called the 'language of theory' and not the 'language of experience' (1973). Our experience . . . is removed from experience altogether by being cast in abstract and theoretical terms. We need a woman's language, a language of experience. And this must necessarily come from our exploration of the personal, the everyday, and what we experience – women's lived experiences.
>
> (Stanley and Wise 1993: 146)

Feminist research is about exploring and documenting women's lived experiences, they say. We should not allow the 'language of theory' to translate and transform women's experience into the 'abstract concepts' beloved by males. In other words, women's accounts of their lived experience are to be taken as valid (even, presumably, if they directly contradict each other) and the researcher's task is to simply accept and document them. Any theoretical analysis of these accounts would be an example of male 'conceptual imperialism' (Stanley and Wise 1993: 162). The suggestion that the application of theoretical concepts is a peculiarly male practice or capacity and that feminist researchers should therefore avoid imposing theoretical categories on the data they gather seems as facile to me as the idea that because most published poetry is by men and so reflects masculine preoccupations, it is a literary form which is incapable of embracing women's experiences and that aspiring women poets should therefore stick to writing greetings card verses.

Equally important, so far as my research with Desiree goes, is the fact that she herself has several different versions of reality. She has an emotional life which shifts and changes, and her accounts of the reality of her work shift and change with it. Moreover, Desiree cannot tell me or accurately describe *everything* about her lived experience. I say this not because I see myself as a scientist, expert or superior being, but simply because people's knowledge of their work life or daily routine rarely takes a very precise or exact form. If a researcher asked me to say how many students knocked on my office door each week, or to sit and describe a typical working day, the information I would give would be fairly vague and impressionistic, because I do not keep a systematic record of such things, not even a mental one. As a researcher, I therefore need to do more than simply ask and accept Desiree's account of her experience. I must try to check it against other versions of reality – that obtained by observation and by systematic monitoring of her clients, that provided by her receptionists and 'hangers on', that achieved through my own observations. In other words, I need to adopt a form of triangulation to check the validity of any one account of her 'lived experience'.

Finally, I would argue that as a researcher who wishes to try to explain events, experiences and processes as well as to describe them, I need to employ theory and to apply theoretical concepts to the material I gather. The two different feminist positions on prostitution which I outlined above, for example, are useful in focusing attention on issues of power, consent and control. They provide a conceptual framework within which I can try to understand some of the stories which Desiree tells me about clients and my observations of events in her house. If I did not apply such concepts to, say, the occasion on which Desiree exacted her revenge on a difficult client by beating him far longer and far harder than he actually wanted, then the accounts I produced would be nothing more than journalistic descriptions along the lines of 'A Day in the Brothel' or perhaps similar to extracts from Desiree's own diary, if she happened to keep one.

Reflexivity

This book has argued strongly for reflexivity in the research process, that is, an awareness of the ways in which the researcher, as an individual with a given social identity, impacts upon that process. Even at this early stage of the research, I am conscious of the fact that my identity as a woman affects the data I collect. To begin with, it is only because I am woman that I am able to participate as a receptionist. A male researcher would not be able to answer the phone without putting Desiree's business at risk, and even if he did, men would be unlikely to say the kind of things that they say to women receptionists (asking for example, whether they will be able to 'come in her face', whether they need to bring a vibrator because they are 'quite small, only four inches' and so on). A male researcher could hardly show punters in or give them cups of coffee and chat to them. In other words, there are parts of the social world which are invisible to men simply because they are men, just as there are certain experiences which no woman is ever likely to have first hand.

There are, no doubt, male researchers who could establish a rapport and obtain worthwhile information in the same setting, but I do also believe that it is easier for me, as a woman, to establish a rapport with Desiree and her receptionists, and that they would probably tone down the extremely crushing remarks they make about male sexuality and men in general if I were a male researcher. I have already observed, however, that making contact with other prostitutes in order to widen the sample might be easier to achieve were I a man. The fact that I am a woman also makes me wary of taking up certain offers and 'leads'. I am more reluctant than a male researcher would be to interview one of Dick's friends in any setting other than the safety of Desiree's house or my own office, even though this increases the risk of him refusing to be interviewed. It is likewise important to note that both Desiree and I are white women. This common 'racialised' identity also has an effect on the data that is gathered. On the one hand, white people often feel able to express views in front of other whites that they would not give voice to in front of a Black person, on the other, white people sometimes reveal sides of themselves to Black people that remain largely invisible to white audiences. I am also aware that if I obtain access to interview Black women working as prostitutes, my 'racialised' identity will impact upon the data I gather.

Furthermore, my class and gender identity probably combine to inhibit Desiree's male hangers on. Take Dick. He may have agreed to talk to me because I am female and because I am 'from the University'. But I am sure that my class identity led him to modify the account of his activities he gave, and to conceal certain things from me. He had previously told Angie, for example, that he did not bother to use condoms with 'girls' he had 'been with before' or 'girls who looked clean'. When I asked him about safer sex, he told me very firmly that he *always* used condoms – 'In fact, I introduce meself to the girls as Mr Condom' he said (and of course, this itself was later contradicted by his statement to the effect that he bargained with condoms). His estimates of how many prostitutes he had sex with on his last visit to Thailand also fluctuated according to who asked him. Desiree was told 50, Angie (who makes her disapproval and disgust for his activities more than evident) was told 40. Dick told me that he had 'gone through' 35. I assume that he would present himself differently again to a male researcher, and very differently to 'the guys' who accompany him on his trips to Thailand.

My class and gender identity as well as my personality also affect the research in other ways. One recurrent problem which Desiree faces stems from the fact that many men obtain enormous sexual excitement by simply entering a brothel and seeing a real, live prostitute. In the past such men would arrive for an appointment, then either sneak into the toilet and wank off, or simply meet her then leave to have a much enhanced wank in their car without paying anything at all. To stop this happening, Desiree instituted a system whereby the receptionists only give her address when clients book a definite appointment, and she charges a set fee for the appointment whether or not they actually receive a massage or sexual service. In other words, once a man turns up on the doorstep, he will not be allowed to leave until he has paid the appointment fee. This, of course, can lead to conflict. The would-be wanker will assert that he did not make an appointment, but called on the off-chance, or that he has no money on him. Now Desiree and her receptionists strike me as tough women. They do not appear to feel intimidated by such men, in fact they often find such encounters hugely entertaining. But I am not renowned for having a fearless disposition, and my version of the reality of such conflicts, my estimation of the degree of aggression being expressed by each party, and even my assessment of Desiree and her receptionists as 'tough', are probably coloured by my own past experiences of verbal and physical conflict. This again underlines the importance of triangulation. I make a point of checking my perceptions of these situations by asking Desiree and her receptionists how they perceived such events.

There are aspects of my social identity and personality which also affect the length and style of interviewing. I curtailed my interview with Dick when he began to masturbate, for example. Another interviewer might have been willing to persist (or to ask him to desist). Other people might also have adopted a more confrontational style of interviewing, directly challenging him on some of his views, and have managed to do so without completely destroying the rapport. My personal interviewing style has always been characterised more by sweet hypocrisy, plenty of nodding and meaningless affirmative noises than by pushy, challenging or incisive questioning. Nuances in interviewing style can have as much to do with personality and self-presentation as they have to do with adherence to a particular methodological school of thought.

The role of luck and chance

Handbooks on research methods seldom mention what seems to me to be something that is absolutely critical to the research process, namely good fortune. I was more than lucky to know Angie, for without her I would not be doing this research and I was fortunate that the prostitute she happened to know happened to be Desiree. These two women's perspicacity, combined with their enthusiasm for the project, makes it possible for me, as a researcher, to find out more than I could possibly hope to discover without them. Desiree's willingness to fill out questionnaires (she requisitions more as they run out) and to have me hanging around her house seems to me unbelievably fortuitous. She is even 'sounding out' various regulars to see whether they would agree to an interview with me. She is, in fact, little short of a dream research subject and I am enormously grateful to her. There is no doubt in my mind that no matter how polished my research skills or how carefully devised my research strategy, without this good fortune, my findings would be more limited.

For me, this is not the first time that luck and chance have exerted an influence over the progress of a research project. My research on employment relations in the privatised water industry (see O'Connell Davidson 1993) was facilitated by the fact that the senior manager who first granted me access to the organisation left the company soon afterwards. The overall effect of this chance event was that I was left with almost unlimited access and freedom to move around the company, interviewing those people I wished to interview, without any accountability to management. I somehow got 'lost'. My presence was accepted, but no one asked to see what I was producing or prevented me from exploring 'sensitive' areas. The fact that luck (or bad luck) and chance can sometimes play a pivotal role in the research process is another reason for emphasising the importance of adopting a flexible approach to research. If researchers are too rigid about implementing a preconceived plan, they may miss opportunities to broaden, deepen or otherwise enhance their data.

POLITICS, POWER AND SOCIAL RESEARCH

This book has stressed the centrality of politics and power to the process and practice of social research. At the most basic level, these issues affect what is researched, by whom and how, through the medium of funding. I intend to put together an application for funding to extend and broaden my research on prostitution. Whether it is succesful depends in part upon the importance that is attached to such research by various funding agencies, as well as upon government policy in relation to funding academic research more generally. At present, I am able to do the research because I am fortunate enough to have a job which both requires and allows me to undertake research. In the current climate, however, most British academics are finding that the government's policy of expanding student intake without simultaneously expanding the universities' resources makes it increasingly difficult to pursue their research interests.

As has been seen, power and politics also intrude on the research process in other ways. My moral and political values mean that I approach the issue of prostitution from a particular angle and view it through a particular lens, for example. Researchers with different values would not necessarily ask the same questions or analyse the data produced in the same way. Moreover, the researcher's social identity (in terms of gender, 'racialisation' and class) affects the research process. Orthodox methodologists tend to overlook the fact that the researcher's relative power in relation to funding bodies, other academics, gate-keepers and the subjects of the research, impacts upon the kind of knowledge that is eventually produced. It is these connections between social identity, social power and social research which lead us to emphasise the need for reflexivity. For as Okely puts it:

> In its fullest sense, reflexivity forces us to think through the conse-
> quences of our relations with others, whether it be conditions of
> reciprocity, asymmetry or potential exploitation. There are choices to
> be made in the field, within relationships and in the final text.
>
> (1992: 24)

Having said this, it is important to reiterate the fact that although social research is necessarily infused by the moral and political values of the researcher, it is not necessarily, and should not be, the simple rehearsal of prejudice. There are better and worse ways of doing research, and if it is undertaken critically, reflexively and competently, a more accurate picture of social reality will be produced. Of course, how this picture is then interpreted, what its implications are taken to be and so on, are moral and political issues.

Finally, we want to return to our emphasis on the interplay between social research and common-sense thinking (social researchers are members of society and therefore draw on a stock of common-sense knowledge and normative and moral values, their research feeds back into this stock of knowledge and value systems), and the fact that social research makes a significant impact not only upon policy but also upon ideological constructs. It follows from this that social research can contribute to social transformation as well as to the maintenance of the existing status quo. A concern with producing critical and reflexive social research may also allow us to begin to transcend the sterile dualisms between objectivism and relativism, structural determinism and methodological individualism, quantitative and qualitative approaches. Marx observed that philosophers had merely interpreted the world, the point, however, was to change it. Of course, all the methods that have been described in this book can be used to support and reproduce existing structures of inequality, but they can all also be employed in the struggle to reveal, challenge and change them. Our hope is that this book will be of some practical use to those readers whose desire is for change.

References

Arber, S. (1990) 'Revealing women's health: re-analysing the general household survey' in H. Roberts (ed.) *Women's Health Counts*, London: Routledge.

Asante, M. (1990) *Kemet, Afrocentricity and Knowledge*, Trenton, NJ: Africa World Press.

Assiter, A. and Carol, A. (1993) *Bad Girls and Dirty Pictures*, London: Pluto Press.

Atkinson, J. (1971) 'Suicide statistics', in A. Giddens (ed.) *The Sociology of Suicide*, London: Frank Cass.

Atkinson, P. (1990) *The Ethnographic Imagination: Textual Reconstructions of Reality*, London: Routledge.

Ball, S. (1981) *Beachside Comprehensive: A Case Study of Secondary Schooling*, Cambridge: Cambridge University Press.

Becker, H. (1963) *Outsiders*, Glencoe: Free Press.

Bejin, A. (1985a) 'The decline of the Psycho-analyst and the rise of the sexologist' in P. Aries and A. Bejin (eds) *Western Sexuality: Practice and Precept in Past and Present Times*, Oxford: Basil Blackwell.

Bejin, A. (1985b) 'The influence of the sexologists and sexual democracy' in P. Aries and A. Bejin (eds) *Western Sexuality: Practice and Precept in Past and Present Times*, Oxford: Basil Blackwell.

Belliveau, F. and Richter, L. (1970) *Understanding Human Sexual Inadequacy*, London: Hodder & Stoughton.

Bennetto, J. (1992) 'Gang rape of men "seldom by gays"', *Independent on Sunday*, 18 October.

Berelson, B. (1952) *Content Analysis in Communications Research*, New York: Free Press.

Bergler, E. and Kroger, W. (1954) *Kinsey's Myth of Female Sexuality: The Medical Facts*, New York: Grune & Stratton.

Bleier, R. (1984) *Science and Gender: A Critique of Biology and Its Theories on Women*, New York: Pergamon Press.

Bocock, R. (1986), *Freud and Modern Society*, Berkshire: Van Nostrand Reinhold.

Bruyn, S. (1966) *The Human Perspective in Sociology*, New Jersey: Prentice Hall.

Bryman, A. (1988) *Quantity and Quality in Social Research*, London: Unwin.

Bryman, A. and Cramer, D. (1990) *Quantitative Data Analysis for Social Scientists*, London: Routledge.

Budd, R., Thorp, R. and Donohew, L. (1967) *Content Analysis of Communications*, London: Collier-Macmillan.

Bulmer. M. (1982) *The Uses of Social Research: Social Investigation in Public Policy-Making*, London: Allen & Unwin.

Burgess, R. (1983) *Experiencing Comprehensive Education: A Study of Bishop McGregor School*, London: Methuen.

Burgess, R. (1984) *In The Field*, London: Allen & Unwin.

Callaway, H. (1992) 'Ethnography and experience: gender implications in fieldwork and texts' in J. Okely and H. Callaway (eds) *Anthropology and Autobiography*, London: Routledge.

Cannon, L., Higginbotham, E. and Leung, M. (1991) 'Race and class bias in qualitative research on women' in M. Fonow and J. Cook (eds) *Beyond Methodology: Feminist Scholarship as Lived Research*, Bloomington: Indiana University Press.

Chartham, R. (1971) *Advice to Women*, London: Tandem.

Cicourel, A. (1976) *The Social Organisation of Juvenile Justice*, London: Heinemann.

Connell, R. (1992) 'A very straight gay: masculinity, homosexual experience and the dynamics of gender', *American Sociological Review*, vol. 57, pp. 735–51.

Cromwell, P., Olson, J. and Avery, D. (1991), *Breaking and Entering: An Ethnographic Study of Burglary*, Newbury Park, CA: Sage.

Davis, A. (1982) *Women, Race and Class*, London: The Women's Press.

Demos, J. (1982) *Entertaining Satan: Witchcraft and the Culture of Early New England*, Oxford: Oxford University Press.

Denscombe, M. and Aubrook, L. (1992) 'It's just another piece of schoolwork: The ethics of questionnaire research on pupils in schools', *British Educational Research Journal*, vol. 18, pp. 113–31.

Denzin, N. (1970) *The Research Act*, Chicago: Aldine.

Denzin, N. (1990) 'Researching alcoholics and alcoholism in American society' in N. Denzin (ed.) *Studies in Symbolic Interaction*, no. 11, pp. 81–107.

de Vaus, D. (1991) *Surveys in Social Research*, London: UCL Press.

Durkheim, E. (1964) [1895] *The Rules of Sociological Method*, Glencoe, Illinois: The Free Press.

Durkheim, E. (1952) [1897] *Suicide*, London: Routledge & Kegan Paul.

Dworkin, A. (1987) *Intercourse*, London: Secker & Warburg.

Edwards, S. (1981) *Female Sexuality and the Law*, Oxford: Martin Robertson.

Ehrenreich, B. and English, D. (1976) *Complaints and Disorders: The Sexual Politics of Sickness*, London: Writers and Readers Publishing Cooperative.

Eisenbud, J. and Mead, M. (1948) 'Kinsey report scored from social and psychological point of view', *New York Times*, March 31.

Ellis, Havelock (1987) 'Love and Pain' in S. Jeffreys (ed.) *The Sexuality Debates*, New York: Routledge & Kegan Paul.

Farganis, S. (1989) 'Feminism and the reconstruction of social science' in A. Jaggar and S. Bordo (eds) *Gender/Body/Knowledge: Feminist Reconstructions of Being and Knowing*, New Brunswick: Rutgers University Press.

Fielding, N. (1981) *The National Front*, London: Routledge.

Fielding, N. (1982) 'Observational research on the National Front' in M. Bulmer (ed.) *Social Research Ethics*, London: Macmillan.

Flandrin, J-L. (1985) 'Sex and married life in the early Middle Ages: the Church's teaching and behavioural reality' in P. Aries and A. Bejin (eds) *Western Sexuality: Practice and Precept in Past and Present Times*, Oxford: Basil Blackwell.

Fonow, M. and Cook, J. (1991) *Beyond Methodology: Feminist Scholarship as Lived Research*, Bloomington: Indiana University Press.

Freud, S. (1974) *Two Short Accounts of Psycho-Analysis*, Harmondsworth: Penguin.

Gebhard, P. and Johnson, A. (1979) *The Kinsey Data: Marginal Tabulations of the 1938 to 1963 Interviews Conducted by the Institute for Sex Research*, Philadelphia: Saunders.

Geerz, C. (1973) *The Interpretation of Cultures*, New York: Basic Books.

Gelsthorpe, L. (1992) 'Response to Martin Hammersley's paper', *Sociology*, vol. 26 no. 2, pp. 213–18.

Giddens, A. (1978) *Durkheim*, Glasgow: Fontana.

Giddens, A. (1982) *New Rules of Sociological Method*, London: Hutchinson.

Giddens, A. (1984) *The Constitution of Society*, Cambridge: Polity Press.

Glaser, B. and Strauss, A. (1965) *Awareness of Dying*, Chicago: Aldine.

Glaser, B. and Strauss, A. (1967) *The Discovery of Grounded Theory*, Chicago: Aldine.

Glasgow University Media Group (1976) *Bad News, vol. 1*, London: Routledge & Kegan Paul.

Glesne, C. and Peshkin, A. (1992) *Becoming Qualitative Researchers: An Introduction*, New York: Longman.

Goffman, E. (1959) *The Presentation of Self in Everyday Life*, Harmondsworth: Penguin.

Goffman, E. (1961) *Asylums*, Harmondsworth: Penguin.

Gold, R. (1958) 'Roles in sociological field observations', *Social Forces*, vol. 36, pp. 217–23.

Government Statisticians' Collective (1993) 'How official statistics are produced: views from the inside' in M. Hammersley (ed) *Social Research: Philosophy, Politics and Practice*, London: Sage.

Griffiths, D., Irvine, J. and Miles, I. (1979) 'Social statistics: towards a radical science' in Irvine, J., Miles, I. and Evans, J. (eds) *Demystifying Social Statistics*, London: Pluto Press.

Gummesson, E. (1991) *Qualitative Methods in Management Research*, London: Sage.

Hammersley, M. (1985) 'From ethnography to theory: a programme and paradigm in the sociology of education', *Sociology*, vol. 19, pp. 244–59.

Hammersley, M. (1990) *Reading Ethnographic Research*, London: Longman.

Hammersley, M. and Atkinson, P. (1989) *Ethnography: Principles in Practice*, London: Routledge.

Hammond, M., Howarth, J. and Keat, R. (1991) *Understanding Phenomenology*, Oxford: Basil Blackwell.

Hargreaves, D. (1967) *Social Relations in a Secondary School*, London: Routledge.

Harre, R. (1979), *Social Being*, Oxford: Basil Blackwell.

Harvey, L. (1990) *Critical Social Research*, London: Allen & Unwin.

Herman, J (1981) *Father–daughter Incest*, Cambridge: Harvard University Press.

Hessler, R. (1992) *Social Research Methods*, St. Paul: West Publishing.

Hickson, M., Roebuck, J. and Murty, K. (1990) 'Creative triangulation: Toward a methodology for studying social types', *Studies in Symbolic Interaction*, vol. 11, pp. 103–27.

Hill Collins, P. (1991) 'Learning from the outsider within: the sociological significance of Black feminist thought' in M. Fonow and J. Cook (eds) *Beyond Methodology: Feminist Scholarship as Lived Research*, Bloomington: Indiana University Press.

Hindess, B. (1973) *The Use of Official Statistics in Sociology*, London: Macmillan.

Hochschild, A. (1983) *The Managed Heart*, Berkeley: University of California Press.

Holsti, O. (1969) *Content Analysis for the Social Sciences and Humanities*, Massachusetts: Addison-Wesley.

Homan, R. (1991), *The Ethics of Social Research*, Harlow: Longman.

Hughes, J. (1990) *The Philosophy of Social Research*, Harlow: Longman.

Humphreys, L. (1975) *Tearoom Trade: Impersonal Sex in Public Places*, Chicago: Aldine.

Irvine, J., Miles, I. and Evans, J. (eds) (1979) *Demystifying Social Statistics*, London: Pluto Press.

Isay, R. (1993) *Being Homosexual: Gay Men and their Development*, Harmondsworth: Penguin.

Jackson, M. (1984) 'Sex Research and the Construction of Sexuality: A Tool of Male Supremacy?' in L. Coveny, M. Jackson, S. Jeffreys, L. Kaye and P. Mahoney (eds) *The Sexuality Papers: Male Sexuality and the Social Control of Women*, London: Hutchinson.

Jackson, M. (1987) '"Facts of Life" or the Eroticization of Women's Oppression? Sexology and the Social Construction of Heterosexuality' in P. Caplan (ed.) *The Cultural Construction of Sexuality*, London: Tavistock.

Jaget, C. (1980) *Prostitutes – Our Life*, Bristol: Falling Wall Press.

Jaggar, A. (1989) 'Love and Knowledge: Emotion in feminist epistemology' in A. Jaggar and S. Bordo (eds) *Gender/Body/Knowledge: Feminist Reconstructions of Being and Knowing*, New Brunswick: Rutgers University Press.

Jeffreys, S. (1990) *Anticlimax*, London: The Women's Press.

Jodelet, D. (1991) *Madness and Social Representations*, Hemel Hempstead: Harvester Wheatsheaf.

Keat, R. (1979) 'Positivism and statistics in social science' in J. Irvine, I. Miles and J. Evans (eds) *Demystifying Social Statistics*, London: Pluto Press.

King, A. (1993) 'Mystery and imagination: the case of pornography effects studies' in A. Assiter and A. Carol (eds) *Bad Girls and Dirty Pictures*, London: Pluto Press.

Kinsey, A., Pomeroy, W. and Martin, C. (1948) *Sexual Behavior in the Human Male*, Philadelphia: W. B. Saunders.

Kinsey, A., Pomeroy, W., Martin, C. and Gebhard, P. (1953) *Sexual Behavior in the Human Female*, Philadelphia: W. B. Saunders.

Kitsuse, J. and Cicourel, A. (1963) 'A note on the uses of official statistics', *Social Problems*, vol. 11, pp. 131–9.

Krafft-Ebing, (1914) *Psychopathia Sexualis*, 14th edn, Stuttgart: Enke.

Krippendorff, K. (1980) *Content Analysis: An Introduction to its Methodology*, London: Sage.

Kuhn, T. (1970) *The Structure of Scientific Revolutions*, Chicago: University of Chicago Press.

Kulis, S., Miller, K., Axelrod, M. and Gordon, L. (1986) 'Minority representation of US departments', ASA Footnotes, vol. 14, no. 3.

Lacey, C. (1966) 'Some sociological concomitants of academic streaming in a grammar school', *British Journal of Sociology*, vol. 17, pp. 245–62.

Laqueur, T. (1990) *Making Sex: Body and Gender from the Greeks to Freud*, Cambridge: Harvard University Press.

Layder, D. (1993) *New Strategies in Social Research*, Cambridge: Polity Press.

Layder, D. (1994) *Understanding Social Theory*, London: Sage.

Levine, M. and Siegel, K. (1992) 'Unprotected sex: understanding gay men's participation' in J. Huber and B. Schneider (eds) *The Social Context of Aids*, London: Sage.

Lewins, F. (1992) *Social Science Methodology*, Melbourne: Macmillan Education Australia.

Lewinsohn, R. (1958) *A History of Sexual Customs*, London: Longmans.

Lloyd, C. and Walmsley, R. (1989) *Changes in Rape Offences and Sentencing*, Home Office Research Study 105, London: HMSO.

Lofland, J. (1971) *Analysing Social Settings*, Belmont, CA: Wadsworth.

Lukes, S. (1978) 'The underdetermination of theory by data', Aristotelian Society, Supplementary vol., LII, pp. 93–107.

Macdonald, J. (1971) *Rape: Offenders and Their Victims*, Illinois: Charles C. Thomas.

Macfarlane, A. (1990) 'Official Statistics and women's health and illness' in H. Roberts (ed.) *Women's Health Counts*, London: Routledge.

McKeganey, N., Barnard, M. and Bloor, M. (1990) 'A comparison of HIV-related risk behaviour and risk reduction between female street working prostitutes and male rent boys in Glasgow', *Sociology of Health and Illness*, vol. 12, pp. 274–92.

Magee, B. (1973), *Popper*, London: Fontana.

Malamuth, N. (1986) 'Sexual arousal in response to aggression: Ideological, aggressive and sexual correlates', *Journal of Personality and Social Psychology*, vol. 50.

Malinowski, B. (1929) *The Sexual Life of Savages in North-Western Melanesia*, London: Routledge & Kegan Paul.

Manning, P. (1992) *Erving Goffman and Modern Sociology*, Cambridge: Polity Press.

Mapplethorpe, R. (1982) *Black Males*, Amsterdam: Gallerie Jurka.

Mapplethorpe, R. (1986) *The Black Book*, Munich: Schirme-Mosel.

Marsh, C. (1982) *The Survey Method: The Contribution of Surveys to Sociological Explanation*, London: Allen & Unwin.

Marx, K. (1980) 'Preface to a contribution to the critique of political economy' in *Marx and Engels, Selected Works, vol. 1*, London: Lawrence & Wishart.

Masson, J. (1984) *Freud, The Assault on Truth: Freud's Suppression of the Seduction Theory*, London: Faber & Faber.

Masters, W. and Johnson, V. (1966) *Human Sexual Response*, Boston: Little Brown & Co.

Matthews, E. (1956) *Right from the Start: How a Baby Comes into the World*, London: Rockliff Publishing Corporation.

May, T. (1993) *Social Research: Issues, Methods and Process*, Buckingham: Open University Press.

Mayhew, P., Elliot, D. and Dowds, L. (1989), *The 1988 British Crime Survey*, A Home Office Research and Planning Unit Report, London: HMSO.

Mayntz, R., Holm, K. and Hoebner, P. (1969) *Introduction to Empirical Sociology*, Harmondsworth: Penguin.

Medea, A. and Thompson, K. (1974), *Against Rape*, New York: Farrar, Straus and Giroux.

Mercer, K. (1993) 'Just looking for trouble: Robert Mapplethorpe and fantasies of race' in L. Segal and M. McIntosh (eds) *Sex Exposed: Sexuality and the Pornography Debate*, New Brunswick: Rutgers University Press.

Merton, R. (1967) *On Theoretical Sociology*, New York: Free Press.

Mezey, G. and King, M. (1992) *Male Victims of Sexual Assaults*, Oxford: Oxford University Press.

Miles, I. and Irvine, J. (1979) 'The critique of official statistics' in J. Irvine, I. Miles and J. Evans (eds) *Demystifying Social Statistics*, London: Pluto.

Miles, N. and Huberman, A. (1984) *Qualitative Data Analysis*, Beverly Hills: Sage.

Milgram, S. (1974) *Obedience to Authority*, London: Tavistock.

Millman, M. and Kanter, R. (1987) 'Introduction to another voice: feminist perspectives on social life and social science' in S. Harding (ed.) *Feminism and Methodology*, Milton Keynes: Open University Press.

Mitchell, J. (1979) *Psychoanalysis and Feminism*, Harmondsworth: Penguin.

Moser, C. and Kalton, G. (1979) *Survey Methods in Social Investigation*, London: Heinemann Educational Books.

Nagel, E. (1961) *The Structure of Science*, London: Routledge & Kean Paul.

Narayan, U. (1989) 'The project of feminist epistemology: Perspectives from a nonwestern feminist' in A. Jaggar and S. Bordo (eds) *Gender/Body/Knowledge: Feminist Reconstructions of Being and Knowing*, New Brunswick: Rutgers University Press.

Nichols, T. (1979) 'Social class: official, sociological and Marxist' in J. Irvine, I. Miles and J. Evans (eds) *Demystifying Social Statistics*, London: Pluto.

Oakley, A. (1981) 'Interviewing women – a contradiction in terms' in H. Roberts (ed.) *Doing Feminist Research*, London: Routledge.

O'Connell Davidson, J. (1991) The Employment Relation: Diversity and Degradation in the Privatised Water Industry, Ph.D. thesis, University of Bristol, Bristol BS8 1UQ.

O'Connell Davidson, J. (1993) *Privatization and Employment Relations: The Case of the Water Industry*, London: Mansell.

O'Connell Davidson, J. (1994) 'The sources and limits of resistance in a privatised utility' in J. Jermier and W. Nord (eds) *Resistance and Power in Organizations*, London: Routledge.

Okely, J. (1992) 'Anthropology and Autobiography: Participatory Experience and Embodied Knowledge', in J. Okely and H. Callaway (eds) *Anthropology and Autobiography*, London: Routledge.

Parr, D. (1975) 'The state of sexology today' in S. Jacobson (ed.) *Sexual Problems*, London: Paul Elek.

Parsons, T. (1951) *The Social System*, Glencoe: Free Press.

Pateman, C. (1988) *The Sexual Contract*, Cambridge: Polity Press.

Patton, M. (1990) *Qualitative Evaluation and Research Methods*, London: Sage.

Phizacklea, A. (1983) 'In the front line' in A. Phizacklea (ed.) *One Way Ticket: Migration and Female Labour*, London: Routledge & Kegan Paul.

Pink Paper, The (1994) 'Surprise results in gay sex survey', issue 312, 28 January: 77 City Garden Row, London N1 8EZ.

Polsky, N. (1967) *Hustlers, Beats and Others*, Chicago: Aldine.

Pomeroy, W. (1972) *Dr Kinsey and the Institute for Sex Research*, London: Nelson.

Popper, K. (1963) *Conjectures and Refutations: the Growth of Scientific Knowledge*, London: Routledge & Kegan Paul.

Porter, R. (1989) *A Social History of Madness*, London: Wiedenfeld and Nicolson.

Radford, T. (1992) 'Hours of boredom and bigotry turn off sex researchers', the *Guardian*, 12 February.

Ramazanoglu, C. (1992) 'On feminist methodology: male reason versus female empowerment' *Sociology*, vol. 26, no. 2.

Reinharz, S. (1985) *On Becoming a Social Scientist*, New Brunswick: Transaction Publishers.

Report of the Inquiry into the Removal of Children from Orkney in February 1991, (1992)

Roberts, C. (1989) *Women and Rape*, Hemel Hempstead: Harvester Wheatsheaf.

Roberts, N. (1992) *Whores in History*, London: Grafton.

Rock, P. (1979) *The Making of Symbolic Interactionism*, London: Macmillan.

Rogers, A. (1993) *Experiencing Psychiatry*, London: Macmillan and MIND.

Rose, G. (1982) *Deciphering Sociological Research*, London: Macmillan.

Rose, J. (1992) *Marie Stopes and the Sexual Revolution*, London: Faber & Faber.

Rosenau, P. (1992) *Post-Modernism and the Social Sciences*, Princeton: Princeton University Press.

Rosenhan, D. (1973) 'On being sane in insane places', *Science*, no. 179, 19 January, pp. 250–8; reprinted in M. Bulmer (ed.) (1982) *Social Research Ethics*, London: Macmillan.

The Rota (1973) Introduction to John Stearne's *A Confirmation and Discovery of Witch Craft*, University of Exeter.

Roy, D. (1973) 'Banana time: job satisfaction and informal interaction' in G. Salaman and K. Thompson (eds) *People and Organizations*, London: Longman.

Ruse, M. (1988) *Homosexuality*, Oxford: Blackwell.

Russell, B. (1976) *The Impact of Science on Society*, London: Allen & Unwin.

Russell, D. (1986) *The Secret Trauma: Incest in the Lives of Girls and Women*, New York: Basic Books.

Ryan, B., Joiner, B. and Ryan, T. (1985) *Minitab Handbook*, Boston: PWS-Kent.

Samson, C. (1993) 'The fracturing of medical dominance in British psychiatry', paper presented to the American Sociological Association Conference, Miami Beach, August.

Schofield, M. (1968) *The Sexual Behaviour of Young People*, Harmondsworth: Penguin.

Scholte, B. (1972) 'Toward a reflexive and critical anthropology' in D. Hymes (ed.) *Reinventing Anthropology*, New York: Pantheon Books.

Scott, J. (1990) *A Matter of Record*, Cambridge: Polity Press.

Scully, D. (1990) *Understanding Sexual Violence*, London: HarperCollins.

Segal, L. (1990) *Slow Motion: Changing Masculinities, Changing Men*, London: Virago.

Segal, L. (1993) 'Sweet sorrows, painful pleasures: Pornography and the Perils of Heterosexual Desire' in L. Segal and M. McIntosh (eds) *Slow Motion: Changing Masculinities, Changing Men*, London: Virago.

Segal, L and McIntosh, M. (1993) (eds) *Sex Exposed: Sexuality and the Pornography Debate*, New Brunswick: Rutgers University Press.

Sherry, N. (1989) *The Life of Graham Greene*, volume 1, 1904–1939, London: Jonathan Cape.

Shipman, M. (1988) *The Limitations of Social Research*, London: Longman.

Silverman, D. (1985) *Qualitative Methodology and Sociology*, Aldershot: Gower.

Simon, J. (1969) *Basic Research Methods in Social Science*, New York: Random House.

Simpson, A. (1987) 'Vulnerability and the age of female consent: legal innovation and its effect on prosecutions for rape in eighteenth century London' in G. Rousseau and R. Porter (eds) *Sexual Underworlds of the Enlightenment*, Manchester: Manchester University Press.

Slattery, M. (1986) *Official Statistics*, London: Tavistock.

Small, S. (1991a) 'Attaining racial parity in the United States and England; We got to go where the greener grass grows', Sage Race Relations Abstracts, vol. 76, no. 3, May, pp. 3–55.

Small, S. (1991b) 'Racialised relations in Liverpool: A contemporary anomoly', *New Community*, vol. 17, no. 4, pp. 511–37.

Small, S. (1994) *Racialized Barriers*, London: Routledge.

Smith, D. (1988) *The Everyday World as Problematic*, Milton Keynes: Open University Press.

Smith, G. (1993) *Fibrenetics: A Fresh Start for Life*, London: Fourth Estate.

Soothill, K. and Jack, A. (1975) 'How rape is reported', *New Society* vol. 32, no. 663: 702–4.

Soothill, K. and Walby, S. (1991) *Sex Crime in the News*, London: Routledge.

Stanley, L. and Wise, S. (1983) *Breaking Out*, London: Routledge.

Stanley, L. and Wise, S. (1993) *Breaking Out Again: Feminist Ontology and Epitsemology*, London: Routledge.

Stearne, J. (1973) *A Confirmation and Discovery of Witch Craft*, University of Exeter: The Rota.

Stoller, R. (1991) *Pain & Passion: A Psychoanalyst Explores the World of S & M*, New York: Plenum Press.

Stopes, M. (1987) 'From *Married Love*' in S. Jeffreys (ed.) *The Sexuality Debates*, New York: Routledge & Kegan Paul.

Stouffer, S. (1950) 'Some observations on study design', *American Journal of Sociology*, vol. 55, pp. 355–61.

Strauss, A. and Corbin, J. (1990) *Basics of Qualitative Research*, California: Sage.

Thompson, K. (1991), *Readings from Emile Durkheim*, London: Routledge.

Thompson, P. (1983) *The Nature of Work*, London: Macmillan.

Trigg, R. (1989) *Reality at Risk: A Defense of Realism in Philosophy and the Sciences*, New York: Harvester Wheatsheaf.

Troyna, B. and Hatcher, R. (1992) *Racism in Children's Lives*, London: Routledge.

Webb, B. (1987) 'The teaching of children as to the reproduction of life' in S. Jeffreys (ed.) *The Sexuality Debates*, New York: Routledge & Kegan Paul.

Weber, M. (1966) *The Theory of Social and Economic Organization*, New York: Free Press.

Weeks, J. (1985) *Sexuality and its Discontents. Meanings, Myths and Modern Sexualities*, London: Routledge & Kegan Paul.

Weeks, J. (1986) *Sexuality*, London: Tavistock.

Wellings, K., Field, J., Johnson, A. and Wadsworth, J. (1994) *Sexual Behaviour in Britain*, Harmondsworth: Penguin.

Wickware, F. (1948) 'Report on the Kinsey Report', *Life*, no. 25, August.

Wilkins, J. (1967) 'Suicidal Behaviour', *American Sociological Review*, vol. 32, pp. 286–98.

Wilson, E. (1993) 'Feminist fundamentalism: the shifting politics of sex and censorship' in L. Segal and M. McIntosh (eds) *Sex Exposed: Sexuality and the Pornography Debate*, New Brunswick: Rutgers University Press.

Winch, P. (1980) *The Idea of a Social Science*, London: Routledge & Kegan Paul.

Index